Sociology After the Crisis

SOCIOLOGY
After the Crisis

Charles Lemert

■ WestviewPress
A Division of HarperCollins*Publishers*

Published in 1995 by the United States of America by Westview Press, Inc., 5500 Central Avenue, Boulder, Colorado 80301-2877, and in the United Kingdom by Westview Press, 12 Hid's Copse Road, Cumnor Hill, Oxford OX2 9JJ

Library of Congress Cataloging-in-Publication Data
Lemert, Charles C., 1937–
 Sociology after the crisis / Charles Lemert.
  p. cm.
 Includes index.
 ISBN 0-8133-2543-9 (hc.)—ISBN 0-8133-2544-7 (pb.)
 1. Sociology. 2. Sociology—History. 3. Social problems.
1. Title.
HM51.L356 1995
301—dc20   95-15689
                                                                            CIP

The paper used in this publication meets the requirements of the American National Standard for Permanence of Paper for Printed Library Materials Z39.48-1984.

10   9   8   7   6   5   4   3   2   1

To Geri,
with whom no crisis lasts for long

Contents

Introduction

Whatever you have heard, or have come to think, sociology is of vital importance to all individuals desiring to come to some workable terms with their world.

Sociology After the Crisis is a book for those who care about sociology, or those who are at least intrigued by it. I am well aware that even such generous qualifications as these limit the population of likely readers. But not so much as some might suppose. All authors entertain more or less conscious fantasies about the ideal readership of their books. Mine, I will admit, are immodest. I would hope that the book might be read not just by professional sociologists and students of sociology but also by an even larger number of persons who are working seriously to come to terms with the primary circumstances of their daily lives.

Those circumstances have changed in recent years. Today, many no longer think it possible to speak of daily life as though it were gently surrounded by the nurturing cocoon of a "world." With rare exception, most individuals live in several different worlds. In these worlds they come up against still more, and different, worlds inhabited by others in whose values and behaviors they recognize little that is familiar and much that is alien, sometimes frightening. To those who view themselves and their local manners as normal and mainstream, this is a disturbing, even infuriating, condition—one that signals the end of customary and cherished ways. The worlds of daily life are, at the least, less stable, and often less hospitable, than once they were.

That most people live in a social environment of this sort is, I believe, a matter of historical reality. It is nothing less than the salient social, political, cultural, and moral reality that has suddenly darkened the bright hopes of Western civilization. Clouds of its coming were faintly, and ironically, visible already at the moment of the West's greatest promise in the two decades following World War II. Just when the United States led a triumphal redevelopment of Western economic and social principles, then also began the first movements of resistance against the colonial world system of the European and American powers. Beginning in 1947 with Gandhi's successes in India against the British, people in other colonized regions in Asia, Africa, the

Middle East, the Caribbean, the American South, and elsewhere within the Euro-American world system won their independence. Even where their freedom has been spoiled by economic disaster, the effect has been a continuing state of near global resistance to the idea that one or another Western power ought to rule a well-integrated world.

This is the crisis alluded to in the book's title. In its most general form, it is no less than a crisis over the very idea of the world's wholeness, its peace and integrity. More concretely and practically, this is a crisis in the lives of individuals frightened or enraged (or both) by the hard necessity of encounters with the ideas and habits of others who seem to disrespect that which one holds dear and true. Some consider this crisis the end of all that is good. Others view it as a liberation from past oppression. Neither, by definition of the situation, is completely right or wrong. Some might call this the crisis of differences, referring thereby to the remarkable intrusion of multicultural thinking and politics into high academic discourse as well as the cultural politics of public life. Others might call it the crisis of values, most famously (but not by any means exclusively) the crisis of family and related values. Whatever the name, only those remotely sequestered from public opinion could not know of this crisis and in some way be affected by it.

As a simple, though dramatic, illustration of its nature, one might consider the case of Sanyika Shakur, also known as Monster Kody Scott, author (in 1993) of *Monster: The Autobiography of an L.A. Gang Member.* Few are likely to understand fully, much less appreciate, the life he has led. "I have lived," he says, "in South Central Los Angeles all my life." And,

> I was recruited into the Crips at the ripe old age of eleven. Today I am twenty-nine years old. I am a gang expert—period. There are no other gang experts but participants. Our lives, mores, customs, and philosophies remain as mysterious and untouched as those of any "uncivilized" tribe in Afrika. . . . I have pushed people violently out of this existence and have fathered three children. I have felt completely free and have sat in total solitary confinement in San Quentin state prison. I have shot numerous people and have been shot seven times myself. I have been in gunfights in South Central and knife fights in Folsom state prison. Today, I languish at the bottom of one of the strictest maximum-security state prisons in this country. (p. xiii)

Monster (Shakur's original street name) is unrepentant of his violence. Neither he nor those outside his world would disagree that Sanyika Shakur is (or was) a monster of some kind. He, however, views what he has done as nothing but the righteous actions of those engaged in a war. Those he murdered were, to him, hostile enemies on a battlefield drawn through one of America's most notoriously violent ghettos. Kill or be killed is the first moral rule of such a world. To read Monster Kody Scott's story with a sympathetic eye is to be persuaded, at least to some surprising degree. Kody Scott considers the battle in South Central L.A. not importantly different from any other military struggle, save that the combatants, if they survive, can never go home. Home, such as it is, is war.

That he is sincere in ways others can understand was evident to viewers of a 1994 CBS News *Sixty Minutes* interview during which Scott broke painfully into visible tears when speaking of his biological father, a well-known sports celebrity, who had abandoned him from the first. When he struggled to wipe away the tears, Scott's hands, bound by prison shackles, could not reach his sad eyes. Even a monster grieves over a lost father.

Quite apart from what you might think about such a man, it would be hard to deny that such men exist and that for them life is, at the very least, constant warfare in both the literal and figurative senses. They, and others at comparable odds with the normal comforts of middling and elite societies, represent the crisis to which sociology must address itself. In worlds in which killing presents itself as a small boy's surest path to respect and survival, the usual expectations of decency lose their force, even and especially among those who most despise the violence. This condition, which surely exists today in American cities and across the globe, is one that creates a crisis at the very heart of the traditional dreams of a good, progressive human civilization. Sociologies of all kinds must take this condition into account.

Before leaving Monster Kody Scott too quickly, I would like to use his understanding of his world to illustrate another of the premises of this book. His view of life as an inescapable and murderous struggle for survival could very properly be called a sociology. It is, in his terms, a coherent account of the social world into which he was born of a good mother and an abandoning father—a world he felt he could not resist. Though professional sociologists might use the more formal language of social disorganization, social pathology, and the urban underclass, Sanyika Shakur's own street-derived eloquence leaves no room for doubt that one is in the presence of a sociology of some compelling kind. The unreachable tears he could not wipe away tell also of an unbreachable human desire he shares with most of us to feel, understand, and be understood. This desire, I believe, is the first resource of all good sociologies.

This idea is not my own. One way or another each of the great founding sociologists and social theorists of the late nineteenth century drew on this same resource. Max Weber (1864–1920), Émile Durkheim (1858–1917), Karl Marx (1818–1883), and Sigmund Freud (1856–1939) are the most enduring, recognized sources of modern sociology. Each was a writer whose ideas drew on the most basic of human feelings and understandings. This is one of the reasons

Sociology After the Crisis regularly refers to them. I try to keep these classic thinkers fresh, if not central, to the book's discussion to show how they collectively invented, and were limited by, the original terms of sociological talk.

All of these four classic writers on modern society made an impression that endured across the subsequent century to the present time, and none of the impressions they made was confined to the narrow, professionalized interests of academic or other technical fields (though of course each also influenced academic fields like sociology). *Sociology After the Crisis* pays attention to them, therefore, not just because they are fathers but more because their ideas, even the most technical ones, were so alive to the most urgent moral concerns of their worlds.

But, I should add, this is not a book *about* these classic thinkers any more than it is simply another book of social theory. I justify the attention paid them on other grounds. Sociology today very much needs to take stock of itself. While this surely involves the invention of new ideas, or their appropriation from other fields, it also requires a serious reconsideration of sociology as it is, for better or worse. If we are to imagine what sociology might become, we must, I think, be willing to work through where sociology came from and how it became what it is. This is hard, sometimes painful, work. But it must be done.

The vital importance I claim for sociology owes to the conviction, mentioned earlier, that sociology, the professionalized academic discipline, is first and foremost a necessary and very practical aspect of public life. I mean by this something that ought to be perfectly evident to everyone. Unfortunately it is not, and, to be frank, I cannot say with complete confidence why not. It is not so strange to speak of laypersons as having a "psychology," by which one may mean either that their psychological nature is of a certain remarkable type or that an individual is capable of a definite psychological orientation to the conduct of daily life. Both such senses could very accurately be applied to Monster Kody Scott, who both has and is able to discuss the psychology of an urban warrior. Such psychologies may or may not have any particular relation to the concepts and terms of professional academic psychologists. In somewhat similar ways, it is common to speak of practical histories (think of the hundreds of family histories being composed at this very minute), and even of practical economics. Who can afford not to have an economic theory of one's relative market position, even if it is only a "home economics"? And it goes without saying that almost everyone has a politics of some kind, but these are usually as little informed by professional political science as home economics is by academic economics.

In similar ways people have a "practical sociology"—by which I mean that normal aspect of human social life in which persons desire to feel, understand, and talk coherently about their social worlds without prior instruction. Is not this the desire that arises more or less consciously along with the beginning of language use and the young child's struggle for psychic independence? How and why would individuals desire to speak, or entertain themselves as separate from the parenting forces of infancy, were it not for a desire to feel, understand, and say something workable about life with others? My oldest son was not yet three when his newly born brother was brought home. Matthew marched on his own still new legs to Noah's crib, peered through its side, turned disdainfully to me and his mother, and said: "*What* is that?" Big feelings, small thoughts, and a passably good attempt to understand the changes to come in a world he had had entirely to himself.

Sociological competence of this sort is more similar to linguistic competence than anything else. Normally, a child comes into language all at once, more or less in the second year of life, from which moment he or she possesses the linguistic knowledge sufficient to daily life. Later, teachers may provide the fortunate with instruction in grammar and vocabulary. While these required subjects do not make a linguistics, they are the rudiments out of which a professional linguistics constructs its technical knowledge. Is it not much the same with sociological competence? Though it comes later perhaps and more slowly than linguistic competence, it too comes as though all at once, and pretty nearly as ubiquitously among all normals. Matthew, upon meeting his brother, knew somehow that even though (to use Kody Scott's expression) he might have wanted to push the kid out of this existence, he was instead obliged to use words. This he did, competently, with only the most casual prior instruction from play group parents and the like.

Sociological competence, however it may arise, is universally required for social survival. Though the differences among these competencies vary from culture to culture much as languages do, it seems nearly beyond discussion that sociological competence is as fundamental to human existence as any of the others. One might get along without a politics, or even an economics; and some practical psychologies are evidently unworkable. But who can get by without a capacity to feel, understand, and speak coherently about one's social world? I once, years ago, met a door-to-door representative of what was to me a strange religious sect. Somehow (I was never sure how) he managed to induce in me a willingness to invite him inside, even to accept return visits. The man's religious ideas were, to me, so beyond comprehension that I experienced his "psychology" as (I must say it) crazy. But his sociology was just fine.

He knew exactly how to get my attention and keep it an inordinate number of times.

Many sociologists have described the practical basis of sociological wisdom, notably Erving Goffman, Harold Garfinkel, Herbert Blumer, and their followers and colleagues, among many others. Also, in their way all of the classic social thinkers appreciated sociology's practical origins in daily life. Freud surely did. Weber's sociological method was nothing if it was not an attempt to build sociology on the basis of the native social capacity for human understanding. Durkheim's theory of social knowledge and moral life would make no sense without the prior conviction that everything people know about what they believe they ought to do is fixed by practical life in the social community. And what was Marx's economic sociology about if it was not about his desire to account for the central existential question of modern life: How is it that men and women in their practical lives under capitalism are normally unable on their own to understand why and how things are so much worse than even they suspect?

So, if the idea is so sensible and has been around in one form or another for so long, why does it deserve the attentions of a good portion of this or any other new book? I confess that the explanation I currently believe does serious grief to my own ideological biases. For the better part of the last decade, academics, including sociologists, have been subjected to a barrage of public attacks, beginning with the criticisms leveled by Allan Bloom in *The Closing of the American Mind*, which appeared in 1987. Since then, there has been a steady stream of tracts of various kinds with titles like *Profscam, Illiberal Education, Killing the Spirit*, by authors who, whatever else may recommend them, were not in these instances overly eager to do the hard work of basing their complaints on a careful study of the actual ideas of those they attack. But the grief I must do my own biases is to admit that at least one of their critical points must be taken seriously.

Sociology is among those academic fields that have, in part at least, lost vital contact with their most important values, with their reason for being. In 1987, the same year as Bloom's *The Closing of the American Mind*, Russell Jacoby published *The Last Intellectuals*. I hated that book when I first read it. It seemed all too preoccupied with the stylistic failures of academic discourse and not sufficiently appreciative of the important, if indirect, contributions academics make to public life. But over the years, I could never get around Jacoby's claim that sociologists are among those who have ceased to be the kind of public intellectuals whose professed values are of evident social worth.

Although *The Last Intellectuals* ignored most of those new public intellectuals who are neither white, nor male, nor necessarily straight, Jacoby was, in this respect, right about much of professional sociology. One of the more important ways in which academic sociology has lost immediate contact with its reason for being is through its loss of the sense of practical and moral seriousness that all of its major classic thinkers had. I do not mean to say that today's professional sociologists are by their nature impractical, and certainly not that they are amoral. But I do believe that the field itself has, temporarily I hope, given up its necessary relation to its only and primary natural resource: the moral concerns not just of individuals in their daily lives but of the hard-to-grasp whole of the worlds of which sociologies must today speak. Though writers like Robert Bellah (and his associates), Steven Seidman, Richard Flacks, Patricia Hill Collins, Judith Stacey, Alan Wolfe, and Dorothy Smith, among many others, are encouraging a return to these questions, these are but the first steps in the deep, patient reworking of the moral basis of sociology itself.

Sociology was founded by a generation of thinkers who cared very much for sociology (or its near equivalent, in the cases of Marx and Freud) *because* they cared deeply about the world as a whole. They had the advantage over us today of believing their own mystifying convictions that there was, all too simply, one true world of which the modern "West" was the historically progressive embodiment. Yet, it could be said that today *we* have the advantage. It is increasingly difficult to hold such a worldview with impunity. There are too, too many vocal, public, and persuasive voices insisting properly that their worlds are as real, plausible, and necessary as the West's and that these worlds are just simply different. A simply singular world is now contested as one simply different and thus many. To anyone caught drowsing over the past twenty or thirty years, this may seem to be a new and sudden development. But, as I said earlier, this crisis of world recognition has been coming for at least a generation. Now it is here.

This is one implication of one of this book's major themes. In the early chapters I develop the idea that from the beginning sociology has been caught up in (without recognizing) its desire for the lost worlds modern society leaves in the wake of progress. From the first, sociologies have been imaginative efforts to re-create the present and its future out of the dreamy residues of longings for a perfect past. For the classic sociologists of the late nineteenth century, those worlds were the primitive or traditional pasts lost to the industrial order. Confused about what they lost, they dreamt of possible new societies that would again bring a perfect human peace—a healthy division of labor, a classless society, a rehumanized rational society. But for us today, even that one world in which early sociology was made and to which it spoke is itself lost. Even if, over the long course of history, the present crisis of seeming incommensurable differences is somehow resolved into a new kind of world peace, it is highly improbable that the predominantly white people in the Euro-American cultures (with all our several similarities to the norms we believe in) will ever enjoy the relative cognitive and social peace that once obtained in the world their sociological (and other) fathers built.

But I should continue to ease away from the notion that these fathers had it all that easy. *Sociology After the Crisis* also concerns the reality of the lost worlds with which *they* had to struggle. It is widely understood that the first sociologists were principally preoccupied with the scientific and moral task of explaining and healing the felt divisions caused by the disappearance of the world *their* ancestors were born into. For them, it was the last vestiges of the traditional order in which—as Durkheim, Weber, Freud, and Marx all observed—religion covered the social consciousness with a powerful resistance to change in the form of a devotion to the sacred cosmos. They, perhaps even more acutely than we, felt the pangs of this lost world, if only because theirs had been so fixed for so much longer than ours—for a millennium, more or less, in their case; for just a century or so in ours.

The reality of the lost world with which they had to contend was more than the reality of historical facts and moral anxiety. It was a reality that came to be central to their sociologies and, thus, to the sociologies we inherit today. One of the reasons I devote so much attention to Durkheim in this book is that he, perhaps more than any of them, felt and thought the acuteness of this loss in ways that serve as a near perfect illustration of what sociology was at the beginning, has become, but seems will never quite be again. Durkheim, who left the traditional world of his rural, religious fathers to found sociology in Paris, grieved over this loss. The moral preoccupations of his sociology were, I believe, those arising from an unconscious longing for what had been lost—to him personally, but more importantly to all men in modern society as he understood it. In the discussions of Durkheim in particular I try to make the admittedly controversial point that the very idea *society*, with all of its ornate indefiniteness, is an idea indebted to the ideal of the lost world for which all sociologies, not just Durkheim's, long.

This ideal is, in a sense, another fundamental aspect of all sociologies, both professional and practical. What else could be the vision of a good society but the vision of that for which one longs? We have known for a very long time that future utopias are always based on past experience. This is a truism. What has not been particularly well considered, and especially not by sociologists, is the idea that this longing for a future world is the inescapable condition of any sociology, whether professional or lay. Such longings, one suspects, must arise very nearly at the same time as the first appearances of sociological competence in early life, in those years when small children must learn to suppress their deep, primary feelings in order to know how to live acceptably in whatever world is presented to them. Matthew, age two and months, must have had the desire to keep for himself the primitive world in which he alone was the center of his parents' overly eager, thus awkward affections. But he could not and would not have been able to even if he had had no brother. When actually faced with a baby rival, he surely had this desire to keep his world and had also the coordinate desire to crash the kid out. But he did not. This is the price of first admission to society. Today, as grown men, the brothers love each other as brothers sometimes can. Miracles like this are the most basic stuff of society itself. The active suppression of overly aggressive (and sexual) impulses for the sake of righteous membership is the normal route to sociological competence. In Monster Kody Scott's case, the rule remains the same, the details being changed: In worlds where disrespect and abandonment prevail, some growing boys feel they must act on those terrible impulses in order to protect their meager, hollow places in a lonely world of lost fathers. It is not, I suppose, quite this simple. But neither is the task of sociologies of whichever kind all that much more complex.

At its best, even professional sociology has understood this near-law of the social life, which was especially well put in C. Wright Mills's famous phrase "the sociological imagination." He meant something slightly different from what I mean. But by defining the task of sociology as that of bridging the emotional and intellectual divide between an individual's experience of the world and realistic knowledge of its historical structures, Mills was right to use the metaphor of imagination. The brilliance of this figure of speech is that it expresses so parsimoniously the essential attributes of a good enough sociology, whether professional or practical.

In the last half of the book (particularly in Chapters 5, 6, 7, and 8) I advance the proposal that sociologies all boil down to deliberations on three necessary, and inseparable, themes: *selves, structures,* and *measures.* It would be foolish of me even to begin to explain here what takes four chapters in the book. But I can, and probably should, say that I am entirely serious in this proposal. In other words, this amounts to saying that sociologies are the serious attempts of persons of varying qualifications to measure the moral and social distance between themselves and the big, power-ridden structures of the modern world. And this can only be done by the courageous exercise of the sociological imagination. Whether an urban warrior is taking the measure of himself in a kill-or-be-killed world or a professional sociologist is taking the measure of correlations between exposure to violence and its devastating effects on early childhood development, the imagination is the means by which a sociology measures the reality.

Mills and Alvin Gouldner (the other sociologist to whom I refer at the beginning of the book) were right in other ways as well. They both aspired, though differently, to serve as prophetic voices whatever the cost (and it cost them both dearly). They were, thus, public intellectuals, though with a special sense of that vocation. They both felt that sociology was less a professional qualification than a survival skill for life in the world. More recently, in a 1994 book *Representations of Intellectuals,* Edward Said favorably invokes both Mills and Gouldner among other morally acute public intellectuals. Like them, Said argues forcefully for the need today of a return of such prophetic voices to the public realm, but, also like them, he is clear that the public social critic (or sociologist) must be as clear about his or her personal life as about the structured worlds being critiqued.

Though it might have fit better earlier, I have left one prefatory word to the end because it concerns a subject easily misunderstood, and, on this, I do not want to be mistaken. The reader will encounter in the latter half of the book references to writers and sociologists who are not nearly so well known as the four great classic men to whom I have referred. These others include Anna Julia Cooper (1858?–1964), W.E.B. Du Bois (1868–1963), and Charlotte Perkins Gilman (1860–1935). Today, each, respectively, is a classic figure in three separate traditions of social thought—Black feminism, African American and Pan-African social thought, and what must today be called, rather awkwardly, white feminism. It is not for reasons of correct appearances that I recommend Cooper, Du Bois, and Gilman, among many others of similar fates and experiences. They were not "unknown" until recently without a reason—and this too is part of sociology's history. If not to "us," they were very well known to others. All three, and others like them, were important public intellectuals, writers, and activists without whose efforts, and the efforts of those with whom and for whom they worked, the world would not be what it is today. They were not known for the reason that they were either scrupulously excluded or not plainly visible from within the culture sociology meant to explain and save. One simply cannot understand sociology today without a knowledge of its repressed and ignored public intellectuals like

Cooper, Du Bois, and Gilman. I mean by this at least two things, both essential to the book.

First, I mean that sociology from the beginning was *both* a prophetic voice criticizing modern society *and* a believing adherent to the promise of modern culture. Sociology thus, in both its professional and popular forms, participated in that culture's witting and unwitting exclusions. Sociologically speaking, whatever is is what it is because it excludes. This too is an obvious but poorly examined near-law of social order. What modern Western culture is is a complexly organized and shared attitude whereby the complexity of social life is made to seem utterly simple by being identified with the grand achievements of a relatively small number of the members of but a few of the world's worlds. Very probably all cultures of whichever kind do just the same. But the phenomenon becomes important when one culture exercises powerful control over worlds other than its own. How, then, sociology has participated in the cultural exercise of this sort of power must be considered in order to take true account of its historical nature. This can be done, I believe, without unduly rubbing its nose in its own dirt. The exclusion of sociologists like Cooper, Du Bois, and Gilman was, straightforwardly, just part of what sociology had to do to become sociology.

Second, and finally, *Sociology After the Crisis* is meant to provoke discussion of what sociology might become after the crisis. Sooner or later, things will settle into their place and whatever that is will then be the world of the worlds. We do not know what those new circumstances will be, or how much they will be different from or similar to that to which many had grown accustomed. This is why I do not consider the postmodernism question in any more than a passing fashion. At least insofar as sociologies are concerned, it is far too soon to say what the world will become. This, I think, is a time of working through how we got to where we are. I don't know of any other way to get to wherever one is going, at least not amid the hard, slow realities of social living.

It seems to me that one of the good ways to go back and work through includes that time-tested method of trying to see ourselves as others see us. The excluded writers to whom I refer may not have preoccupied themselves with what the dominant, excluding culture was doing and thinking. But it certainly was the case, and always will be, that individuals in the more socially precarious position will necessarily be the better guides to the true nature of those of whom they must be wary.

Hence, another disturbing aspect of the crisis: Wariness and caution in social affairs, as in sociology, have replaced comfortable certitudes and reassuring confidences. But things could be worse. Not all of us have to deal with a world like Kody Scott's, even if understanding such a world, and ones like it, is probably where the future of sociologies lies.

Charles Lemert
Killingworth, Connecticut

Chapter 1

After the Crisis

Aʙᴏᴜᴛ ᴀ ɢᴇɴᴇʀᴀᴛɪᴏɴ ᴀɢᴏ, more or less, a sociologist wrote a book he called *The Coming Crisis in Western Sociology*. Today many might be shocked by the audacity of its assumptions: that sociology was a subject of general human interest, that a crisis in sociology would be central to the cultural and political crises then already defining social life, that resolution of such a crisis would require a renewal of sociology in which critical reflection on one's personal life would join and inspire rigorous analysis of the big, historical structures of society.

Few of the many who read that book in the early 1970s could have anticipated how right it would be about the coming crisis. Nor could they have known, then, how wrong it would be about the fate of sociology. The crisis came. It defines social life worldwide today. Yet, somehow, sociology has lost its way, if not its promise.

It is time, possibly, to think seriously of the nature and fate of sociology. Perhaps we are near the time when the crisis either will be at its end—or, will have become the way we live. What then, after the crisis, will be the place of sociology?

In 1970, when Alvin Gouldner's *The Coming Crisis in Western Sociology* first appeared, the United States was still at war with communism. The war in Vietnam was both the cause and the effect of moral and political turmoil at home. On May 4 in the year this book was first available on college campuses, young men of the Ohio National Guard were ordered to fire into a crowd of unarmed students protesting the war at Kent State University. Four students were killed, nine others were wounded. In the investigation following, one of the commanding officers testified that he ordered his troops to fire because he felt they—his troops!—were at risk.

Indeed, it was a time when millions of American citizens felt themselves in danger against irrational forces. Ten days later, in a similar incident, two students at Jackson State College in Mississippi were killed by the police. That spring, college campuses across the United States were disrupted by many thousands of protests, strikes, rebellions, and worse. Some remember the then president of the United States, Richard M. Nixon, snarling, "These bums, you know, blowin' up the campuses."[1] Crisis was everywhere. Since the urban riots in the middle 1960s and the waves of domestic crises in 1968, danger was a normal state of feeling and fact in deviant times.

The crises in American society and much of the Western world were very much on Alvin Gouldner's mind when he wrote *The Coming Crisis*, which began with these words:

> Social theorists today work within a crumbling social matrix of paralyzed urban centers and battered campuses. Some may put cotton in their ears, but their bodies still feel the shock waves. It is no exaggeration to say that we theorize today within the sounds of guns. The old order has the picks of a hundred rebellions thrust into its hide.[2]

Thousands of young women and men read that book in 1970 as part of a struggle to figure out what had become of the hopes that had moved them through much of the preceding decade. By 1970, it was already difficult to keep a clear sense of the social faith that inspired so many of their generation to think and act as though the world could and would soon be better.

It was by then even difficult to remember an earlier book, similar to Gouldner's, that had appeared just as the 1960s were beginning. In 1959, C. Wright Mills had published *The Sociological Imagination*. This was the clearest, most enduring statement of Mills's many recommendations to the New Left, by which name the growing student movement signified its resolve to change the world politically as well as socially. In it, Mills defined the sociological imagination in terms persuasive to young men and women already familiar with an increasing number of social criticisms of American life in the years following World War II. In fact, ten years before Mills's book, in 1950, David Riesman's *The Lonely Crowd* was one of the first books to suggest that American society had lost its moral edge.[3] A decade later, Mills had reformulated this theme for the generation of young people coming into their own just as the 1960s were beginning. *The Sociological Imagination* opened with words especially reminiscent of Riesman's *Lonely Crowd:*

> Nowadays men often feel that their private lives are a series of traps. They sense that within their everyday worlds, they cannot overcome their troubles, and in this feeling, they are often quite correct: What ordinary men are directly aware of and what they try to do are bounded by the private orbits in which they live; their visions and their powers are limited to the close-up scenes of job, family, neighborhood.[4]

The social imagination Mills envisioned was not so much an academic attitude as a practical moral vision meant to enable "its possessor to understand the larger historical scene in terms of its meaning for the inner life and the external career of a variety of individuals."[5] In 1970, in almost the same language, Gouldner would conclude his *Coming Crisis* by recommending a reflexive sociology that he defined as a personal and political orientation to life that would "*transform* the sociologist, to penetrate deeply into his daily life and work, enriching them with new sensitivities, and to raise the sociologist's self-awareness to a new historical level."[6] Though the idea of a reflexive sociology was aimed at professionals, it was rooted (as was Mills's sociological imagination) in the practical prescription that individuals are most free when they reflect on themselves, though always with an historical eye.

Mills, near the beginning of the 1960s, and Gouldner, near their end, understood the world and the place of sociology in it in much the same way. Both took seriously the political and economic crises of their times. As a result, for both, sociology was more than a professional academic practice. To them, sociology was—before and above all else—a practical survival skill necessary in order for men and women to live with power and pleasure in the modern world. Yet the worlds they each saw, a decade apart, were remarkably different. Mills's was a world closer to Riesman's lonely, alienated, conformist crowd. At the end of the 1950s people felt in their guts a gnawing sensation, poorly understood, that something was wrong—that the world was not just as it should be. Gouldner's in 1970 was already a world in flames. Yet, both Mills and Gouldner and their readers held fast to the moral conviction that structural changes in society's political and economic life were necessarily linked to the intellectual and moral sensibilities of the personal life. Though Mills may have been the first to propose this moral formula, *personal politics* became the code word of the new social movements that forced the social crisis of which Gouldner spoke in 1970.[7] The civil rights and Black power movements, like the antiwar, feminist, gay-lesbian, and other movements that followed, had complex and differing agendas. But in those early days they shared a concern to set politics in a vital relation to the personal.

Both C. Wright Mills and Alvin Gouldner influenced a generation of people who were still young in the years between 1960 and 1970. Yet, neither, had he survived,[8] would be a hero in the 1990s—at least not without first having undergone a fundamental change of character. In their day, Mills and Gouldner were both very much men from an earlier era. Both, in fact, thought of the thinker, the political man, and the sociologist as though they were of masculine gender. Their moral ideals, like their language, assumed a world in need of virile virtues—tough thinking for tough times. Throughout their lives, each thought of himself in the mythology of his youth—Mills, as the frontiersman from Texas; Gouldner, as the street-tough kid from the Bronx. In adult life, Mills played with real guns and rode motorcycles; Gouldner had at least one notorious fistfight. Though each in his way was a uniquely American exaggeration, each believed in the Western ideal of the intellectual as a moral force in the world.[9]

Many believe today that the moral worlds of Mills and Gouldner are dead; that even the faith they had in knowledge's ability to force the hand of power is hopelessly naive. Today, tough men are widely considered a problem. Then, in the 1960s, they were still considered the solution. Ironically, on one crucial point both Mills and Gouldner would probably have agreed more with Talcott Parsons, the sociologist whom both fiercely attacked, than with those today who argue that the time of the modern world is past; that modernity's political and cultural values no longer suited a changing world. In 1971, the year after Gouldner's *Coming Crisis,* Parsons said: "Talk of the 'postmodern' society is decidedly premature."[10] Nothing in the writings of Mills and Gouldner suggests they would have disagreed. Their worlds were closer to Parsons's than to the social reality of those today who think the postmodern is, if not already here, at least the coming crisis of *our* time.

This may be why Mills and Gouldner, and many others influenced by them, could not have imagined the situation of sociology today. They could not, then, fully imagine the extent to which the world would change. In the 1960s, sociology was in the streets with those who challenged the old order. Mills and Gouldner were exactly right about this. Mills, in 1959, helped make it happen. Gouldner, in 1970, tried to remake sociology because it had happened. True to their sociologies, Mills imagined it and Gouldner reflected on its personal and social meaning. Still, neither imagination nor reflexivity was sufficient for them to anticipate just how potent the ideal of practical, political sociology might be. It is not that professional sociologists did not directly influence the events of the 1960s. Many did. But not even C. Wright Mills, whose ideas were read by student revolutionaries in the early 1960s, could be considered *the* major source of radical social theories. It was the other way around. Mills, later Gouldner and others, were influential among students and other intellectuals because they put words to a story millions already knew. Although told in many and various themes, it was the story of the world changing in ways that, years later, would come back to haunt and challenge even the best bright academic social theorists. But it was sociology just the same—especially by the standards of Mills's sociological imagination.

If, as Mills taught, sociology is an act of the social imagination in which individuals reflect critically on the relations between their "personal troubles" and "the public issues of social structure,"[11] then sociology occurs wherever such imagination takes place. In this sense, sociology in those days was breaking out all around the world. At first the critical voices were heard in the 1950s in towns and cities in Africa, Asia, and the American South. By 1968 few parts of the globe were unaffected by some sort of sociological imagination.[12] New social thinking circulated, increasingly, from place to place. The collapse of the European colonial empires was already well under way in Asia and Africa in the late 1940s. Soon ideas from these distant places had their effects in Europe and, most dramatically, America.

In 1960 the Student Nonviolent Coordinating Committee (SNCC), which soon became a principal force in the African American freedom struggle, was organized in Raleigh, North Carolina, through the leadership of Ella Baker, a veteran of civil rights struggles since the 1930s. The students were, mostly, Blacks—themselves veterans of the lunch-counter sit-ins earlier that year—protesting exclusion from restaurants and other public accommodations. SNCC's 1960 founding statement contained an explicit vision of a new societal order:

> Through nonviolence, courage displaces fear. Love transcends hate. Acceptance dissipates prejudice; hope ends despair. Faith reconciles doubt. Peace dominates war. Mutual regards cancel enmity. Justice for all overthrows injustice. The redemptive community supersedes immoral social systems.[13]

SNCC's nonviolent social theory was borrowed from the political and moral philosophy of the Reverend Martin Luther King Jr. and others in the Southern Christian Leadership Conference (SCLC) who had been influenced by the example and teachings of the leader of India's decolonizing movement, Mohandas Gandhi.[14] Judeo-Christian values were mixed with Third World revolutionary ideals.

A year later, in fall 1961, Tom Hayden was in Atlanta, Georgia, working as a Students for a Democratic Society (SDS) field secretary while his then wife,

Casey Hayden, was working with the YWCA and SNCC.[15] Throughout the early 1960s, Hayden, like many whites in the student New Left, learned his politics through experience in the civil rights movement in the South. The year after his first associations with SNCC, Hayden drafted the Port Huron Statement, which became SDS's sociological imagination for the student generation:

> We are people of this generation, bred in at least modest comfort, housed now in universities, looking uncomfortably to the world we inherit. . . . When we were kids the United States was the wealthiest and strongest country in the world; the only one with the atom bomb, the least scarred by modern war, an initiator of the United Nations that we thought would distribute Western influence through the world. Freedom and equality for each individual, government of, by, and for the people— these American Values we found good, principles by which we could live as men. Many of us began maturing in complacency. . . . As we grew, however, our comfort was penetrated by events too troubling to dismiss.[16]

First among those troubling events was the discovery of racial bigotry in the American South. Though, obviously, the Port Huron Statement was written by, and for, predominately white students in the elite colleges and universities outside the South, it was influenced by the events in the civil rights movement.

The post–World War II civil rights movement soon, however, took another turn, influenced, again, by Third World intellectual and political philosophies. In 1961, Frantz Fanon—a native of Martinique, a French-trained psychiatrist practicing in Africa—wrote *The Wretched of the Earth,* one of a growing number of social theories of the black, decolonizing revolution that were increasingly read in Europe and the United States. Though he was cultural light-years from the world of C. Wright Mills and the SDS students, Fanon wrote with sociological imagination of the issues that explain the troubles of colonial subjects in rebellion:

> Decolonization never takes place unnoticed, for it influences individuals and modifies them fundamentally. It transforms spectators crushed with their inessentiality into privileged actors, with the grandiose glare of history's floodlights upon them. . . . Decolonization is the veritable creation of new men. But this creation owes nothing of its legitimacy to any supernatural power; the "thing" which has been colonized becomes man during the same process by which it frees itself. . . . In decolonization, there is therefore the need of a complete calling in question of the colonial situation.[17]

There could hardly be a more perfect application of Mills's ideal of joining reflexive biography to the critical history of social structures.

Thinking like Fanon's soon came back to the Euro-American world. By 1965–1966, the nonviolent civil rights movements had collapsed, giving way to a new, more aggressive social theory of the world. SNCC kept its name, but changed its thinking as it liberated itself from the more integrationist philosophies of SCLC and the early civil rights movement. Thus began what today is called identity politics. SNCC in the mid-1960s now believed that

> Racism has functioned as a type of white nationalism when dealing with black people. We all know the habit that this has created throughout the world and particularly among nonwhite people in this country. . . . Therefore any re-evaluation that we must make will, for the most part, deal with identification. Who are black people, what are black people, what is their relationship to America and the world? . . . It must be repeated that the whole myth of "Negro citizenship," perpetuated by the white elite, has confused the thinking of radical and progressive blacks and whites in this country. The broad masses of black people react to American society in the same manner as colonial peoples react to the West in Africa, and Latin America, and had the same relationship—that of the colonized toward the colonizer.[18]

As Fanon used sociological imagination to define the hope of the colonized, so SNCC and other Black revolutionaries applied Fanon, and theorists of the colonial situation, to the European and American situations.

In 1967, for example, C.L.R. James (a native of colonial Trinidad, writing at the time in London) described Stokely Carmichael—the inventor of the slogan "Black Power" and the most conspicuous SNCC leader in the U.S.—as the leader of the latest wave of Black world leaders:

> We must see Fanon as the political activist and writer who is saying that now we have actually achieved independence we have to fight against not only the old imperialism creeping back: we have to carry on a desperate all-out struggle against those native leaders who may have fought for independence. . . . We do not see Fanon correctly if we do not see him as a natural development after what [George] Padmore represented, and Padmore as the political stage of the wide avenue opened by Du Bois and Marcus Garvey. . . . It is only now that we are able to see what Stokely and the advocates of Black Power represent. They stand on the shoulder of their ancestors. . . . Too many people see Black Power and its advocates as some sort of portent, a sudden apparition, as some racist eruption from the depths of black oppression and black backwardness. It is nothing of the kind. It represents the high peak of thought on the Negro question which has been going on for over half a century.[19]

Then, in 1969, in another turn of social theoretical events, the Black Panther Party Platform, one of the most radical expressions of Black power, reversed the course of decolonizing thinking in an outrageous concluding declaration:

> Prudence, indeed, will dictate that governments long established should not be changed for light or transient causes; and, accordingly, all experience hath shown, that mankind are more disposed to suffer, while evils are sufferable, than to right themselves by abolishing the forms to which they are accustomed. But, when a long train of abuses and usurpations, pursuing invariably the same object, evinces a design

to reduce them under absolute despotism, it is their right, it is their duty, to throw off
such government, and to provide new guards for their future security.[20]

In the same year, at Woodstock, Jimi Hendrix performed with similar irony
his unforgettably eerie rendition of the American national anthem. Thus, it
could be said that by 1969 this one line of practical sociological imagination
had come full circle—from Judeo-Christian values to Gandhi to SCLC to
SNCC to the theorists of decolonization in Africa and the Caribbean to Black
power in the U.S. to a new wave of Pan-African thinking to the Black
Panthers, who used the American Declaration of Independence to attack the
American state, then still the symbol of Western culture's world power.

This was but one of many lines of thinking and action along which those
upon whose backs the West was built were turning things around. It was political rebellion, certainly, but much more. Social thought on the world's mar-
gins was turning European and American culture inside-out, upside-down. In
that decade, sociological thinking of the sort imagined by Mills and later by
Gouldner had already become a worldly practice rooted in wave after wave of
liberation movements everywhere in the world. But what neither they nor
other professional sociologists who thought as they did were able to imagine
was what few of them could have foreseen in those days.

By the end of the 1960s, the world was on the verge of changes in the very
nature of things social. Feminisms and gay-lesbian political movements, then
just emerging, would become major cultural forces in Euro-American public
and intellectual life. Marxism, then riding high, would eventually collapse as a
political force and recede as an influential social theory. The Cold War, still
the major preoccupation of Western politics, would end. Europe and the
Pacific Basin, then still economically weakened by war, would rise to challenge
the United States. World politics, then neatly organized between core and peripheral players, would become the oddly defined field of uncertain forces it is
today. State powers, then dominant in the West and expectant in Africa and
Asia, would shrivel before the renewed power of ethnic loyalties and other
forms of identity politics. Technology and drugs, the oddly coupled sources of
new consciousness in the sixties, would become sources of violence and dete-
rioration in villages and cities where weapons and beepers defend and sell the
drugs that kill. World health, then considered improving and a near attainable
human right, now is threatened by worldwide epidemics of violence, AIDS,
starvation, and homelessness.

These, and more, combined—churning somewhere in the deep structures
of modern life—are part of the crisis that came and comes, still. Not all is bad,
though much is. The important thing is that there is every good reason, now,
to think that the world as such is somehow put together (if it is put together at

all) in a way different from what was considered normal for the several centuries prior to the events that unfolded in the 1960s.

In 1960, when John F. Kennedy was elected president of the United States, there was, for many, more reason than ever to think of the twentieth as the American century. By 1968, Lyndon B. Johnson, trapped between the war in Vietnam and political rebellion at home, repeated again and again, "Come let us reason together"—a far cry from Kennedy's "We can do better!" Today, more than a quarter-century later, there is no political leader anywhere who can say that with conviction. Were the truth told, few political leaders believe there is a "We" of sufficient coherence to hear an appeal to reason together. Where there is reasonable hope, if any, it is more likely in the sober vision of Czech president Václav Havel:

> Man's attitude to the world must be radically changed. We have to abandon the arrogant belief that the world is merely a puzzle to be solved, a machine with instructions for use waiting to be discovered, a body of information to be fed into a computer in the hope that, sooner or later it will spit out a universal solution. . . . The world today is a world in which generality, objectivity and universality are in crisis. . . . Sooner or later politics will be faced with the task of a new, postmodern face. A politician must become a person again, someone who trusts not only a scientific representation and analysis of the world, but also the world itself. He must believe not only in sociological statistics, but also in real people. He must trust not only an objective interpretation of reality, but also his own soul; not only an adopted ideology, but also his own thoughts; not only the summary reports he receives each morning, but also his own feeling.[21]

The crisis, as Havel sees it, presents itself through the simple, moral measures he describes.

World crisis may first appear in dramatic, bloody manifestations—as it did for Havel in his youth when the Soviet tanks rolled into Prague in 1968, as it did for others elsewhere torn by bombs and police dogs. It may lead through prison—as it did for Havel, Nelson Mandela, and untold thousands of students and poor people in Africa, Latin America, the American South, China, and the former East bloc nations. If in the end, however, crisis crosses whatever warp keeps the different from the familiar, then it is possible that a world thus transformed can be recognized for what it is only by such simple gestures as those Havel proposes. Since it has been a very, very long time since any world change comparable to the one some think is now occurring, it is by definition true that none of us has any direct experience of any such thing. Knowing what that changed world might be would thus require, if not speculation, trust—less in the statistics, more in the world one feels and imagines.

This too entails a form of sociological imagination, but one that somehow lets in the unkind proposition that whatever is to be might not be what we had been taught to expect and, therefore, now desire.

▼ ▼ ▼ ▼ ▼

Whatever the future may offer, if and when the crisis passes, its promises will not be divined from the knowable past. The hour for revising earlier ideas or romanticizing a prior golden age is long past. It is possible, however, to benefit from the spirit that Mills and Gouldner, and much later Havel, embodied: *Think and feel, hard and honestly, about the world as it is, and our place in it.* But obviously this entails, as Gouldner put it, a transformation of the deeper sensibilities, including those determining how and what we feel and do no less than how we think. If such a transformation in our deepest personal faculties is indeed required, then it is required because the deeper structures of the world as such have changed.

Thus, many of those a generation ago who participated in, and reflected upon, the early social and political movements that may have brought us to this end were not in a position to see the world as it has become. Martin Luther King Jr. never dreamed that the racial divide would be worse, not better. Few in the early student movement would have predicted that their children would adhere more, not less, vainly to the hope that a college degree would save one's economic life. Frantz Fanon could not have supposed that the new humanity decolonizing the world in his day would be cut down in such great numbers by disease, starvation, and civil wars. Stokely Carmichael and the early feminist and gay or lesbian proponents of identity politics knew there would be resistance, but probably not that the cultural battle lines would be drawn so harshly. The Black Panthers might not have imagined that American state power would wither into the present spectacle of military brilliance cloaking economic confusion.

Nor, important to say, could C. Wright Mills, Alvin Gouldner, and many of their readers have anticipated that, as right as they were about the importance of sociology in practical life, they could be wrong about the sociological assumptions they took from the professional science to which they were still loyal. Behind their respective visions of the sociological imagination lay the classic sociological ideas that, somehow, the world works in a definite, logical way: If, as the formula goes, the social world is a series of big, enduring structures—markets, polities, nation-states, class systems, and the like—then (one concludes) the human individual was somehow outside and against these big structures. For them, given this logic, the individual moves toward greater power in social life if he or she rethinks the relation between those structures and the individual life. Knowledge, including sociological knowledge, was still the source of the imagination that would liberate.

It is not so much that such a logic is inherently wrong, and certainly not that knowledge of the sort Mills and so many others imagined is useless to the desired end. Rather, it may be that the world is differently structured. It may be, now, that the world cannot any longer be well apprehended *if* one thinks of it as a series of big structured things against the little person. This is where those who think like Václav Havel may think the world differently, perhaps more accurately. His view, at its best, is not that we must give up on the world but that we should give up on certain, traditional *ideas* of the world—in particular all those ideas that teach us to imagine it as though it were, if not seamless, at least sutured under the surface by a common and universal thread.

Were Havel, and others who think as he does, right in this supposition, then the effect of it on sociology would be powerful—to some devastating, to others interesting. It would mean, at the least, that sociologists would be on less certain ground when they suppose that the task of the sociological imagination—whether practical or professional—is to weave the thread of knowledge into a universal whole of some kind. Sociology, then, would be more, and something other, than the act of the enlightened (perhaps engaged) moral subject capturing (perhaps judging) the truth of big, objective structures. That there are huge structured things crucial to what we call society is beyond dispute. That, simultaneously, there are different and unique individuals and social groups nurtured or hurt by those structures is also beyond reasonable argument. The question, however, is a prior one.

What, if any, might be the nature of the relations between and among social things? And how, if at all, can they be known? These, more or less, are the questions with which the high modern world began in the eighteenth century. For a long while, there had been a broad, seemingly universal, accord that the answers were readily knowable if not absolutely known. But that broad accord, such as it was, relied to a surprising degree on a set of global political and economic arrangements that, in turn, supported the moral culture that encouraged the accord. When such arrangements change, the culture associated with them loses at least some of its universal appeal. It has. Then also, the moral accord on which we base our assumptions about how the world is constituted, and can be known, very likely meets frustrating, and surprisingly vocal, opposition. It has.

Thus, finally, *if* there is reason to entertain any of these propositions, then sociology will want to consider them. This, after all, is the business of sociology. That its original assumptions may be open to current doubt does not mean that it is any less responsible to its vocation: to figure out the social world that is, then to tell others about it.

Chapter 2

Sociology as Theories of Lost Worlds

I T ALL BEGAN WITH the first storyteller of the tribe." So said Italo Calvino speaking of men, storytelling, and the moral reponsibilities of daily life. He continued:

> Men were already exchanging articulate sounds, referring to the practical needs of their daily lives. Dialogue was already in existence, and so were the rules that it was forced to follow. This was the life of the tribe, a very complex set of rules on which every action and every situation had to be based. The number of words was limited, and, faced with the multiform world and its countless things, men defended themselves by inventing a finite number of sounds combined in various ways. Modes of behavior, customs, and gestures too were what they were and none other, constantly repeated while harvesting coconuts or scavenging for wild roots, while hunting lions or buffalo, marrying in order to create new bonds of relationship outside the clan, or at the first moments of life, or at death. And the more limited were the choices of phrase or behavior, the more complex the rules of language or custom were forced to become in order to master an ever-increasing variety of situations. The extreme poverty of ideas about the world then available to man was matched by a detailed all-embracing code of rules.[1]

Thus began practical sociology in an attempt to overcome an original poverty of ideas about the world.

Sociologies, having thus begun, are proper to an imaginary space between real worlds such as they are and those lost sometime in a past. Sociologies, both practical and professional, were (but may no longer be) the struggle of men (in all the meanings of the word, acknowledged and suppressed) to rid themselves of the choking effect of rules. Certainly, from its first beginnings in modern culture, especially in the late nineteenth century, professional sociology has been similarly preoccupied with these dilemmas of the human condition.

Italo Calvino's remarks were first delivered as a talk in Turin, Italy, in 1967 just when European and North American cities were on the verge of the most massive, and widespread, political and cultural turmoil to break out since World War II. His words are the sociological observations of a man who, though not a professional sociologist, posed the right questions. Calvino, a writer, lived by the imagination. What allowed him, at a time of pending crises in the West, and without professional qualifications, to imagine so precisely the reality of sociology?

▼ ▼ ▼ ▼ ▼

Twenty-five years later, in late 1992, on one of his last days as president of the United States, George Bush spoke at Texas A&M University. As retiring world leaders have every right to do, Mr. Bush told the story of his presidency. The speech was, in effect, an informal sociology of the world during his lifetime. Though less elegant in scope and style, Mr. Bush's speech was in its way like Calvino's. What appeared unusual about Bush's sociology, if I may continue to put it this way, was that it was the social theory of a lost world, of the world order that many had come to believe had passed away, or was, at least, in some difficult last stage of its life. In fact, President Bush's story, in being a passable sociology of his times, was a story many others could have told in their way:

> In thirty-six days I'll hand over the stewardship of this great nation, capping a career in public service that began fifty years ago in wartime skies over the Pacific. And our country won that great contest but entered an uneasy peace. You see, the fires of World War II cooled into a longer cold war, and one that froze the world into two opposing camps: on the one side, America and its allies—and on the other, the forces of freedom, thus, against an alien ideology that cast its shadow over every American.[2]

This story was not easily told. In these first lines Mr. Bush slipped on a badly tangled metaphor. From the fire of real war the world cooled into a cold that froze the opposing camps: "on the one side, America and its allies—and on the other, the forces of freedom"! At first, one supposes the confusion is nothing more than Mr. Bush's chronic trouble with spoken English. But the speech itself is about a confusing turn of events. Not many, however high or low their office, know how to tell it straight. How, indeed, does one account for the end of the Cold War without using the language of Cold War?

Though a president, Mr. Bush spoke with the difficulty most people experience when describing a changing world. In his case, it was hard to say which was the side of freedom—America and its allies? the dark alien ideology? The political facts of the collapse of the Soviet Union were, indeed, that the "forces of freedom" (Boris Yeltsin's standing against the tanks in the summer of 1991) had brought down the Communist Party (at least for a time). But, in the story as customarily told and known to Bush, Yeltsin had been, strictly speaking, in the other camp. The most essential principle of Cold War social theory was that America was the force of freedom. To make narrative matters worse, Bush had then to explain how, precisely, this force for freedom, now exhibited on the other side, had come to assert itself out from under the dark shadows of an alien ideology. If such a force is real in human history, then—by its own logic—it must be either natural to all human creatures or, somehow, distinctly American. If the former, then the collapse of communism is readily explained. If the latter, then it is not. Bush, the last of the cold warriors, obviously believed the latter. A few paragraphs after opening, he said:

> My thesis is a simple one: Amid the triumph and the tumult of the recent past, one truth rings out more clearly than ever. America remains today what Lincoln said it was more than a century ago: the last best hope of Man on Earth.

But, if America is indeed the world's last best hope, how could freedom have sprung robust in Moscow against the tanks in late August 1991?

Bush was telling his story of a world that had just lost a long-standing claim to reality. But that world was already lost to reality by the time Bush gave his speech. It would be wrong, therefore, to hold it against him or anyone else who could not make complete sense of it. When telling the story of one's world anyone can come up against this problem. Whatever is, or was, real is seldom precisely comfortable within the terms of the story.

▼ ▼ ▼ ▼ ▼

Sociologies, it could be said, are stories people tell about what they have figured out about their experiences in social life. This is the most basic sense in which sociology is always an act of the imagination.

What distinguishes a sociology from other endeavors to imagine the meaning of human life is that a sociology, whether practical or professional, intends to give special attention to the social. As a result, the first problem a sociology encounters is that the general object of its attentions is nearly impossible to define, mostly because it lacks a readily observable set of things to which a definition might refer. The social is different in this respect from, for example, that which serves as the object of specialized interest to a psychology. Even when psychologists disagree on the proper name for their defining field of objects—brain, learning, mind, behavior, cognition, human development, the unconscious—they are able to indicate some object more or less readily imaginable because it is felt to be palpably concrete. I may not understand much of what a professional psychology means to say about the biochemistry of brain physiology, but I have little trouble imagining what a brain is and what, in principle, its neurology might be about. Neither the word "social" nor its cognate, "society," inspires the same degree of confidence in the commonsense imagination. Ironically, this very fact makes the field of social life to which a sociology pays attention even more a reality reliant on the imagination. There are thinkers who consider this an inherent weakness of the enterprise, but such a view is ungenerous.[3] One cannot anymore hold a sociology to account for the inherently uncertain nature of its object than an astrophysics for the far more impetuous uncertainty of its. No one ever actually sees those bright, distant, dead stars. A sociology, likewise, need not be embarrassed by the greater definiteness of other fields.

This is not to say that attempts to understand and describe society, or the social, are practices lacking a serious attitude toward reality. A very great deal of reality, social and otherwise, subsists mostly in the imagination (and some realities, such as the power of lost fathers, only exist there). Everyone knows, beyond much reasonable doubt, that there is a sphere of social things out there that affects human life in powerful ways. Whatever we may call them, these social things are usually considered more immediate forces than, say, those that owe to the alignment of stars warped in distant times and spaces. From this view, a sociology, while deficient in respect to its definiteness, is enriched by its association with important and powerful aspects of the human environment.

Society, one could say, is that layer of our environment which uneasily settles the area just beyond the limits of what humans are able to know with their ordinary senses. "Society," accordingly, is not anything we can feel, smell, touch, see, or hear—at least not directly. Yet, we can think it, talk about it, and use it—and its gross constituent parts—in order to explain the lives we and others lead. How and why, for example, such strange, but normal, social practices as breakfast? How, were we to figure it out, could breakfast make sense without the social arrangements we never see that bring some of us each day our daily bread?—to say nothing of those ancient rules lost in time that imposed the fast broken arbitrarily at dawn? In this still quite abstract sense, society is not, after all, that much different from, once again, the brain. For it is not, of course, the mass of brain tissue kept viable in saline solution that is definite to a psychology. Brain tissue can be the general object of a psychology only to the extent that psychologists imbue it with scientific significance by means of coherent talk about its (presumably causal) relations to learning or perception. So, society (however much less definite a thing it is) is a meaningful resource for explanation only when, through a series of sometimes complicated procedures, it is made to bear a relation to those phenomena ordinary persons can truly sense, directly.

A sociology is, perhaps, somewhat more like an economics that stipulates what is commonly called a "market" as the general name for its field of significant objects. Such a market is said to provide the nurturing environment in which prices rise and fall in some relation to the supply and demand, of and for, commodities. In this sense, an economist's "market" is little different from a sociologist's "society"—neither in itself is a particularly concrete thing; both, thereby, work primarily in the imagination.[4] Yet, an economics, while lacking the advantages of a more concrete neurophysiology of the brain, still has the upper hand over a sociology. While the economist's market is unlike any real market in which, face-to-face, people negotiate prices for valuable goods, it is still a sphere of social life ordinarily encountered each day one pays the current price for red peppers or regular, unleaded fuel. By contrast, even though most people encounter, on the same daily basis, indications of the prestige others do or do not attribute to them, somehow such a societal mechanism is felt to be less concrete. A sociology is very well able to describe the relation between an individual's social status and the complicated system of statuses by which a society somehow determines who gets which status for how long and why. This system, additionally, can be discussed in relation to other socially structured things such as the structures defining occupations, incomes, values, and class differences. But none of these larger societal things is generally considered to be as directly related to ordinary life and experience as are the market structures determining prices. We are not soon likely to witness a segment of the evening television news reporting the daily composite index of social prestige rankings. We do, however, get precise, numerical, and regular reports on the cost-of-living index and stock market values of selected industrials, usually just before the sports scores and weather reports.

In many ways this is a surprising fact. The amount of prestige accorded us in society affects our lives every bit as much as do prices, and much more than the weather or football results. One day, suddenly, for no apparent reason, those whose opinions of us were taken for granted rise to greet us with surprising enthusiasm, or, they remain inexplicably silent upon our entry. Are not such measures of the daily rise or fall of one's prestige vitally important to the individual? Does not one's prestige determine in a most fundamental way one's ability to afford the costs of life? Is it not well known that the poor, having little prestige, pay more, not less, for their daily bread? Yet, such social things as prestige are usually not considered to be as real as economic things. Similarly, though all known theories of economic markets are every bit as reliant on the tutored imagination, a sociology is considered the less real or less concrete activity. In this respect, it is most like history, which has no definite field of objects (unless one wants to refer to time, which, by contrast, makes market and society seem as concrete as brain tissue). Histories, however, are seldom subjected to public scorn as are economic or social theories. It is probable that the public's willingness to allow histories this relative immunity from close scrutiny owes to a general recognition that we require a healthy supply of meaningful stories about our pasts.

▼ ▼ ▼ ▼ ▼

Whatever may be the differences among the activities by which humans interpret their worlds to themselves, there is one important habit of nomenclature practiced commonly, if not universally. Many, if not all, types of human knowledge tend to use the same term to define those features of reality that most abstractly account for their better organized and evidently distinct spheres. With rare exception these are called *structures*. In some psychologies, the brain may be taken as the mass of structures in relation to which mental life is supposed to make sense. In most economic theories a market of some kind serves an analogous purpose. Thus, in a sociology, society is the imagined mass of structures without which a great deal of group life would make no sense. Much the same is said of the far less certainly structured relations in interstellar space-time that make qualified sense of what is usually called the universe.

When they are used to organize what is said about the meaning of social, natural, and most physical events, structures have the following qualities:

1. Structures endure over time.[5]
2. They are thought of as salient—that is, if not actually big, at least powerful in relation to that which they structure.
3. Their salience is commonly considered a consequence of their capacity to endure over time; thus, durability is a normal way of describing the reality of structures.

4. Yet, enduring structures are seldom directly observable in their entirety; and, they are never fully *present.*[6]
5. Structures, therefore, tend (usually if not always) to be products of the human imagination.[7]
6. Finally, as a corollary of the preceding, the reality of structures is always a discursive fact; that is, structures lack concrete significance until we say something about them—in talk, writing, or other forms of communication about the nature of such things in themselves.[8]

In short, among social things structures are never present—neither in time nor being. Neither markets nor societies nor anything of this kind is visible as such. The reality of social structures, insofar as it can be grasped, is in what is said about them.

Thus considered, sociologies are unavoidably theoretical. Being necessarily concerned with structures, sociologies are the activities whereby the structures of worlds lost to immediate consciousness are made tentatively real. Whatever evidence sociologies may refer to (no matter how technical or informal) makes sense only when someone tells it in some kind of a story. Even "s = 1/i" and other formal statements make scientific sense only when the story they condense is told.[9] Sociologies, thus, are much like histories, with one important difference. Historical imagination reconstructs the past. The structured worlds of which histories speak are lost in the sense that, even when a history is told for the purpose of criticizing or explaining the present (or giving direction to a future), the story (by agreement) is of that which transpired in a definite past time. Sociologies, by contrast, purport to tell the stories of social worlds as they are, presently. Among professional sociologists, this is the usual reason given for distinguishing between sociology and the two fields with which it shares the most in common, history and anthropology. But if one steps outside the circle of academic interests, it becomes plain that the distinction is not remarkable, for one fundamental and unavoidable reason.

All attempts to explain with reference to a structure are, necessarily, reconstructions of worlds that may or may not any longer be present. This is most especially true in astrophysics, where the described structural relations are often of worlds long since dead. It is obviously true of histories and anthropologies, but also of sociologies whose structures persist in present time as only the considered talk of those who imagine them. No socially structured thing can be observed as such in its present. Or, it might be said, sociologies seek to distinguish themselves from other forms of social knowledge by the not entirely unreasonable practice of thinking of their structures as structures-presenting-themselves in the present.[10] It is reasonable to think this way only with a sense of humor in the face of the ironic fact that there is no other way to think of enduring social structures.

Sociologies, for example, discuss the family as though it were a definite and stable structure. Yet, there is every reason to believe that the family most often talked about in discussions of such issues as family values is a structure that exists in the present at best precariously. In the United States, the two-parent-(of-different-genders)-plus-a-variable-number-of-children-but-no-other-kin-(not to mention: living-together-and-at-least-minimally-sheltered)-family is far from the norm. Whatever the kin structure in American society *is,* if there is one, it is unlike the imagined structure. It is possible, historically, that such a structure, if it ever was *the* family structure for industrialized societies, may actually have been normal for a very short time only in the years immediately following World War II. Today, among persons living in domestic units of some kind, scarcely half are in families of this sort, and the number is shrinking rapidly, especially among Blacks.[11] How many of today's domestic arrangements might be called a family without doing violence to what is normally meant by the term is another question still. In what sense, for example, is a typical lesbian-headed household with children an "American family"? What is to be made of the fact that one of the newest, most rapidly growing "family" units is the never-married, single householder? Are unsheltered families still families in the "American" sense? We have no certain way to determine just what exactly is the demographic average family form. This is so partly because demographers rely on census reports often taken years before the sociologists have anything to say about the trend in family structures.

More to the point, this is so for sociologies of all kinds, because their social worlds are like the astronomer's universe—at best, virtual realities; at worst, ones dead years before. In some cases a sociology describes a world that has been destroyed, literally, of which one of professional sociology's contemporary classics, *The Urban Villagers,* is an example. The working-class neighborhood of Boston studied in this book was literally destroyed during the research—lost, in effect, to urban "redevelopment."[12] In other cases, like attempts to interpret the structure of family in the recent modern world, the uncertainty of the world is a methodological condition. But, in all instances where people, for whatever purposes, purport to tell the story of a social world, their only real reference can be to the virtual world in the story, whatever else they may tell themselves or others. Sociologies, therefore, are always theories of possibly, even probably, lost worlds. For all intents and purposes, wherever this kind of talk about structures takes place, the world is *at least* lost to the story itself. Social reality, in this sense, is always in the story. Former president George Bush's discursive dilemmas were, in this respect, part of his normal sociology.

▼ ▼ ▼ ▼ ▼

From the beginning even the best professional sociologists had to face, often against their wills, the perverse reality that all social worlds are lost. This is the way in which, in their earliest days, professional sociologies were attentive to practical ones.

Émile Durkheim (1858–1917) was the first professional sociologist, but not by any means the first sociologist. He was among the first to organize sociology as an academic field in the modern university. Practical sociology, in the sense of attempts to talk about the social world, was practiced throughout the modern era since at least the eighteenth century. But professional sociology did not come into being until quite late in modern times; not until after the modern research university was well organized in the United States and Europe beginning in the 1860s.[13] Though the first successfully institutionalized professional sociology was in the United States, at the University of Chicago in the 1890s, Durkheim's role in the organization of academic sociology was memorable because he provided the classic definition of the field. To this day, among academic sociologists, no definition of sociology's subject matter and object field is more compelling.

In 1894, in *The Rules of Sociological Method,* a small book written for the express purpose of organizing the scientific foundations of sociology, Durkheim first stated his famous definition of a *social fact* as

> [a] any way of acting, whether fixed or not, capable of exerting over the individual an external constraint; *or:* [b] which is general over the whole of a given society whilst having an existence of its own, independent of individual manifestations.[14]

The striking feature of Durkheim's definition that caused it to be remembered must have been that it served practical and professional sociology equally well. Durkheim himself was quick to say that he invented the concept social fact, thus defined, because a distinctively social type of fact was necessary if there was to be an academic field by the name of sociology. Though the term "sociology" had been widely used in France since the days of Henri de Saint-Simon (1760–1825) and Auguste Comte (1798–1859), neither of Durkheim's predecessors thought of sociology as a field of academic specialization.[15] It was Durkheim, more than anyone in Europe, who dedicated himself to making sociology a formal university science.[16] His definition served this purpose well. For sociology to be an academic science it needed to claim a special kind of fact, one "having an existence of its own, independent of its individual manifestations."

Three years after *Rules,* in 1897, Durkheim's next major book, *Suicide,* was published. This book was written in order to demonstrate the power of this definition, thus the salience of sociology itself, as he had advertized it in *Rules.* By applying his sociology to a human phenomenon that in common sense one might think of as an irrational act of the individual, Durkheim made a brilliant tactical strike against those who would resist the idea of sociology's distinctive scientific value. *Suicide* succeeded. For many, it remains today a model of careful empirical study, clever theoretical analysis, and respected accounts, not just of suicide but of the tragic effects modern society can have on people. *Rules* and *Suicide,* along with Durkheim's first book, *Division of Labor in Society* (1893), established Durkheim's reputation, which he soon converted into a position of prominence in Paris, where he taught, wrote, and led the famous Durkheimian school of sociology until his death in 1917. Except for the University of Chicago's Department of Sociology, no other school of sociology at the time had achieved so much public and academic success as Durkheim's.

But, unlike other of the great social theorists of the classical age—Karl Marx (1818–1883), Max Weber (1864–1920), Sigmund Freud (1856–1939)—there was little about Durkheim's personality or personal style that might explain his enduring importance as a sociologist. Though he took a courageous public position against the military in the Dreyfus affair and was a public figure of note in Third Republic France, neither he nor his writings were of the sort that would excite public imagination. There is little among Durkheim's writings to compare with the memorable public lectures of Weber on science and politics in Munich in 1918 or with Marx's 1848 *Manifesto of the Communist Party* or with Freud's numerous popular lectures on psychoanalysis. Though Durkheim's ideas were widely known and debated in France, it is hard to say why, at least at first reading. The explanation of this anomaly of Durkheim's public success over the years lies less with Durkheim than with sociology itself.

A sociology will not endure for very long, nor rise to public notice, if it fails to capture something important in popular experience. A sociology need not *be* popular. But, to endure, it must make compelling sense *in* public, even if ordinary people (so-called) do not read it. The first volume of Marx's *Capital* (1867) was infinitely more technical than his and Engels's 1848 *Manifesto* yet, reading them, one can readily see the sense common to both and thus appreciate how even those without expert knowledge of political economy could read (that is, get the point of) *Capital.* There is no known instance of a professional sociology, no matter how technical, achieving a durable recognition without first expressing something powerful in the collective lives of those about whom it claims to speak.

A most famous instance of this rule in the post–World War II era was the sociology of Talcott Parsons (1902–1979). Parsons's writings are nearly impossible even for the trained eye to read, objects of scorn to many fellow sociologists (notably Mills and Gouldner), abstract beyond words. Yet, the sociology of Parsons dominated a great deal of social science through the 1940s, 1950s, and well into the 1960s. Even today, hardly anyone who comments on social thought or popular culture in that era fails to mention Parsons.[17] Why? Certainly, among other reasons, because Parsons's academic sociology in the 1950s expressed the popular social hope that—after a half-century of war, holocaust, and economic crises—perhaps America had finally discovered the moral key to a world without conflict. Durkheim's success in the pre–World War I period, and his lasting importance, owes to a similar reason. Durkheim, like Parsons after him, believed in the possibility of the conflict-free society. Both wrote professional sociologies that, while seldom read outside scientific circles, could be read in ways that seemed to ring true to what people in society felt and wished. Those who think professionally about society are also men and women who go somewhere at the end of the day to live however they live with whomever, and to read the daily news; even to worry as we all do. Whatever membrane separates professional social science from ordinary life is at best semipermeable, if not downright sievelike. This is especially true of sociologies of all kinds.

Even Durkheim, whose professional life among the cultural elite of Paris in his day was seemingly well sheltered, knew well enough the personal troubles of people in France, Europe, and the modern world. At least, he had his own practical theory of those troubles. That theory, in its most elementary form, informed most of what he did, even the most technical of his scientific studies. Easily overlooked, Durkheim's practical sociology appears refracted already in the first part of his definition of a social fact as "[a] any way of acting . . . capable of exerting over the individual an external constraint." Like many modern people (in his day and ours), Durkheim felt society was a constraint on the individual. In this formal definition in his book on methodology, this belief is disguised—dressed up for presentation in his new science, which, he says at the end of *Rules,* ought to "renounce worldly success and take on the esoteric character which befits all science."[18] Yet, neither Durkheim himself nor his sociology ever renounced the world. His sociology meant to serve the moral needs of the world as he saw it. Even his idea of social fact served this mission.

The book Durkheim wrote in 1893, the year before *Rules,* was as much a moral philosophy as a sociology. Many years later, anyone reading *Division of*

Labor would be justifiably surprised that a book like *Rules* could follow so closely. This earlier book was his first, full sociology of the modern world. In it, Durkheim expressed his interest in social facts constraining the individual, but, in contrast to the definition of the year following, those facts were here understood explicitly as *moral* facts. In *Division of Labor,* interestingly, moral facts are a subject of concern not because they limit the individual but, just the opposite, because they *fail* to constrain individuals sufficiently well:

> It has been said with justice that morality—and by that must be understood, not only moral doctrines, but customs—is going through a real crisis. . . . Profound changes have been produced in the structure of our societies in a very short time; . . . *Our faith has been troubled; tradition has lost its sway; individual judgment has been freed from collective judgment.* But, on the other hand, the functions which have been disrupted in the course of the upheaval have not had the time to adjust themselves to one another; the new life which has emerged so suddenly has not been able to be completely organized and, above all, it has not been organized in a way to satisfy the need for justice which has grown more ardent in our hearts. If this be so, the remedy for the evil is not to seek to resuscitate traditions and practices which, no longer responding to present conditions of society, can only live an artificial, false existence. What we must do to relieve this anomie is to discover the means for making the organs which are still wasting themselves in discordant movements harmoniously concur by introducing into their relations more justice by more and more extenuating the external inequalities which are the source of the evil.[19]

From the very earliest of his writings to the end, Durkheim's sociology played deceptively on a loose, but definite, relation between things moral and things social. This was not by chance. He was the child of generations of Jewish rabbis who became a founder of sociology at the cost of renouncing the moral tradition of his origins.

From his first great book, *Division of Labor,* to *Elementary Forms of the Religious Life* (1912), his last, Durkheim was preoccupied with the problem found in the contradiction in his famous definition of social facts. The distinct facts of sociology were distinct in Durkheim's mind because the conviction of their generality arose from his (the individual's) experience of their constraining power. The definition in *Rules* seems merely to answer the question "What is a social fact?" But on closer reading of the famous definition (p. 20), one notices that it is in two parts, separated and linked by an "or." One might think of this "or" as a simple organizing connective were it not for the evidence, earlier in the chapter, that the famous definition unites much more than the two analytic components of a formal definition.

The definition of social facts serves double duty. On the surface, in its formality, it defines a science. But, nestled in the not immediately obvious tension between its two parts, the definition hides Durkheim's lifelong attempt to figure out the complicated relation between the moral life and the science of his modern world.[20] The social fact of Durkheim's definition of social facts is that, try as he might, he could not resist the constraining power of his practical morality on his scientific sociology. Earlier in the chapter in *Rules,* before he formalizes his definition, Durkheim makes a statement that merits more attention. Here he speaks of social facts more discursively, appealing, it seems, to the reader's practical, moral concerns:

> As an industrialist nothing prevents me from working with the processes and methods of the previous century, but if I do I will most certainly ruin myself. Even when in fact I can struggle free from these rules and successfully break them, it is never without being forced to fight against them. Even if in the end they are overcome, they make their constraining power sufficiently felt in the resistance that they afford. There is no innovator, even a fortunate one, whose ventures do not encounter opposition of this kind.
>
> Here, then, is a category of facts which present very special characteristics: they consist of manners of acting, thinking and feeling external to the individual, which are invested with a coercive power by virtue of which they exercise control over him. Consequently, since they consist of representations and actions, they cannot be confused with organic phenomena, nor with psychical phenomena, which have no existence save in and through the individual consciousness. They constitute a new species and to them must be exclusively assigned the term *social.*[21]

In this somewhat less formal attitude, Durkheim reveals himself—though surely without wanting to. It is evident that the formal definition, which concludes the chapter, is meant to be the one referenced and used in the science he is intent on inventing. But this long passage leaks meanings that are evidently there though not fully intended. A science of social facts that will shape the future is drawn from an informal ethical judgment of the changed and changing social world. The question implied, but not asked in so many words, is that of the constraint imposed by social facts on individuals: Is it good, or not? The answer turns entirely on the dilemma posed by the opposing forces of his science and his morality.

When they serve as the necessary foundation of Durkheim's science the constraining facts are unequivocally good. But, when Durkheim seeks to illustrate in a looser, more rhetorical style, he comes to the example of the most salient figure in classic social theories of the modern world, the industrialist. Like Marx's Mr. Moneybags (in *Capital*) and Weber's capitalist entrepreneur (in *Protestant Ethic and the Spirit of Capitalism*), Durkheim's industrialist is the figure of, and for, that social individual who both made and now represents the modern world itself. Marx thought of him as the greedy owner of capital, and Weber considered him the ascetic entrepreneur caught eventually in the cage of his own calculations. But Durkheim saw him in the industrialist, as the cultural hero embodying the moral dilemma, and hope, of modern man. For all intents and purposes, Durkheim ignored the difference between the industrialist and, himself, the prototypical sociologist: "Even when in fact I can struggle free from these rules and successfully break them, it is never without being forced to fight against them." Marx's capitalist does not struggle, and Weber's entrepreneur does nothing, in the end, but struggle. But Durkheim's modern man (like Calvino's) struggles to break free from rules. Thus, when Durkheim frees himself from the formal rules in order to illustrate in common language the beneficent constraints of social facts in daily life, he comes quickly to modern man himself struggling to be free from the fact of those same constraints.

At first, this is not surprising. Among the great classical social theorists, Durkheim's Enlightenment inheritance was the least contested. He was the direct descendent not just of Comte and Saint-Simon but of Montesquieu and Rousseau.[22] Durkheim's modern man, quite naturally, would be expected to struggle against the constraining rules. The industrialized man's moral purpose is, precisely, to free himself from the "opposition" of prior rules. This is the constraining force that in science is a good but in moral life is at least a dilemma. He said, to recall, in *Division of Labor:* "Our faith has been troubled; tradition has lost its sway; individual judgment has been freed from collective judgment." One year before *Rules,* the opposition of traditional rules was good in the complicated sense that its loss frees modern man too much. In *Rules,* constraint was good in an entirely different sense, that of the unambivalent virtue of the facts upon which his sociology depended.

The contradiction nestled in Durkheim's definition of social facts springs from its lair to run wild in his other works, earlier and later—*Division of Labor* and *Suicide.* Each, it can be shown, is a book built on misrecognitions of the very facts upon which it relies. Each in its way is good sociology to the ironic extent that it exceeds, or refutes, Durkheim's formal definition of professional sociology. Neither can be explained fully by recourse to such standard interpretive methods as the author's scientific logic because the misrecognitions in each are less a matter of error than of the necessary contradictions of a moral theory of modern man.

Durkheim published the first of these two books, *Division of Labor,* one hundred years exactly before George Bush, upon leaving the presidency, told his contradictory story of the end of the modern era. Durkheim, writing earlier in that era, was in the same unwitting predicament as Bush. Neither was able to resist the constraining facts of the modern world. Each had his theory of a lost world, theories that similarly fell short of the reality of which each spoke. Thus, both suffered not the indignity of error but the ordinary conditions of doing sociology.

Surprisingly, one of the normal ways people of all kinds exercise their sociological imagination is by regularly reading and discussing the classics. In the simplest of terms a classic text is one from a prior lost world that, for any number of reasons, continues to promote discussion well after its time is past.

Each of Durkheim's major books is considered a classic among one or another group of social theorists. For this reason, the books are read and reread—often less to extract direct scientific information than to root subsequent social theory in some tradition, usually in order to explain to one's own world of fellow theorists just who one thinks he or she is. The classics people read and talk about become part of their public identities.[23] Thus, reading the classics is an inherently conserving activity in which readers situate themselves in some relation to a tradition without which they would become less in some way. As a result, it is not only possible but likely that subsequent readers of classics will overlook what they are not looking for in the first place. Since, in addition, the writers of classics are themselves identified with a tradition (even if it is the tradition they are in the process of inventing), they too will be predisposed to "miss" something. Inevitably (perhaps necessarily), the circulation of ideas, including social theories, flows in and around what is unsaid.[24]

Durkheim's *Rules* and *Suicide,* for examples, are reread by theorists looking for an origin to certain traditions of scientific sociology. Those who cherish them are seldom inclined to reread *Division of Labor* with the same loyalty. Those who read *Division of Labor* are somewhat, but not considerably, more inclined to read *Elementary Forms of the Religious Life,* which today is considered an important classic for the study of culture, generally not an important subject to those who identify themselves with *Rules.*[25] And so on. The same is so with all great classic writers and their books. Some read the young Marx; others the mature one. Some read Freud on sex, others his drive theory, others his interpretation of dreams. Some read *Hamlet,* others *Much Ado About Nothing.* What is there depends on what one reads, which, in turn, usually depends on what the authors read and said or did not say.

To read all of Durkheim's classic books is, therefore, to take the risk of being astonished by what one might have assumed was there somewhere but turns out to be missing. Durkheim, the most important definer of professional sociology, neglected to provide an explicit, general theory of society. Though quick to define sociology's facts, and sure in his diagnosis of the dilemmas of modern society, Durkheim says relatively little about the general structural object comprising those facts and that dilemma—society itself.

One might not notice Durkheim's omission were it not for the fact that other of the classic writers—Weber in particular, Marx in his way, even Freud—occupied themselves with the invention of a general and explicit theory of society. Some might say that the *Division of Labor in Society* was Durkheim's general theory of society. But his ideas on society in that book were either dropped or substantially revised almost immediately, even by the time he got to *Rules* the next year, certainly by the time of *Suicide* in 1897. It is true that *Suicide* is an implicit theory of the moral crisis of modern societies, and thus a continuation of the moral concerns of *Division of Labor*. But *Suicide,* as it turns out, is largely preoccupied with suicide rates, leaving to the imagination the general thing, society, that may under varying conditions be said to compel the act of self-murder. There is, however, something of a general theory of society in *Elementary Forms,* which is not entirely what it claims to be (a study of religion). *Elementary Forms* is at least as much a study of the social foundations of human knowledge. It is here, and only here, that the reader finds the thin outlines of a general theory of society, most memorably in the phrase that completes the logic of the definition of social facts: "Society is a reality *sui generis.*"[26] But what strikes most is the preemptory universality of the definition. It is drawn from analysis of the most elementary societies, applied therefrom to all others, including the modern—as if his studies of the 1890s describing the differences between traditional and modern societies no longer mattered. They did, of course. But still, there is something odd here in the fact that nearer the end of his life Durkheim, in his most bold and coherent book, could so readily think of society not just as the source of knowledge and culture but as the simple undifferentiated thing-in-itself for which the most elementary of totemic societies was a sufficient model.

How could he do this? Why was it necessary? The answers were already evident in his first book. In *Division of Labor* Durkheim first introduces his famous expression *collective conscience,* about which much is said because of its double meaning. Like the moral purposes nestled in his definition of facts, this expression enjoys a similar double play by virtue of the French term *conscience,* which covers the two meanings: moral conscience and consciousness—the former a moral quality, the latter a state of mind (in this case, a state of the collective mind). Thus: "The totality of beliefs and sentiments common to average citizens of the same society forms a determinate system which has its own life; one may call it the *collective* or *common conscience.*"[27]

After diagnosing the hidden in the definition of social facts in *Rules,* one is rightly suspicious of this definition in *Division of Labor.* Its first phrase is the language of the science to be defined (a rhetorical reversal of the pattern in *Rules*). Here Durkheim writes of the power of beliefs and sentiments *as though* the collective conscience were common to all societies without regard to their historical variations. As it turned out, it was not. This loss (his "loss of faith") is the moral theme of *Division of Labor.* The phrase, along with the suspicion it evokes, is entirely convenient to Durkheim's study of the differences between two historic forms of social organization that, in their differences, put at issue the status of the collective mind—most particularly, whether the collective mind, moral and conscious, is common. This, in fact, is the crisis of which Durkheim spoke at the end of the book, and the crisis best known by his most famous concept, *anomie.*

In *Division of Labor,* Durkheim's *society* occurs in two, distinct forms: The traditional is mechanical; the modern is organic. By the former Durkheim meant to suggest the more elementary or primitive societies in which the social consciousness is common, simple, undifferentiated—hence, like mechanical parts, fixed in their relations or, in Calvino's words, defined by an "all-embracing code of rules." By the latter societal form, he meant modern societies in which the advanced state of the division of social labor creates a different type of collective life—one in which the solidarity among the parts is organic in the sense that various parts of biological bodies enrich the bodily whole by their different functional gifts. The idea of the modern society as organic is clearly meant to describe the reality of social differences arising when the original collective life with its powerful common conscience gives way to the modern division of social labor.

It could be said that Durkheim's *Division of Labor* is a social theory of social differences, which, in a sense, was the subject of all classic modern sociologies. In the culture of the late nineteenth century, social differences were principally understood as class differences with which European societies, especially France, had struggled politically throughout the century. Then, differences due to race, gender, sexual orientation, or colonial life were, for the most part, not thought through, certainly not as they are today. With Durkheim, thus, that the more mechanical societies of his day were almost exclusively non-white and non-European and were in many cases colonized goes without mention. When, at the end of *Division of Labor,* he bemoaned the loss of traditional faith, Durkheim clearly had in mind not the traditional life of the most elemental societies but Europe and France before the modern era, under the ancien régime. That the European dark ages might have come under the same, or different, social laws as the dark continents of Africa or Native America and aboriginal Australia (from which he drew his evidence in *Elementary Forms*) was not well considered. The dark past of *Division of Labor* was ancient Israel, but in *Elementary Forms* it was aboriginal Australia and North America.[28] The effect of an equation of false similarities is to erase the differences of race Durkheim does not see. Such blind spots in Durkheim's social vision were, like his doubled definition of social facts, less an error than a condition of his sociology.

Durkheim, thus, found himself in a most demanding, if not impossible, circumstance. He was required to explain social differences, the dominant structural fact of modern society, while under the moral constraint to explain away the evident reality of those differences. In other words, he was forced by the cultural logic of his times to resolve those differences, the reality of which he could not deny. His solution was to interpret class wars less as a social fact of modern life than as corruption of the modern division of labor.[29] Class divisions could not be a social fact, by his definition, because they most evidently disrupted that condition by which social facts were defined: the generality of constraining force. So long as there are class differences, the *sui generis* society cannot uniformly constrain its members. Durkheim, therefore, had to deal with differences of this kind, which he did with so much finesse that the reader might not at first detect the awkward moves required to protect the collective conscience in a divided society. For example:

> In sum, since mechanical solidarity progressively becomes enfeebled, life *properly social* must decrease or another solidarity must slowly come in to take the place of that which has gone. *The choice must be made.* In vain we shall contend that the collective conscience extends and grows stronger at the same time as that of individuals. . . . *Social progress, however, does not consist in a continual dissolution.* On the contrary, the more we advance, the more profoundly do societies reveal the sentiment of self and of unity. *There must, then, be some other social link* which produces this result; *this cannot be other than that which comes from the division of labor.*
>
> If, moreover, one recalls that even where it is most resistant, mechanical solidarity does not link men with the force as the division of labor, and that, moreover, it leaves outside its scope the major part of phenomena actually social, it will become still more evident that social solidarity tends to become exclusively organic. *It is the division of labor which, more and more, fills the role that was formerly filled by the common conscience.* It is the principal bond of social aggregates of the higher types.[30]

In this summary of the argument of *Division of Labor* it is apparent that Durkheim's moral vision—that is, the practical demands of his sociology—overwhelms his science.

Durkheim must, now, account for the salient differences structured into modern life without the very term by which society is defined, collective conscience. Thus, he must say what he must not have wanted to say, namely: that the division of labor "must" be that which the common conscience once was; or, roughly: that common social life in modern society is founded, somehow, in the nature of differences. This *must* be so because "social progress does not consist in continual dissolution."

But what is to made of this "must"? Everything! It is the necessary term that accounts for that which is missing. If there are social facts, there *must* be society. If social progress, there *must* be something to take the place of the collective conscience. Since modern society is divided (and the conscience cannot be truly common), that division of labor must now be the source of society. Durkheim's "must" poses as a logical corollary when, everyone knows, it is more a conjecture.[31] His "must" is the link to what one must turn to when evidence and reason are exhausted. "Le coeur a ses raisons que la raison ne connait point" (The heart has reasons which reason knows nothing of).[32] Durkheim's "must" stands at the limit of social facts. It is the clue to contradictions hidden away in an otherwise calm, progressive sociology. When, at the end, in *Elementary Forms*, Durkheim returns to the collective conscience, he returns in order to explain knowledge itself. There, in the book that drew its reasons from the logic of the most elementary social forms—the aboriginals of Australia and North America—that is, those societies that could not reasonably be said to be the traditional of Europe. In this last great book, Durkheim attributes all knowledge, including the proud and hopeful knowledge of modern man, to society. Society is the collective force from which derive the collective representations, which in turn account for the categories of human knowledge. But this neat formula relies on a prior refusal to see what is plain to see. This formulaic society, a *sui generis* reality, was most real not among his own European fathers but among those whose racial as well as social differences from white Europe were so evident that one failed to speak of them only when preoccupied by some greater moral task, such as inventing sociology in order to save modern progress.

It is apparent that in summing up his grand theory of knowledge, Durkheim, though unable to speak of them, still harbored dark thoughts about the unity of collective life, thoughts that were, again, displaced:

> In summing up, then, we *must* say that society is not at all the illogical or a-logical, incoherent and fantastic being which it has too often been considered. Quite to the contrary, the collective consciousness is the highest form of the *psychic life*, since it is the consciousness of the consciousness.[33]

But Durkheim, one can see, is too deeply implicated to extricate himself at the last. If society is the "highest form of psychic life," then is it not also "fantastic"? Durkheim's society is, in fact, a product of the "psychic life," thus of the imagination.[34]

Durkheim's sociology was a theory of lost—hence fantastic—worlds. He would have been horrified to contemplate that he of all people could not outrun so base and seemingly psychological a fantasy. It was against just this that he had wished to found his sociology. Durkheim had, however, set for himself, and sociology, an impossible task. Societies, though real in their effects, are also imaginary. Yet, in denying this fact, and much else, Durkheim was nothing less than a modern man—modern culture being that which struggles inconclusively with social differences.

Having broken with the rules of the first men, moderns like Émile Durkheim and George Bush find it difficult to tell their stories.

Chapter 3

Modernity's Riddle and Durkheim's Lost Fathers

MODERN CULTURE HAS ALWAYS WRAPPED itself around a riddle as though to hide that which it could neither avoid nor explain. Sociologies, having come into their own with special urgency in the modern era, are caught up in this dilemma of their native culture.

Near the end of *Monster: Autobiography of an L.A. Gang Member*, Sanyika Shakur, aka Monster Kody Scott, recounts the moment when he learned he was not who he had thought he was. The scene of his recollection is solitary confinement, the Hole, at Chino State Prison in California. Alone in the dark, forced to sleep on a concrete floor among the rats, Shakur remembers an earlier confinement when he was still a youthful offender.

On one of her regular visits to the youth detention center, his mother came in tears. Though he was already hardened to crime and violence, she spoke as a mother to her son: "Baby, I got something to tell you. Something you are old enough to know now." What she had to tell him was that the man he had thought was his father was not. Scott was not Kody's father. Suddenly Kody knew who he was not. He was not, for one, loved by this man he had been given to believe was his father. Scott had denied Kody any real affection and regularly excluded him from the deeper intimacies of the family circle. Now Kody knew why. His mother and Scott had divorced when Kody was a small boy, but memory of the rejections still hurt.

On that painful visit, his mother told Kody, aka Sanyika, that he was in fact the son of a famous sports personality who had refused to have anything to do with him. The baby Kody had been twice despised by the fathers who should have loved him—by Scott for the fact that Kody was the issue of an affair during an early break in the marriage; by his true biological father, who insisted only that he be aborted.

As the memory of his mother's visit fades, Shakur describes the Hole:

> I fell into a rough sleep and don't know how long I'd been out when someone started beating on the steel covering over the window in my door.
>
> "Get up," said the voice, distinctively American. "Get up!"
>
> Irritated by being awakened, and generally mad, I shouted back, "What, muthafucka, what?"
>
> "Hey, I got some paperwork for you to sign, Scott."
>
> "I ain't signin' shit, and my name ain't no fuckin' Scott!"
>
> Not only did I refuse to sign, I refused to talk anymore. Why? What else could they do to me if I didn't? I stretched my sheets out as best I could and tried to go back to sleep, but I couldn't. . . . As I lay there I could hear rats scurrying across the floor.[1]

If his name "ain't no fuckin' Scott," then who is he?

Little boys who lose their fathers are right to be mad. Long before they recognize who they are by accepting a name as theirs, children need at least to feel they belong in the world. Those deprived of that security must deal with the painful anger at their loss. Some, like Kody, grow into monsters. Others deny the pain and very often pretend that nothing in fact was lost. With notable exceptions, modern culture has been the latter kind of child.

In the simplest, most commonsensical, terms, to have an identity is to be able to recognize a rightful place for oneself in a social world. Though the alleged securities of premodern social life are overrated, at least then social life imposed a more certain sense of whomever one was considered to be, for better or worse. In traditional societies individual identities were locked more securely in a social place. Even when, as in the now famous case of *The Return of Martin Guerre*,[2] an individual sought to misrepresent himself among village people in traditional times, his true identity could not be hidden. In such a time, an imposter could not successfully pass as someone he was not. By contrast, one who presents a false identity in a more modern, urban world, where all are virtual strangers, can more readily cover a false identity (if at the terrible cost of social isolation). In the modern world, as Georg Simmel put it, the stranger is not "the wanderer who comes today and goes tomorrow, but rather the man who comes today and stays tomorrow—the potential wanderer, so to speak, who, although he has gone no further, has not quite got over the freedom of coming and going."[3]

In the late nineteenth century, when sociology was inventing itself as a profession as well as the practice of everyday life, there was a widespread fear that all would become strangers to one another and that the world had become one in which one's name counted for nothing, like Kody Scott's. Under such circumstances, wherever they prevail, a person is at risk of not knowing who he or she is. It is a common fate that our identities, which we very often consider something quite private within ourselves, are in fact dependent, in Blanche DuBois's famous line, on the kindness of strangers. Identities are social things.[4]

Among its many disruptions, the high modern world of the late nineteenth century disturbed the expectation that good, bourgeois people could count on their place in the world. Against their deepest wishes that it would be otherwise, they had to concede that what Marx called class struggle, and many others including Durkheim call the division of social labor, presented individuals of their kind with a world of differences. The world no longer invited them to think of themselves as securely fixed and good within it. Modernity was the culture that sought to solve this problem by its grand moral promise that human progress would in time give everyone his (!) place, his due sense of himself. Professional sociology was among those sectors of modern culture that encouraged this progressive hope.

Meanwhile, the practical sociological thinking of many others pressed the urgent question: *Who am I really, if so much of this world is so utterly different from what I had been taught to think I am?* It was a dilemma, a riddle, not entirely different from Kody Scott's. This existential riddle wore doggedly at the high purposes of professional sociology. It kept sociology in palpable, if generally unwanted, contact with the lost worlds that both inspired and frustrated the sociological imagination.

More than any of the classic social theorists, Émile Durkheim devoted himself to founding and defining *a* sociology that could become *the* sociology of modern life. With the possible exception of Max Weber, none of them was as temperamentally suited to the precise definition as a way of beginning endeavors of this kind. By contrast, Marx and Freud were too much interested in getting to the mysterious bottom of things to allow their conscious logic to be the foundational pillar of any project.

Thus, again, an irony: that among those still famous classic thinkers, the one who in his professional sociology most resisted the fantastic and the imaginary could not keep them out. Durkheim was, therefore, precisely correct (or correct enough) in his science. A sociology is, indeed, about facts that constrain the individual *even when* the individual resists them. There could be no sociology without them; of which there could be no better proof than Durkheim himself, who in his life as a professional sociologist wanted to be the one who proved there were social facts that did not rely for explanation on the individual. Yet, he was a practical enough moralist that he could not resist the constraining force of the moral riddle of modern life, which entails, among other things: *Modern societies are different from all others because, being divided themselves, difference is what makes them modern.* As science, modern sociologies were obliged, somehow, to explain difference with difference. As moral theory, modern sociologies had, somehow, to justify the good of difference as a (now) natural state of life. The riddle within the riddle was what to do with the different demands of science: *If science could produce the truth, then moral differences would fade; if, however, moral differences were taken with final seriousness, none would be true.* Difference, in other words, challenged the liberal, cultural foundations of modern life.

More, once again, than any other of the great nineteenth-century thinkers, Durkheim attempted to solve both sides of the riddle in one formula, beginning with his famous definition of social facts. Durkheim was, thereby, one of the most modern of the classically modern social theorists. Weber, by contrast, took the easier path of separating the science from the morality, only to find that they could not be kept apart if his sociology were to be subjectively adequate to real, moral men. Thus, both Weber's scientist and his moral man were caught in the drudgery of rational calculations, hoping for that which they could not calculate.[5] Marx, from the beginning in the 1840s, never tried to keep them apart, placing his science and his morality in a deferred, final resolution. He was, in one respect, the most formally classical of the four. Marx's modern man, having lost his original humanity in history, could regain it only at the end of history, for which modern capitalism alone among the historical forms of social division, its contradictions being so severe, could be the historical preparation for the revolutionary solution.[6] Even Freud, who among the four was the least comfortable within the terms of modern moral culture, could not resist the desire to found a science that could treat the original differences. Through the transferential relation of analyst and analysand, the simple remedy of freely associated (that is, unconstrained) speech was thought to cure the defenses against allowing the unconscious truths to enter the conscious life.[7]

Surprisingly, among these four, Durkheim and Freud sought the most similar solutions to modernity's riddle. While Marx turned his science into a practical ethic and Weber struggled vainly to keep science and values separate, Durkheim and Freud both invented a science they thought could cure the moral ills of modern man. Each specifically imagined the science he invented might heal modern man's constrained social existence. Each viewed modern man as separated from his original state of freedom—from preoedipal desire, in Freud's case; from the original collective conscience, in Durkheim's. Though Marx, in particular, shared this classically modernist theory of original loss, his solution was the mirror image of theirs from the point of view of the relation of science to morality. Freud and Durkheim both, in their ways, believed that science could provide the moral solutions. Marx envisioned a resolution of the lost, but desired, freedom in a pragmatics of the moral life—in history, not in science.

Yet, though both believed in the moral truth of science, Durkheim and Freud ultimately occupied the extreme opposite ends of the same theoretical space. Freud's was a science based on the proposition that everything that occurs to the conscious mind is, to some significant degree, a perversion of the deeper, more real, but less observable, truth of modern man's life. Durkheim, more the heir of Enlightenment hope, believed wrongly that everything real was more or less visible. To Durkheim this surely seemed the better, and only reasonable, attitude to take. Yet, unbeknownst to him, the effect of taking it required an unconscious move in order to make it real: For the real to be visible in a divided society, then the good *must* be *in* differences themselves, which could only, by consequence, mean that the good is in social progress. As he said in *Division of Labor,* "[If] social progress [is not to] consist in continual dissolution, . . . [then] the more we advance, the more profoundly do societies reveal the sentiment of self and of unity."[8]

Durkheim's was actually the preferred, liberal solution in the political and economic world of modern life. He was, thereby, not just the original sociologist but very nearly the prototypical modern man in his belief that social progress is the source of moral hope. This conviction, it turned out, had all the advantages one could want, save one. The end toward which progress moves cannot be infinitely deferred. Eventually, society must come back to the divisions in modern society in order morally to heal them and scientifically to explain them.

Durkheim's solution to the riddle did not succeed because it could not—either in his sociology or in his moral theory of modern life. He did no better, no worse, than the other classic social theorists. But the earnestness with which Durkheim held to his conviction that a new science could solve the riddle of modern life illustrates best of all the depths to which this riddle structured modern culture. *Modern societies are different from all others because, be-*

ing divided themselves, difference is what makes them modern. Durkheim, like many moderns, believed that the differences that make and shake the foundations of modern life were a new, more progressive form of common life. He understood that the social differences were just as salient in modern times as the collective conscience was for its time. Yet the puzzle was how to recover the latter's original social good in the modern division of labor. For Durkheim, as for many moderns, the solution was to stipulate future progress as the final standard for the good society. The silent contradiction in that standard was that it could only be one projected back to an original good lost to the present. In Durkheim's case, the price of a real—that is, present and good—society was the denial of its very condition of existence, its differences.

▼ ▼ ▼ ▼ ▼

There are many sociologies, practical and professional. But they all work, in some way, with the same question Durkheim asked behind his definition of social facts. What exactly is the relation between individuals and the constraining fact of society? At the beginning of *Suicide,* the book in which he tried to deal most forthrightly with that question, he put the issue this way: "There can be no sociology unless societies exist, and . . . societies cannot exist if there are only individuals."[9] At first, the logic seems compelling. But, as in the definition of sociology, the logic rests on an assumption that may not bear scrutiny. He defined a social fact as "any way of acting, whether fixed or not, capable of exerting over the individual an external constraint." But this cannot be so. Facts, normally understood, are not the constraining forces but the representations of them. There is, for example, an important difference between the social forces, whichever they are, that may constrain individuals to commit suicide and the facts that represent the occurrence of those forces. Thus, Durkheim says: "Indeed we must not forget that what we are studying is the social suicide-rate."[10] Strictly speaking, *Suicide* is, therefore, a study of suicide-rates, thus of social facts, not of suicide itself.

What is at work here is the effect of what Durkheim cannot talk about: society. It is society that constrains. But Durkheim is not able to speak directly about society, only about its representations, facts. Thus, this line from the passage at the beginning of *Suicide* makes sense only if one substitutes "society" for "sociology," thus producing the statement: "There can be no [society] unless societies exist, and . . . societies cannot exist if there are only individuals." Thus put, one sees immediately the importance of sociology in Durkheim's practical morality. Sociology—professional sociology, that is—is the key to everything. Without sociology, as he has defined it, Durkheim is limited, perhaps prohibited, from talking about the central moral issue of modern life.

What is the relation of individuals to society? He answers with a statement that makes sense *only* if professional academic sociology were the real thing constraining individuals, which it is not. When the statement's real meaning (so to speak) is uttered, it becomes nonsense. Obviously, it is only sociology that cannot exist if there are only individuals. The phrase "societies cannot exist if there are only individuals" may be true, but it makes sense, on its own, only as a moral question. Only an academic sociologist, or some similarly occupied social philosopher, would wonder about the analytic relation between such a thing as "society" and another, the "individual." The practical moral question of that relation is different altogether: Is it good that societies constrain individuals? And if so, why? This is the question asked, and answered, in *Suicide* and throughout his early writings, even when Durkheim thought he was asking the more scientific question.

Sociology is a science constrained, sometimes in spite of itself, to ask the moral question of the good entailed in the individual's relation to society. Even when a sociology tries, with motives as sincere as Durkheim's, to define its science on its own factual terms, it cannot because the facts of social life always necessarily refer back to the practical question. Indeed, there would be no value whatsoever in scientific sociology if the practical question did not first exist. The only good reason to have the science is if, in Durkheim's terms, a psychology of individuals is insufficient to an answer. It makes little practical difference whether there is or is not a realm of social life above what individuals see and feel in daily life *unless* there is a moral dilemma; that is, unless the constraint of those social things is, somehow, a problem for breathing and moving real individuals.

This, then, clarifies the two most general facts about sociology: (1) A sociology, even when it is a science, is first and foremost a practical, hence moral, activity; (2) sociologies do not become activities of any great urgency until individuals encounter the riddle of modern life, which can now be simply put: *If things social are different, then who am I?—that is, if my world is divided, where do I fit in?* The reason sociologies are theories of lost worlds is found in these two general facts.

If things social are different, then who am I? For all practical purposes, the question only arises in modern societies because only then and there is difference considered a structured (that is, enduring, hence salient) feature of social life. Were it the case that individuals lived in social relations they had no reason to consider different (or, as it is often said, Other), then very probably the need for a sociology would not arise. For only when the structured social life is different (both from the individual and in and of itself) is there any reason to worry, one way or another, about its constraining power. If the social world appears to be the same as oneself, then it can be more safely assumed that one knows who one is.

This would all be "mere" theory, as it is often said, were it not for the fact that, so far as it is known, all human individuals do at some time in their experience encounter those elemental social conditions in which the social is *not* felt to be different. One such experience is, of course, that of infancy and early childhood. The other is in later life when the individual, having been told the tales of his family and community, "remembers" what it was like in earlier, simpler times. The former is direct experience; the latter indirect. The two are linked directly in social experience. Individuals tell and hear, thus imagine, that they remember the stories of earlier times because they all experienced such an earlier, elementary time—a time when, in Durkheim's terms, the collective consciousness was, for all intents and purposes, the same as the individual's: not different, thus not modern. In this sense, we were all once, to use the awkward but necessary word, primitives.

In *There Are No Children Here*, Alex Kotlowitz tells the story of two boys trying to survive in one of Chicago's most dangerous public housing projects. Lafeyette, then age ten, said: "If I grow up, I want to be a bus driver." The "if" suggests one of the reasons Kotlowitz took the book's title from an observation by Lafeyette's mother: "But, you know, there are no children here. They've seen too much to be children."[11] Children whose lives are interdicted (one might say "constrained") by poverty, violence, and the threat of death are known to experience severe disruption in the normal and necessary patterns of childhood development.[12] When a child says, "If I grow up . . . ," he is, it might be said, expressing a social theory at too young an age. Normally, childhood is a time when the individual requires a familiar environment, similar to, if not entirely the same as, what he feels himself to be. Children deprived of such a time usually experience difficulties, often serious ones, as they grow. Lafeyette understood that the world in which he actually lived was different and hostile to his desires. Yet, he retained the child's capacity to dream. He understood the American dream of growing up and being something good, against which he had to pose an "if." Such a dream is normal, though its contents vary from culture to culture. All children eventually must leave that dreamworld sooner or later, by gentle or harsh transition.

Curiously, there are no children in most sociologies, and none at all in Durkheim's. Had it not been for Freud, there would have been few children at all among the classic social theorists.[13] But, it is clear why, except for those few in some of his suicide rates, Durkheim's sociology had no children. The child in his scheme would have been outside, before the social. The child was among those social things Durkheim could not have thought because of his view of man: "Man is double, that is because social man superimposes himself upon physical man." To which Durkheim adds immediately this astonishing remark:

> If this dissolves, if we no longer feel it in existence and action about and above us, what is social in us is deprived of all objective foundation. *All that remains is an artificial combination of illusory images, a phantasmagoria vanishing at the least reflection;* that is, nothing which can be a goal for our action. Yet, this social man is the essence of civilized man; he is the masterpiece of civilization. Thus we are bereft of reasons for existence; for the only life to which we could cling no longer corresponds to anything actual; the only existence still based upon reality no longer meets our needs.[14]

For Durkheim, sociologically speaking, there is nothing real outside the social because there is no individual without the social. Man is either social, or some rudimentary physical creature left to the phantasmagoria of pure imagination.

For Durkheim, the small preverbal child is not social, therefore not sociologically real. The idea is astonishing because the opposite could be just as true according to his theory. The small child is, in social fact, the individual most completely constrained by the social, beginning with the total social environment provided (in his middle-class European culture, surely) by that other social individual who, also, does not exist in his sociology: the mother-woman.

Here, Durkheim is faced with a particularly hard set of facts. Women exist. They certainly existed in his study of suicide rates. Yet, according to his implicit theory of society as the collective conscience, it is only man who is double, only man who is civilized. Woman exists, but she is not social. "[The] two sexes do not share equally in social life. Man is actively involved in it, while woman does little more than look on from a distance."[15] Though more social than the child, the woman (without whom, in real life, the child cannot be social) is similarly outside social life, thus outside Durkheim's sociology.

Woman, in particular, must be less than social. Otherwise, society, as Durkheim thought it, could not be what he imagined it to be. For society to be *the* thing in itself—to be sui generis, thus the social fact of sociology—society *must* be one of two things: Either society is integral, that is, one in and of itself as in the elementary collective conscience, or it is sufficiently one as in his vision of a progressively moral organic society. Durkheim's society, thereby, could not tolerate real, unyielding, constraining differences. Durkheim's sui generis society was, thus, the elementary society of the lost past of modern society. Modern society depended, in his view, entirely on the ability of modern life to progress to an organic unity in which the differences felt in such social divisions as class struggle would be overcome in a greater bodily unity of equal, if separate, contribution. Thus, similarily, he says, of woman:

> The female sex will not again become more similar to the male; on the contrary, we may foresee that it will become more different. But these differences will become of greater social use than in the past. Why, for instance, should not aesthetic functions become woman's as man, more and more absorbed by functions of utility, has to renounce them? Both sexes would thus approximate each other by their very differences. They would become socially equalized, but in different ways. And evolution does seem to be taking place in this direction.[16]

In modern life, the differences are overcome by functional equalities. In this case a woman has the aesthetic function, man the utilitarian. She makes the home and other things beautiful; he works and makes the world.

Thus the deep structural contradiction in Durkheim's sociology. He wants a sociology that will solve the riddle of modern life, one that overcomes differences while acknowledging them as real. But he cannot account for differences in society except by his unacknowledged leap of the imagination. Women, like class divisions, are not morally real. The differences they represent resolve themselves in social progress. But what is social progress? Nothing less than the achievement, in modern life, of that state of social consciousness which most nearly approximates the one now lost to consciousness, the elementary or primitive.

Durkheim's society was indeed a "phantasmagoria vanishing on the least reflection." However much he wanted it otherwise, Durkheim's theory of society was that of the social world lost to the present, recaptured in the hope of progress. But not real in the sense of being there, present. What was most real, for him and the social theorists, was a world divided by differences. Then, in Europe, differences of class. In the United States, this too, but also palpable differences of race. And, in both, differences between men and women.

▼ ▼ ▼ ▼ ▼

With all the best intentions, Durkheim was forced to discredit two historic figures, both of whom were salient in his life and his society. Without this move, his sociology would have failed. But his discrediting was not harsh. Both of them were given their place—one as the heroic figure of the modern primitive; the other as the sign of the primitive modern yet to be. These figures were the Jew and the woman. The one was the figure of his own lost childhood, the other of society's future perfect.

Among the accounts of Durkheim's early childhood is the following:

> David Émile Durkheim was born on 15 April 1858 at Épinal, capital town of the department of Vosges, in Lorraine. His father, Moïse Durkheim, had been the rabbi of Épinal since the 1830s and was Chief Rabbi of the Vosges and Haute-Marne; his grandfather, Israel David Durkheim, had been a rabbi in Mützig (Alsace), as also had his great-grandfather Simon Simon, appointed in 1784. His mother, Melanie *née* Isidor, was the daughter of a trader in beer (or horses). He grew up within the confines of a close-knit orthodox and traditional Jewish family, part of the long-established Jewish community of Alsace-Lorraine that was notable for providing France with many army officers and civil servants at the end of the nineteenth century. Durkheim, however, was destined for the rabbinate and his early education was directed to that end: he studied for a time at a rabbinical school. Yet he soon decided, while still a schoolboy, not to follow the family tradition.[17]

The collective conscience Durkheim knew as a child was that of Jewish life and law. He would not, however, have become a sociologist had he not renounced those traditions. This act may, or may not, have been the central drama of his early life. But it is unlikely to have been one whose effects were not powerful moral constraints on Durkheim the individual. In some important way, he became what he was because he had lost the collective conscience of his childhood, for which he sought a new morality in the science of modern life. But, Durkheim the child could not have been far away, ever.

Though Durkheim said nothing of his own childhood and little of children in his sociological writings, he said quite a lot about Jewish people and their traditions. In *Division of Labor,* for one striking example, the Jews were the basis for another of Durkheim's surprising omissions. The crucial technical feature of that book's argument was his use of laws as the visible index of the moral life of the two different forms of social life (a move made necessary by the significant fact that society "does not lend itself to exact observation nor indeed to measurement"[18]). He, thus, stipulated penal laws, which were repressive in their effect, as the observable indicator of mechanical societies. He was, in this regard, of the same mind as Calvino in thinking that the more primitive societies were rule organized, thus repressive of those who broke the mechanical form. Contrariwise, the more modern and organic societies, Durkheim thought, came into sight when the repressive rules of the most ancient societies made way for laws that served more to bind the separated members to the whole. These, of course, arose as the division of labor became more and more organic. Functionally separated members meant that no one member was bound to the common conscience directly, for which the corollary: In the more modern, organic society no individual could insult the social whole gravely. The modern man, thus, was less susceptible to repressive punishment (which Durkheim described as the repulsive gesture of the collective conscience in primitive societies). Accordingly, in organic societies, the rule of law served more and more to restitute the deviant member to the whole. In its most advanced form, contract law is the organic law par excellence. In Durkheim's own words in *Division of Labor,*

> Social life comes from a double source, the likeness of consciences and the division of social labor. The individual is socialized in the first case, because, *not having any real individuality, he becomes, with those whom he resembles, part of the same collective type*; in the second case, because, while having a physiognomy and a personal activity which distinguishes him from others, he depends upon them in the same measure that he is distinguished from them, and consequently upon the society which results from the union.
>
> The similitude of consciences gives rise to juridical rules which, with the threat of repressive measures, impose uniform beliefs and practices upon all. The more pronounced this is, the more completely is social life confounded with religious life, and the nearer to communism are economic institutions.
>
> The division of labor gives rise to juridical rules which determine the nature and the relations of divided functions, but whose violation calls forth only restitutive measures without any expiatory character.[19]

On close inspection, there is something wrong here. It's all too neat. Where there is collective conscience, there is no individual; where there is division of social labor, there is, though in indirect relation to the social whole, to society. But if, in the simpler societies, there is no individual, how can there be a "similitude of consciences"—in either sense of the word?

Part of the problem appears in an odd literary fact of *Division of Labor*. The book contains very few actual social facts. Though published just a year before *Rules* and filled with clues that he was already planning his great empirical study of suicide,[20] *Division of Labor* relies on very few facts. The problem is not simply that it is a book of theory (in spite of the author's empirical intentions). Rather, it is that when he does refer to facts Durkheim gets them wrong. Most astonishingly he is wrong (or at least not exactly right) where he ought to have known better, but perhaps he was constrained by his theory to misrecognize the facts.

Durkheim gets the facts of ancient Jewish law wrong at the crucial point in his argument. In order to prove the theoretical scheme (summarized in the passage just quoted), he turns to history. Given his theory, one would there expect empirical references to "primitives." Indeed, he begins the crucial section: "As far as we can judge the state of law in very inferior societies it appears to be entirely repressive."[21] Durkheim then refers to the unfreedom of the savage. But who is the savage? It turns out to be the original Jews, ancient Israel. His argument establishes the laws of ancient Israel as a principal illustration of repressive law ("the oldest monument of this kind that we have"). Durkheim then summarizes and discusses the four most juridical and priestly books of the Pentateuch—Exodus, Leviticus, Numbers, Deuteronomy—to support the conclusion that in them "restitutive law—cooperative law in particular—holds a very minor position."[22]

What is wrong is that this is not so. The priestly codes of ancient Israel were always developed against the foundational covenant that binds Israel to its God. In fact, it is hard to imagine any interpretation of the very scriptural texts to which Durkheim refers without ultimate reference to the original covenant. As it turns out, the predominant narrative of Exodus, the first of the books Durkheim cites, is restitutive: "Now therefore if you will obey my voice and keep my covenant, you shall be my own possession among all peoples; for all the earth is mine, and you shall be to me a kingdom of priests and a holy nation. There are the words which you shall speak to the children of Israel."[23] The repressive laws of the Pentateuch are morally and religiously incoherent without references to the contract God makes with Israel, and that contract, like modern contracts, is regenerative and restitutive. In fact, in the annual cycle of Jewish ritual life, regeneration and restitution are every bit as salient as atonement and punishment.[24]

Even if one were to allow for the likelihood that in Durkheim's orthodox childhood the collective conscience strongly emphasized the repressive rules in Jewish life, it is hard to imagine how he could have escaped instruction on Israel's founding contract. It is more likely that he was driven in adult life to misremember, or misrecognize, his own Jewish past. The sociology of Durkheim's adult life took on moral assumptions that required a denial of his childhood—either of what he knew in fact, or of what he could have known had he been more free to look clearly. Durkheim was too careful a scholar to have made such a mistake without some good reason. That reason, very likely, was that his sociology was linked in important ways to his personal experience in childhood. It is perfectly clear that his personal story contradicts his sociology. Were it the case that the orthodox Jewish laws of his childhood had constrained so powerfully as to deny those under its influence "any real individuality," then it is improbable, if not thoroughly inconceivable, that Durkheim could have separated himself from the powerful societal force of those generations of rabbis and Jewish law. Conversely, had he, one would expect he would have been severely punished, if not by his father (who died young), then by that community. So far as I know, there is no evidence that he was. In fact, when he died, Durkheim was buried not among France's cultural saints in Père la Chaise in Paris but in provincial Épinal among those he had left to found sociology.

Such was the power of Durkheim's sociology. In order to make it what he thought it should be, he had to misrepresent the experience of his own childhood. The lost world he obliquely reconstructed in his book on the modern division of labor was a product of keen, but entirely modern, imagination. For there to be a society sufficiently sui generis to account for the independent power of social facts, there had to be, at least once, a collective conscience before the altar of which modern men learned the power of that society. Yet, for modern man to live as a free and rational individual, that original society *must* have been replaced by one that allowed an individual sufficient freedom to be "an autonomous source of action" and sufficient *conscience* (in both senses) to be a moral man.[25] Thus, again, the riddle of modern morality: *If things social are different, who am I?* I can only be who I am if I am free enough from the demands of the society to be autonomous, yet somehow moral. That is, the modern man can accept himself as different only by insisting that he is not fully social, not fully constrained by society.

Thus, Durkheim was left in a quandary he sought to repress behind his good theory. If, morally, modern society had lost its original power, then how could there be a sociology based on facts that constrained powerfully? If, in other words, we were to account for Durkheim himself—as sociologist, not as rabbi—we could only do so in one of two ways, neither fully satisfying. Either, his theory of sociology was wrong because, were it right, he would not have been what he was. Or, Durkheim was wrong about that which he ought to have known best—his childhood, his experience as a Jew. The latter is the only plausible choice. But its price is that one must suspect Durkheim's idea of sociology and, thus, very likely, sociology itself. That there is reason to do so became evident in his greatest book on the 1890s, *Suicide,* where the Jew reappears, misconstrued again, at a crucial juncture in that book's argument; and where one must accept as fact that Durkheim's sociology required, among other misadventures, the exclusion of women from society.

▼ ▼ ▼ ▼ ▼

If *Division of Labor* is the book in which Durkheim outlines his moral theory of modern life and its uncertainties, and *Rules* is the book where he outlines his formal program for a sociology capable of resolving those uncertainties, then *Suicide* is the book in which both of these prior purposes come together. As he said in its preface, "The progress of a science is proven by the progress toward solution of the problems it treats."[26] Here he sought to prove two things at once: (1) that sociology's social facts could explain what was apparently the most unsocial of acts, self-murder; (2) that sociology's account of suicide in modern societies confirms the moral responsibility of modern societies to rebind themselves by securing a truly organic division of social labor. Yet, again, the two purposes do not suit each other exactly as Durkheim had hoped.

In order to demonstrate the power of sociology, Durkheim had not only to show that the most individualistic of human acts, self-murder, was caused by social forces but to prove that there was variation among the causes and types of suicide. The theoretical demands on Durkheim were strict: If in a divided modern society suicide and its causes did not vary, then, in the words of his definition of social facts, neither could meet the condition of being "general over the whole of a given society whilst having an existence of its own." In more formal language, unless suicide and its causes varied in a differentiated society, then they could not be variables, dependent and independent, in scientific sociology. Thus, the book's underlying argument (especially in its crucial Book 2, "Social Causes and Social Types") required him to set up his famous, but incomplete, fourfold table of suicide types. Each type of suicide was to correspond to a different cause:

1. *Egoistic suicide* is principally illustrated by the greater rate of suicide among modern individuals in the liberal, more educated, more well-to-do classes—Protestants in particular. This is the type of suicide caused, he argued, not by knowledge or education itself but by the failure of modern society to integrate the individual, thus to prevent him from becoming too individualistic, thereby escaping society's moral protection.

2. *Altruistic suicide* is, presumably, due to just the opposite cause. If egoism is too much individualism, altruism is too much society. The principal examples of altruistic suicide are cases of individuals who kill themselves for the sake of some powerful societal purpose—men in old age, women at the death of their husbands, followers or servants on the death of their chiefs.

3. *Anomic suicide* is most clearly and unambiguously illustrated by its association with times of economic crises. Anomie may lead to suicide when major disruptions in the social order inhibit society's ability to regulate the feelings

and actions of individuals. Lacking moral guidance in difficult times, individuals are deprived of the moral preservation that might otherwise keep them from self-murder.

4. Fatalistic suicide is best known for being the most famous footnote in the early history of sociology.[27] While Durkheim devoted at least a chapter to each of the other types, fatalism appears in a footnote at the end of his discussion of anomic suicide. It was a logical afterthought (one defined "for completeness' sake") and significant for that fact alone. As altruism was to be the opposite of egoism, then, he reasoned, fatalism must be anomic suicide's opposite—instead of too little, too much regulation. Examples of fatalism were hard to come by, he freely admits, though he proposes suicides of young husbands or of married but childless women. In the footnote, he adds: "But it has so little contemporary importance and examples are so hard to find aside from the cases just mentioned that it seems useless to dwell on it." As before, Durkheim was forced by his scientific logic to mention even that which seemed useless.

But was it useless? If that fourth causal type were not there, then what is one to think of the others? If he was correct in defining the preceding three—that is, if his logic rightly isolated those distinct types—then how could there not be this fourth? Had he set out to perform a purely inductive study in which he searched the empirical field for instances from which to infer the types, then the fourth logical type would not be required. But, he had already set out with the assumption that the types *must* exist if sociology is to work in a society of social differences. That fourth type just *had* to be there. Just as altruism (also, weakly developed) had to be there as the opposite to egoism. But the real test of the integrity of Durkheim's four types, and thus of his sociological method, is between those two most clearly modern types, egoistic and anomic.

The problem of Durkheim's method becomes all the more evident in his own summary of the three main types:

Anomie . . . is a regular and specific factor in suicide *in our modern societies.* . . . So we have here a new type to distinguish from the others. *It differs from them in its dependence, not on the way in which individuals are attached to society, but on how it regulates them.* Egoistic suicide results from man's no longer finding a basis for existence in life; altruistic suicide, because this basis for existence appears to man situated beyond life itself. *The third sort of suicide [anomic, that is] . . . results from man's activities lacking regulation* and his consequent sufferings. . . .

Certainly [anomic] and egoistic suicide have kindred ties. Both spring from *society's* insufficient presence in individuals. In egoistic suicide it is deficient in truly collective activity, thus depriving the latter of object and meaning. In anomic suicide, *society's* influence is lacking in the basically individual passions, thus leaving them without a check-rein.[28]

Not only, as Durkheim admits, do egoistic and anomic suicide have kindred ties, but, for all intents and purposes, they may be the same. In the one, society's collective activity is deficient; in the other, society lacks influence. In the one, the individual is too little integrated; in the other, he is too little regulated. In one (egoistic), the principal example is that of the too successful economic man whose success may separate him from society; in the other (anomic), the prime example is that same man when he faces a collapse of his economic order. It is not that there are no differences but that the differences are so slight. What might have been the results had Durkheim had at his disposal a technology that would have permitted a convenient regress of the causes against each other? Did the individual economic man kill himself more or less often in times of social disruption? One supposes more. But Durkheim does not say.

What can be said in retrospect is what is obvious from Durkheim's unqualified use of the word "society" in this important summary statement. For it is in the modern divided societies where suicide is the most interesting sociological fact that his lack of an explicit theory of society is most a problem. If society is the general, powerful, and sui generis thing he thought it was, then the problem of modern societies is that they are too divided for such a sui generis society to be any one thing.

Durkheim's society, thus, was a lost world he constructed in his sociological imagination, for which the most primitive societies (where suicide is not a remarkable fact) were the dreamlike images. This was already evident in *Division of Labor* and would become the central fact of *Elementary Forms of the Religious Life.* For Durkheim to argue strongly that sometimes modern societies allow individuals too much autonomy (thus accounting for egoistic suicide) and that sometimes individuals are insufficiently regulated by society (thus causing anomie and its consequences) was to argue little more than his general moral concern with modernity: The modern social division of labor sometimes causes individuals not to know who they are, or what to do, amid the differences it creates. For Durkheim to argue a strong causal explanation of the variable types of suicide, he would have had to have a stronger theory of society. He did not because the society he imagined, even in modern times, was the lost society of his—and modern man's—childhood.

Once again the Jew and the woman put Durkheim's sociology up against his moral concerns. In *Suicide* the Jew is the all-important figure who confirms the uniqueness of egoistic suicide. In the strongest, most confident, early part of his analysis of this type, it is the Jew who accounts for the unusually high rates of suicide among the educated, well-to-do Protestants. Durkheim here has no problem explaining the higher rates among Protestants relative to Catholics, for the latter are the less well educated, thus less likely to be separated from the social influence of the religious community. But, by this logic, Jews, being on the average even more literate and educated than Protestants, ought to have had even higher suicide rates. Instead, by his calculations, they had the lowest. This could only be, he concludes, because it is neither the religion nor the education that explains excessive individualism but the religious society. Jewish religious society is strong. Thus, among Jewish people, education serves to bind men to their community, while among Protestants it presses men toward individualism and separates them from the religious society. This is the crucial distinction because Durkheim's whole moral and sociological enterprise would be nonsense if, as he says, knowledge were "the source of evil [and not] its remedy, the only remedy we have."[29] Durkheim, therefore, was forced to conclude that the Jew was at one and the same time among the most intelligent, therefore most "modern," of men, *and* a "primitive" in certain respects. "The Jew, therefore, seeks to learn, not in order to replace his collective prejudices by reflective thought, but merely to be better armed for the struggle."[30]

The Jew, therefore, *must* have been for Durkheim the modern primitive. Otherwise, egoistic suicide would have been doomed as a type from the beginning. The cost, however, was that Durkheim, again, was required to renounce himself. If not himself, at least his childhood self. Once again, Durkheim's sociology could not explain Durkheim, the educated Jew who sought to learn precisely in order to separate himself, and all of France, from the "collective prejudices" of the traditional social conscience upon which his vague, but necessary, image of society depended.

Durkheim's science worked at the expense not just of his own original tradition but of the other figure for whom he could not account: *woman.* Woman appears more prominently than one might suppose, given Durkheim's prejudices. Yet, she, in her way, is the crucial test of the theory. Were one to study the suspicion that the four types are logical and nonempirical, it would be possible to test the lack of empirical salience in Durkheim's types by looking for, then comparing, any category of social facts that is constant to all four. If there were one, then it would be possible to determine if the facts associated with the multiple appearance of the social category varied with the general type. There is one, and it is woman.

She is, first of all, common to the two marginal types. The widow is a prime example of altruistic suicide, as the barren woman is one of the two meager illustrations of fatalistic suicide. But she is even more salient in the other two types, where women create major technical problems that Durkheim had to solve to save his theory. In his discussion of egoistic suicide, after the presentation of the Jew as the primitive modern, he turns to the second major instance of egoistic suicide.[31] Just as in the first case, suicide is said to vary inversely with the degree of integration of religious society, so he finds it varies inversely with the degree of integration of domestic society. For Durkheim, there is something about marriage and family life that serves as, in his words, a "coefficient of preservation" against suicide. It is not insignificant that it is here (in the opening section of chapter 3, Book 2) that Durkheim performs his most subtle statistical analysis. In fact, he invents the "coefficient of preservation" (crude by modern standards, but still the only coefficient in the book) seemingly in order to solve a problem in the evidence. The facts were that married life appeared to protect individuals to varying degrees depending on a number of variables, including whether one lived in France or (if in France) in the provinces or near Paris; whether there were children in the marriage or the mate had died; and, of course, whether the individual was male or female. Thus, Durkheim encountered a substantial number of variables, which created technical problems because he had to perform all the calculations by hand. But when he did those calculations he found a persistent, and to him, surprising fact.

Women, at every turn, did not conform. Or, more exactly, it was necessary for Durkheim, the sociologist, to get them to conform, statistically speaking. Among the ways in which the women represented by his suicide rates confused the picture were these:[32]

1. The coefficient of preservation (against egoistic suicide) varies between the sexes depending on the society and marital status.
2. In France, for example, marriage protects women less well than men (though it protects both better than the single life, which Durkheim's translator naively describes as "celibacy").
3. In general, the presence of children protects all married persons more than does simple marriage—considerably for men, partially for women.
4. Still with respect to egoistic suicide, the state of widowhood or widowerhood decreases the immunity for each spouse, but the decrease is in regular proportion to that sex's level of protection in marriage, that is, widowers have higher coefficients of protection than widows.
5. With reference to anomic suicide, marriage protects the wife more than the husband in societies where divorce is more common.

This last point (5) is, of course, cross-societal. How it was arrived at involves a story of its own, one that turns out to have powerful implications for Durkheim's method and theory. By contrast to 1 and 5, conclusions 2 through

4, generally, refer to France (though Durkheim is not entirely careful to limit his generalization). The issue arises because, in the second chapter on anomic suicide, he reports that in the Grand Duchy of Oldenburg, women were more favorably protected than in France, thus posing a problem of difference Durkheim could not neglect (even though he defers his account to the chapter on anomic suicide).

Oldenburg was an important subject in the argument as a whole for three reasons. First, it was the only governmental unit to have kept data that could be converted into the suicide rates represented in his coefficients of preservation. Durkheim, thus, set about to compile (literally, to retabulate, thus invent) comparable data for France so that he could counter the then prevailing argument that, among other things, insisted that marriage protected women *better* than men. Thus Oldenburg was crucial to his use of suicide rates, and his method. Second, however, the Oldenburg data contradicted the French, causing Durkheim to drop references to Oldenburg in Book 2, chapter 3, only to take them up again in Book 2, chapter 5, in the discussion of anomic suicide, where he returned to the data on egoistic suicide (which, in principle, ought to have described an entirely different type). There he accounted for the relative protection against anomic suicide of married women in the Grand Duchy by linking their lower rates while married in Oldenburg to the practice of divorce, which was greater in that Protestant society than in Catholic France. Here the idea apparently was that in societies where there is anomie affecting (by divorce) both the conjugal and family societies, women are better off married, while without the anomic disruption the marriage makes less difference to them. Finally, from this humble statistical beginning, Oldenburg led to the conclusion that had a potent effect on Durkheim's moral recommendations at the end, about which more later.

In other words, straightforwardly put, women are different. More different than, according to the weak general theory of society, they should have been. If society is sui generis—one, general, and powerful—then why are women all that different? Worse yet, if the problem of modern society is anomic disruptions in the social division of labor, then why are not women, with their greater indifference to that society and its negative effects, the solution to its problems? Durkheim had an answer to the former question, but none to the latter (though, as the passage quoted on p. 41 suggests, he seems to have been aware of its implications). In any case, Durkheim's discussions of the difference of women with respect to the two main types of suicide (and thus to the crisis of modern societies) show just how important the difference of woman was to him. These ultimately awkward discussions of women eventually raised serious and unanswerable questions about whether his types of suicide are, in fact, different empirical types. This in turn creates confusion not just for Durkheim's professional vision of sociology but for his practical, moral sociology.

If, as previously observed, there are no fundamental differences among the types of suicide, then there can be no plausible sociology for modern societies. No such differences would mean no variables, which, in turn, would mean both no scientific method and nothing to say about the fundamental social fact of modern society. What then would become of his claim that *social facts* give conceptual life to differing variables and, therefore, to the four distinct types of suicide? The bind is tight. The way out puts the differences among his logical types in grave doubt. For one, Durkheim himself admits that neither the logical afterthought (fatalistic suicide) nor altruistic suicide has any importance to modern society.[33] In addition, as I suggested earlier, the two principal illustrations of the two main types of suicide are, essentially, two sides of the same coin. If excessively individuated economic man is the token of egoism, and the economic man crushed by political and economic crises is the token of anomie, then are not these two recto and verso of the same type? Is not, thus, society's inability to prevent excessive individualism essentially the same as society's failure to regulate its members sufficiently? Or, if they are different, why is it, in the end, when considering practical solutions to the divisions of modern life, Durkheim advises that both egoism and anomie "might be dealt with by the same treatment"?[34] These, in themselves, raise questions hard to answer.

Finally, it is woman who puts Durkheim's whole enterprise in doubt.[35] It is she who not only links the discussions of the two main types of suicide but also forces him to concede (just after he admits the two types are "kindred") that in respect to her the two types have the *same* cause and, thus, *are* the same.[36] When Durkheim returns to the question of widowhood (and to the Duchy of Oldenburg) in the chapter on anomic suicide, he refers back to the discussion of the same subject with reference to egoism, and says: "The suicides occurring at the crisis of widowhood, of which we have already spoken, are really due to domestic anomy resulting from the death of the husband or wife."[37] Is he not saying that egoistic suicide (which ought to be due to a discrete independent variable) is "really" a case of anomie? As generous as one might want to be toward Durkheim, it would be hard to conclude otherwise.

Durkheim surely knew better, just as in some way he knew better about the primitive modern Jews. He made a serious effort to explain this anomaly. But that explanation could be found only by resorting to the weakest, most gratuitous aspect of that theory. When he did, it quickly became evident that even that aspect was more an entailment than a gratuity. The aspect in question was his much-debated theory of the *double man*—one part social, the remainder a rudimentary, passion-filled, and not particularly real individual. Obviously, this crude idea was a consequence of his sociology. If sociology existed for and because of social facts, then it surely could not admit as fact those elements of the individual outside the constraining force of society. Thus, the double bind of his general theory of *modern* societies: On the one hand, if we *must* define them, they are like the elementary society in their moral force; on the other, since we know they are divided by differences, then somehow they *must* eventually progress to a state where the moral demands of society and the individual moral responsibilities of free individuals might discover a steady state of mutual satisfaction. In other words, again, the consequence of resorting to the lost past for a theory of society required a projected, and parallel, resort to a progressive future. At no point are the implications of this bind more terrible than with respect to woman.

The only plausible account Durkheim could give for the difference of women (thus, by implication, for the difference between the two suicides) was in his double-man philosophy. Women, in short, are the lesser social creatures. In fact, the "man is double" idea is introduced first, and necessarily, at the end of the second chapter on egoism at precisely the point where he must account for the striking difference of women. Just after saying "social man is the essence of civilization," he adds his cumulative explanation for those facts that, with respect to suicide, women seem less affected, one way or another, by family life. Durkheim, then, with the double-man idea in mind, enumerates all the lesser creatures of the social world: children, the aged, animals, and women:

> Suicide is known to be rare among children and to diminish among the aged at the last confines of life; physical man, in both, tends to become the whole of man. Society is still lacking in the former [children] . . . ; it begins to retreat from the latter [the aged]. . . . Feeling a lesser need for self-completion through something not themselves, they are also less exposed to feel the lack of what is necessary for living. The immunity of an animal has the same cause. . . .
>
> This is also why women can endure life in isolation more easily than man. When a widow is seen to endure her condition much better than a widower and desires marriage less passionately, one is led to consider this ease in dispensing with the family a mark of superiority. . . . Actually if this is her privilege it is because her sensibility is rudimentary rather than highly developed. As she lives outside of community existence more than man, she is less penetrated by it; society is less necessary to her because she is less impregnated with sociability. She has few needs in this direction and satisfies them easily. *With a few devotional practices and some animals to care for, the old unmarried woman's life is full.*[38]

Please! . . . But, Durkheim has no choice. It is either women or his sociological enterprise. Women have to be inferior. Nothing else can explain the evidence of his suicide rates. Nothing else can save the difference between his types and thus his sociology. It now becomes clear that the man in his "man is double" idea is not a linguistic convention. He is in fact gendered, not generic.[39]

Having been constrained to speak as he does, Durkheim creates another problem for himself. What becomes of man? If the lesser gender is (in France at least) more naturally protected from suicide, what is to be said of gendered man and, more urgently, of modern society? If he is dependent on domestic society for a good coefficient of preservation, then how can he be "the higher essence of civilization"? What, for example, is to be said of the moral authority of that civilization if it is unable significantly to protect married man against anomic suicide where there are high rates of divorce? He begins: "Marriage may very possibly act in an opposite way on husband and wife." Durkheim is being coy. He believes it:

> *For among us love is a far more mental than organic fact.* A man looks to a woman, not merely to the satisfaction of the sexual impulse. Though this natural proclivity has been the germ of all sexual evolution, it has become increasingly complicated with aesthetic and moral feelings, numerous and varied, and today it is only the smallest element of the total complex process to which it has given birth. *Under the influence of these intellectual elements, it has been partially freed from its physical nature and assumed something like an intellectual one.*[40]

So, first, Durkheim speaks as if his subject is generic man rather than the gendered man whose suicides he must explain: "For among *us*. . . . " Here Durkheim describes the essential man as though it were the essential nature of all social beings, which, given his prior definitions of the double man, he ought to be. But, upon inspection, it turns out that this man is sexed (otherwise he would not be), even though his true nature is supposed to be an intellectual one.

Then, Durkheim continues:

> Moral reasons as well as physical needs impel love. Hence, it no longer has the regular, automatic periodicity which it displays in animals. . . . *But just because* these various inclinations, thus changed, do not directly depend upon organic necessities, social regulation becomes necessary. Thus he *must be* restrained by society since the organism has no means of restraining them.

Now, one must ask, which man—the physical or the intellectual? One may note the slight hesitation in "but just because" (and, thereby, recall that in the previous passage this man is only "partially" freed from his physical needs). This, then, is why he must be restrained, and "this is the function of marriage. It completely regulates the life of passion. . . . For by forcing *a man* to attach himself forever to the same woman it assigns a strictly definite object to the need for love, and closes the horizon." This is the concluding section of a paragraph that, near the top, began with a "for among *us*" and, now, in its conclusion, shifts without notice to "a man." Generic man becomes gendered man in a paragraph that begins, "After all, what is marriage?" For gendered man, marriage is a moral necessity. For woman, when she cannot divorce, it is an unnecessary burden.

Durkheim's real question is, therefore, What is man? To which the answer is, He is double. But not as Durkheim had hoped. Gendered man, as the embodiment of civilization, is moral. But, as a real individual in need of marriage for protection, he is physical. What then, one wonders, is the relation between the physical needs of man and those of woman if she is the one who is primitively social and moral? Well, it seems, he is sexual, while she walks the dog—he needs marriage, she does not. "Woman's sexual needs have less of a mental character, because, generally speaking, her mental life is less developed."[41] The "generally speaking" might be a hint that Durkheim senses that what he has had to say does not quite add up.

Where it adds up least, however, is at the very end of *Suicide*. After having presumably demonstrated the social fact of the new science he defined in *Rules,* Durkheim comes back explicitly to his moral vision for the future. There, in the final chapter of Book 3, he returns to woman. In the chapter's recommendations for solutions to the current state of modern society, Durkheim returns to advice he had previously given in the conclusion to *Division of Labor* and, more conspicuously, would give in his famous 1902 preface to that book, "Some Notes on Occupational Groups." Having diagnosed the anomic (and/or egoistic) ills of the modern society, he *must* return to the question of his first book. How, exactly, will the modern division of social labor progress to the point where man will be even better off in his independence than he was in his original dependence on the collective conscience? The answer he provides here, and elsewhere, is that man will benefit from the greater maturity of corporate society:

> [A] more perfected division of labor and its accompanying more complex cooperation, by multiplying and infinitely varying the occupations by which men can make themselves useful to other men, multiplies the means of existence and places them within reach of a greater variety of persons. The most inferior aptitudes may find a place there. At the same time, the more intense production resulting from this subtler cooperation, by increasing *humanity's* total resources, assures each worker an ampler pay and so achieves a balance between the greater wear on vital strength and its recuperation.[42]

Or, as he said earlier: "The corporation has everything needed to give the individual a setting, to draw him out of his state of moral isolation." In the end,

Durkheim can resolve the crisis only with reference to the generic man of *humanity*. He thus keeps close to the convictions he had already formed in his first book. As in the appearances of difference between his two modern forms of suicide, which were most striking in the case of egoistic and anomic economic man, he proposes a solution within the economic order.

Yet, in the previous section he had already begun by admitting: "There is one form of suicide, however, which could not be halted by this means; the form springs from conjugal anomy. We seem here confronted by an antinomy which is insoluble."[43] The confronting problem is the one expected. The "two sexes do not share equally in social life." But, in these concluding pages, Durkheim seems to take a somewhat different attitude toward women, for here appears the passage, quoted much earlier, in which he hints that at least some part of the solution to modern life lies with, if not woman, some new division of labor between men and women:

> The female sex will not again become more similar to the male; on the contrary, we may foresee that it will become more different. But these differences will become of greater social use than in the past. . . . Both sexes would thus approximate each other by their very differences. They would be equalized, but in different ways.

One wonders, after reading the whole of the book, how Durkheim imagines that woman, in her difference, might become equal if her social nature is so rudimentary? He has no definite answer, but like a true liberal, he has a qualified wish:

> Only when the difference between husband and wife becomes less, will marriage no longer be thought, so to speak, necessarily to favor one to the detriment of the other. As for the champions of equal rights for women with those of man, they forget that the work of centuries cannot be instantly abolished; the juridical equality cannot be legitimate so long as *psychological inequality* is so flagrant. Our efforts must be bent to reduce the latter. For man and woman to be equally protected by the same institution, they must first of all be creatures of the same nature.

Is it by chance that the first professional sociologist now resorts to a psychological explanation for woman's inequality?

For Durkheim's theory to add up, he must abandon a good bit of both its scientific and moral content. He seems to recognize, in the end, that woman's difference cannot be attributed to her lesser nature. It might even be, he suggests, that the sexual division of labor needs to stand alongside the corporate life as a possible resource for the progressive division of labor that will heal the hurts of modern life.

He does not say more. Just the same, one learns a great deal about his sociology from the two shadowy figures that haunt his plans for that sociology.

The Jew represents, without fully containing, the primitive past of modern man—the past of the child, and of the childlike time of society, when rules constrained to good moral effect. The Jew, for him, is the primitive modern— chief among those mythic figures from which he draws his imaginary vision of society itself. If the Jew of his past pushes Durkheim somehow into a dream of what modern morality might be, the woman pulls him beyond what he is able to imagine. She alone is the individual who cannot be explained by his science, nor healed by his morality. Yet, she, were she to become equal in her way, might help define the future of hope of a divided society.

If things social are different, who am I? Durkheim's answer might be said to have been: As the Jew, I am the same in a different world. As the man who needs a woman to complete my moral soul, I am, in my difference, dependent. The Jew and the woman—the primitive modern, and the social future perfect—explain the difficulties of this man's earnest and honest desire to invent the original professional sociology.

The sociology Durkheim invented was an act of the social imagination in which he sought to reconcile his modern world to those of his lost Jewish fathers and of his silent, necessary mothers. Faced with the same modernist riddle, most of his successors shared Durkheim's noble, unsettling dream.

Of all the classic, canonized social theorists, Durkheim was the only one to insist so precisely that the social must be a special sphere. Professional sociology might not have thrived in its academic world without his definition of social facts. But the other great social theorists, each more or less the sociologist, refused to define the social as a thing in itself. Neither Weber nor Marx, and certainly not Freud, could imagine social life cut off from the other compelling forces of modern life. It is, therefore, unwise, perhaps impossible, to understand the origins of modern sociology without the interests of all four men— political, legal, economic, cultural, and unconscious, as well as the social.

One of the most striking ironies of Durkheim is that, after him, his sociology led along two paths. One, that from *Rules* and *Suicide,* led directly to modern empirical sociology; that is, the sociology most professionalized, most securely identified in the academic division of labor, and thus the sociology most inclined to believe in social facts—general, independent, and powerful. The other path from Durkheim came much more from *Elementary Forms* and led directly to modern structural anthropology and structuralism, then to poststructuralism, and then, some would say, to postmodernism. Claude Lévi-Strauss, one of the most important founders of this other way, was devoted enough to Durkheim to speak of him in 1960 on the occasion of his inauguration to the Collège de France. What Lévi-Strauss said, in effect, was that he, and the structuralism he was then inventing, could not have been without Durkheim. Yet, the founder of modern structuralism quickly added that he could not have been a Durkheimian without Durkheim's nephew. It was Marcel Mauss who gave up his uncle's exclusive definition of social facts and the social. In *Essay on the Gift,* Mauss demonstrated to Lévi-Strauss's satisfaction that sociology could also be a science of the "down-to-earth man"—in Mauss's words, sociology could also be a science only to the extent that "body, soul, society—everything, merges."[44] In effect, the idea here is that Durkheim, in his desire to make the social real, pulled the social out of reality.

But there is an irony in that irony. Durkheim was right about a great deal. Among which, he was right about what he thought without saying: that the society which is sociology's object of study can only be a theory of a lost world. The best he could do was say, in so many words, that modern society was a reality we can know only if we think of society in complex relation to its elementary and original forms, then examine its present with reference to facts defined by moral concern. He did not, we now know, exactly intend it this way. He has been taken (with good justification) as more of the pure scientist than he was. The more honest and complicated interpretation is that Durkheim's solution to modernity's riddle demonstrated the most important fact of sociology: A professional sociology may indeed require a separate set of facts and rules of its own. But, however well and intelligently one tries to make it a science, it is impossible for any such sociology to outrun the deeper currents of its practical, moral life. Where Durkheim made mistakes (if they can be called mistakes), he made them because he was, in spite of himself, as much the moralist as the scientist.

The question he asks of today's sociology, professional and practical, is this: Can sociology thrive outside its own neatly defined factual world? Can it face directly and honestly the question of modern society, *What am I if this world is different?* Due, perhaps, to the effects of the line of work that led from the *other* Durkheim of *Elementary Forms,* a great deal of current sociology today would say that a sociology has no choice. Sociology does least well when it denies these differences and next least well when it insists on its own factual terrain. It does most well when it accepts its necessary nature: that what a sociology talks about is unavoidably the lost worlds we imagine. This is reality enough.

Chapter 4

The End of Ideology, Really!

Professional sociology, as it came to be in its classic era, claimed to tell the truth of the modern social order, the regime of liberal man. Because that regime was riddled with differences moderns wanted to deny, professional sociology could never quite tell the truth of which it dreamed. The truth of modernity was, therefore, always caught up in distortions. As a result, ideology became a central, if underestimated, question of modern man's social identity.

Who was that man? The question has been asked of the man who so overdetermined the sociologies of classic social theorists like Durkheim's.[1]

In a seemingly different reference the question was asked, late in 1992, by those who may have noticed a haunting news service story from Anchorage, Alaska:

Last Sunday a young hiker, stranded by an injury, was found dead at a remote camp in the Alaskan interior. No one is yet certain who he was. But his diary and two notes found at the camp tell a wrenching story of his desperate and progressively futile efforts to survive.

The diary indicates that the man, believed to be an American in his late 20s or early 30s, might have been injured in a fall and that he was then stranded at the camp for more than three months. It tells how he tried to save himself by hunting game and eating wild plants while nonetheless getting weaker.

One of his notes is a plea for help, addressed to anyone who might come upon the map while the hiker searched the surrounding area for food. The note bids the world goodbye.[2]

Whoever he was, he struggled to survive. Alone in a wilderness, he faced beasts, hunger, injury, and fear. He was courageous against the odds; inventive, but not lucky. He was as well, it seems, a man of decent moral virtue. Just before dying, he wrote: "I have had a good life and thank the Lord. Good bye, and may God bless all." According to these meager first reports, it seems he may even have been a humanist. He died blessing "all."

Months later, after President George Bush had left office, another report identified the man, but told a different story. He was Chris McCandless, a recent college graduate who had had a good life growing up in a white, middle-class Virginia suburb of Washington, D.C. Though he was gifted in the arts and sports, he kept to himself while a student at Emory University in Atlanta. After graduating with honors, he abruptly left his family and the urban civilization he had known. He hit the road under the assumed name of Alexander Supertramp and eventually ended up in Alaska. In April he had set off again, ill prepared, alone in the deep, thawing wilderness. He wanted out of civilization.

Chris was said to have been "a character in the wrong century, born too late for the age of discovery."[3] Sometime during his last days, he scratched a chaotic memoir on the wall of the shelter where his starved body was found:

> Two Years He Walks The Earth. No Phone, No Pool, No Pets, No Cigarettes. Ultimate Freedom. An Extremist. An Aesthetic Voyager Whose Home *is The Road*. Escaped from Atlanta. Thou Shall Not Return, Cause "The West *Is* the Best" And Now After Two Rambling Years Comes the Final and Greatest Adventure. The Climactic Battle To Kill the False Being Within And Victoriously Conclude the Spiritual Revolution! Ten Days & Nights of Freight Trains and Hitching Bring Him to the Great White North No Longer to Be Poisoned By Civilization He Flees, and Walks Alone Upon the Land To Become *Lost* in the *Wild*.[4]

Still, one wonders. Who was that man?

Or, it could be asked, which was the truth about this man? In his diary, Chris McCandless presented himself as an ordinary man, lost in the wild, praying in the face of death for humanity—"I have had a happy life and thank the Lord. Good bye, and may God bless all." But, in his fragmented memoir, the truth of the man seems otherwise. He tells us (or someone) that he wanted out from among us. He wanted to win the spiritual struggle by losing himself in the wild—"He Flees, and Walks Alone Upon the Land to Become *Lost* in the *Wild*." Was one of Chris's presentations of himself more true than the other? Or, could both stories be true?

Back in the culture Alexander Supertramp fled, the bias is strong toward believing there is always some discernible truth about human lives and deaths—some fundamental fact, or at least an ultimate story, that explains everything else. Death and its equivalents frustrate progress toward uncovering that deepest truth in the nature of things social. In such a culture, a conclusive end is effectively the moral opponent of the fulfilling end of progress. Finitude frustrates fulfillment. In such a culture, a death leaves one stranded with scratched signs from which to decipher forever incomplete truths. One supposes that even those closest to Chris McCandless could not have known a final truth about the meaning of his flight from civilization. Nor is it likely that he did.

To moderns, death comes in many forms. Most poignantly, more even than death itself, it comes in the necessity of recognizing the terrible limitations of human knowledge, thus of modern culture.[5] Since the beginning of the modern era, to live has meant to live free, and to live free has been to know. Kant's famous words, "dare to know," are the key to everything.[6] If the culture provokes this hope, then any final limitation on what man can know limits his freedom and thus life itself. Whatever may have been the particular truths of Chris McCandless's life, he can be said to have been a true representative of modern man, in and because of his contradictions. In the odd figurative relation of a Supertramp and the West, the truths common to the two different accounts Chris left as he lay dying are, just as much, truths common to the West today. In the one note, he gave thanks for a good life and blessed all humanity; in another, he understood himself as on a quest for "Ultimate Freedom," for which he fled civilization. Is it possible that this lost man sought the essence of the humanity he blessed by leaving it? That is, could it be that the ultimate freedom is the desire to be wild, at the farthest limit of human civilization—yet, still somehow, remembered by and connected to all men?[7] He did leave notes! For whom? Why?

Whoever this man truly was, he was, in these indeterminate senses, truly modern. The desire for freedom wrenches the modern away from the civilized past into a new world in which all one has is knowledge. A civilized past, for him, is remembered as the wild for which man longs. And, in this freedom, man learns that in the subject's desire to discover the objective truth of his own kind, he is finite. It is not, as it is normally taught, that there is a defining barrier between the civilized and the wild, between the subject and his object. It is more that the two sides of what are thought of as dichotomies actually form a moral space much like the one of Durkheim's double man—a space man enters looking for freedom only to find instead his finitude. There the modern, like Chris McCandless, comes to the riddle Durkheim could not solve. Who am I if things social are so different? All Chris did was to invert the terms of the riddle: *How can I be whoever I am if I do not make myself ulti- mately different?* "An Extremist. An Aesthetic Voyager Whose Home *is The Road*." Straightforward or inverted, it is the same riddle. Who is man, if it is correct to call him that, in such a world?

If it is impossible to determine the final truth of things human and social, then it is necessary to reconsider the relation between truth itself and reality. So strong is the belief in true knowledge as freedom that much of modern culture contradicts its professed hostility to absolutisms by holding fast to the impossible idea that truth can set men free only if the reality of the world is beyond doubt. Modernity wants to have it both ways. But, this cannot be. If daring to know is the source of human freedom, then free "men" will shake the real world in their moral actions if not in their epistemologies.[8] Sociologically speaking, truth is about morality, not knowledge. To be a modern, one must dare to know, which, in turn, requires one to suffer the uncertainties of breaking with absolute truth. Or, in the lan- guage of Calvino and Durkheim, modernity breaks the rules that define the truth of social life. This is the unavoidable condition, and a disruptive dilemma, of modern culture. Modern man cannot possess that which he must seek.

Durkheim's double man—delicately conscious in the social; rudimentary, nearly animal, without—was a fantasy of his desire to save modern life without abandoning its moral need for progress. For Durkheim, only man's double life could explain modern knowledge. In his last great book, he sought to do noth- ing less than correct, complete, and modernize the master philosopher of mod- ern knowledge. Immanuel Kant located the categories of modern knowledge in the transcendental structures of mental consciousness. Durkheim, then, collec- tivized Kant's consciousness in order to relocate knowledge in a quasi-historical structure, society.[9] In *Elementary Forms of the Religious Life*, knowledge is in (and because of) societal consciousness imposed on crude passions. The fan- tasy was that original, elementary collective life would lift man above the limita- tions of his animal nature. Man, thus doubled over his animal nature, was Durkheim's hope of overcoming the structured lawlessness of modern life. Woman, thus tied to nature, could not have been for him anything but Other. Whatever the evidence, however man relied on her, she *had* to be that which man was not. Durkheim was not alone in thinking such thoughts, even though his writings may have been among their purest representations.

Thinking of man as double was not an accident of logic but a condition of modern life. *Who am I if things social are different?* It is one thing to ask the question, another to think in and around it in order to produce knowledge.

Man's knowledge of man is trapped in a contradiction of which the misrepresentations, ignorances, and confusions in Durkheim's sociology are nothing more than visceral bends from diving too deep. Any science of the human is caught in the terms of this riddle. If "who I am" is a moral uncertainty because I am not like the others with whom I suppose myself to be the same, then how am I to define those others in terms I can recognize? One solution is to state the sociological truths elliptically, in language *only* the individual can understand. This may be why it has been said that "for Durkheim, Society is a kind of writing that only he can read."[10] Foucault, in his elliptical style, put this well: "[Man] appears in his ambiguous position as object of knowledge and as a subject who knows: enslaved sovereign, observed spectator."[11] It is not so much the difficulty of knowing the objective essence of that of which one is, but knowing it in its difference from what one is. Alex Supertramp must have known this much at least. He thought of all humanity at that very moment he had achieved the greatest possible difference from it—at the nearness of death on the farthest, wildest edge of its world. Yet, in making himself over as ultimately different, he still could not rid himself of the desire to communicate. He longed, still, to tell the world who he thought he was and then to bless it.

Historically speaking, the idea of a social (or human) *science* is, therefore, oxymoronic—that which can be said and done only as a contradiction. Since, until the past generation, the social sciences attempted to define themselves against a strict scientific logic, it could be said that they put themselves in the circumstance where they could never tell the truth in the terms of their own choosing. The social sciences were faced, and still are, with the task of defining their truths as a tactical way around the impossibility of their strict logic. In Durkheim's case, the tactic was that of overdefining social facts in order to avoid the complications of defining society.

At the time the social sciences organized themselves in the last third of the nineteenth century, science had long been understood as an accomplishment of the ideal of pure knowledge. Science, thus, was the modern heir to Scholastic and Renaissance theologies. It is sometimes forgotten that Kant invented the theory of practical reason in order to save modern morality from the hopelessness it faced upon accepting that it could not prove God's existence.[12] Science was, and still is, often thought of as the promise of union between the pure knowing subject and the positive truths of the object world. By the time of the earliest attempts to organize a science of this sort with man as its object, it was already widely believed that the union was possible. It was, of course, believable because of the centuries-long preparation of the religious life and its thought. Durkheim was exactly right on this. The idea of

modern science, thus of a science of the social, goes back to man's original social experience—the collective experience that man arose from and thus depends on a higher power. "We have established the fact that the fundamental categories of thought, and consequently of science, are of religious origin."[13]
Durkheim did well to explain that this higher power was neither God nor the
spirits but society. It is perfectly understandable why he avoided the third
term, and the corollary it requires, of his sociological syllogism. If, as he said,
man knows because he is social, the social having originally been represented
by the gods, then the corollary must be, Man knows because he believes in the
gods, the gods having been the representations of the social. But for
Durkheim, and the other original social theorists of the modern age, the
corollary was both unspeakable and unthinkable. They thought, one way or
another, that the path to knowledge, thus freedom, was *through* and beyond
the gods. They were not entirely wrong.

Each of the classic social theorists did what he did in relation to what
Foucault once described as the unthought:

> Man and the unthought are, at the archaeological level, contemporaries. Man has not
> been able to describe himself as a configuration in the *episteme* without thought at
> the same time discovering, both in itself and outside itself, at its borders yet also in its
> very warp and woof, an element of darkness, an apparently inert density in which he
> is embedded, an unthought which it contains entirely, yet in which it is also caught.
> The unthought (whatever name we give it) is not lodged in man like a shrivelled-up
> nature or a stratified history; it is, in relation to man, the Other.[14]

The oxymoron in the idea of a social *science* is that when man makes himself
the object of his subjective thoughts, the relation between subject and object
can be purified only by projecting these two contradictory moments onto the
nature of things—that is, by contradicting the very claim modern thought
had so proudly insisted upon as its essential truth. The modern was to have
been that for which no Other was required.

Modern social thought could not avoid its own essence. The subject as object to itself had to be made to take the place in historical Being which God
had held in Being itself. Otherwise, God would have remained the only truth
of man. Man, the subject-object, did not, therefore, escape finitude. When
God and his kings reigned, man was subordinated to higher, supernatural
truths. But, when man became subject of the object world, man, having become that higher truth, was subordinated still—to his own nature. Finitude in
the modern world is not ever being able to know oneself purely. It might be
said punningly, subjects always object to themselves when the self they see as
object is different from what they had wished. To overcome this objection
(that is, to double over oneself), modern man made himself a virtual substi-

tute for God and his various manifestations throughout human history.[15] *Subject-object* thus became the center of things on the condition that one try never to tell this truth in public. Modern social thought was, thus, wholly dependent on the willingness of its adherents to keep secrets. Occasionally, some deviant or another would come along and break the code.

Alex Supertramp, for example, could not escape, and would not repress, these facts of modern life. At the end of the world, he still wanted to be known and remembered back home. He wanted, in spite of himself, to be at least recognized as human *because of,* and not in spite of, his efforts to make himself different. He betrayed the lie that civilized human subjects belong to an objective reality that is Other to the wilderness.

▼ ▼ ▼ ▼ ▼

The classic social theorists—Weber, Marx, and Freud, as well as Durkheim—are not, therefore, original sources of sociological truth. They are classic as much for their vulnerability to failure as for their successes. They are still read because, even today, one reads in them the unthought—the not always conscious reality of modern social life.

Though they all faced the uncertainties of the unthinkable, others of the classic thinkers tried different ways around it. Durkheim succeeded in making a sociology, but he could not avoid founding it on the fantasy of man doubling back to his origins.

Among the four, Max Weber was, in one respect, closer to Durkheim in being among the most modern of thinkers. They both believed that society could be thought directly. But, unlike Durkheim, Weber chose a more oblique path. If Durkheim tried to invent and define a positive sociology, Weber tried to invent a positive technique whereby the social subject's inner meanings could be read as clues, if not facts, in elective affinity with the world's objective structures.

In Weber's most famous book, *The Protestant Ethic and the Spirit of Capitalism,* the structure of the modern world was, in very large measure, accounted to a meaningful affinity between a new subject of history, the rational man, and the economic practices of capitalism he structured disproportionately in the West wherever Calvinism's word had spread. Yet, Weber, like Durkheim, still worked within the new modern formula. If anything, Weber took it with greater (certainly more explicit) seriousness than Durkheim. Just the same, by trying to work everything necessary in relation to the subject and its object world, Weber came quickly up against the unthought and unthinkable. If, for Durkheim, the Other was Woman (and her anthropological kin— the Jew, the animal, the aged), for Weber it was the East. Everything in Weber's

facts was oriented (so to speak) to the West—to the capitalized, protes-
tantized, rationalized regions of the world. Yet, he thought, the more history
moved West, the more it trapped itself in its own calculations. Somehow, the
East always haunted Weber.[16] He was, for whatever reason, more open in seeing and more honest in saying what he saw. Durkheim, by contrast, was so
drawn to solve the modern world's moral dilemma that he could not see the
corollary of his convictions: Society—therefore knowledge—not only originated but was still fixed, dependent on the primitive past.

Weber, much unlike Durkheim, preoccupied himself with studies of the
past, and the East, and their religions. Always, he found there that which was
lost, and the only hope. If what was lost in the iron cage of rationality was the
spirit-filled sensuality of traditional life, then what remained as the only hope
of the future was the charismatic figure—the ancient religious prophets of the
Far and Near East in whom subjective meaning and objective truth were so
powerfully united that the calculated reason of this world might break open
into freedom. With Durkheim, social truth was progressive. With Weber, it
was, if at all, explosive. For Weber, progress in the West had locked in the human and threatened the passions. In those most memorable words at the end
of *Protestant Ethic,*

> No one knows who will live in this cage in the future, or whether at the end of this
> tremendous development, entirely new prophets will arise, or there will be a great re-
> birth of old ideas and ideals, or, if neither, mechanized self-importance. For of the
> last stage of this cultural development, it might well be truly said: "Specialists without
> spirit, sensualists without heart; this nullity imagines that it has attained a level of
> civilization never before achieved."[17]

Weber did not fear so much as fend off the passions of human life. He wanted
in many ways to free them. Sensuality *with* heart! His many fascinations with
the irrational[18]—with music, with the religious prophets, with charismatic
authority, with the inner subjecthood of method, with the passions of scientific calculations—were to him a courageous move toward the unthought of
modern life. Too much the modern rationalist to enter again, after years of
mental torment, the irrational, Weber nonetheless kept the courage to think
the unthought through the irrational—to make it a positive, if displaced, feature of his sociology. Though Weber sought to rationalize the inner subjective
meanings, no one who knew him, and knew what he had gone through,[19] is
likely to have supposed that he was convinced that the inner life could ever be
thought through. Durkheim, in effect, denied the Jew, and effaced Woman,
without whom, both, he could not have been. Weber, by contrast, vainly built
the cage of his sociology of interpreted reasons, all the while admitting and

exploring the hope that the unreasonable power of the mysterious, enchanted religious truths of the past and the East would once again break in.

Freud, alone, named the Other in so many words. Beginning with *The Interpretation of Dreams,* Freud built his theory of social life on a foundation that confounded modernity's own foundational couplet. Just the same, even in Freud, the subject as object to itself organized the general definitions of the realistic limits of unconscious life. Against the unconscious, Freud set the false reasonableness of conscious life. He pictured that life as a constant battle within the analytic geography of the psyche, between id and superego for control of the ego. Where Durkheim believed the social conscience dominated the animal passions to make an individual human, Freud put the two against each other, making the unconscious an active, if displaced, force in the action of the human self. And as his theory developed, Freud stipulated the two, opposed positive instincts—death and life, aggression and love—as the object field of analytic science.[20] Like Durkheim in believing a science could solve the modern world's moral divisions, Freud was unlike Durkheim in the power he lent to the unthought. In this respect, Freud was the very opposite of Durkheim in frankly defining that which his theory aimed to explain.

Freud, in effect, made the unthought a partial, positive foundation of his science. Yet, this required a displacement of normal methods of science. All of the rules governing the interpretation of dreams and other expressions of the unconscious mind could not, in the end, disclose Freud's object world. Displacement, inversion, and condensation were the explicit governing rules for the interpretation of expressive materials produced by the unconscious mind. But, the most essential truth of the unconscious mind was that it was the repository of the Other—of all the dark thoughts that could never be said (some, not even in session). Psychoanalytic truth, insofar as it is attainable, is always displaced and distorted by the patient's life-seeking resistances. Freud, thereby, worked at the limit of modern thought. Yet, perhaps because he pursued that limit so far, like Alex Supertramp, he was not able to define the central issues of modernity's social life.

Freud has been largely ignored by sociologists surely because they recognized in what he said that which would threaten the artificially pure theoretical space of the social. Freud made the convincing best case against Durkheim's insistence on the purity of sociology. Freud, among the classic social theorists, could have best diagnosed Durkheim's characterological forgetting of his Jewish past, his mother, and women. These forgettings were symptomatic of the need any subsequent pure, professional sociology would have to leave something out, significantly. Freud might have concluded that Durkheim's repressed was a defense necessary to the organization of his adult life.

Durkheim was, in this sense, the near perfect harbinger of professional sociology inasmuch as, since Comte, organized sociology had promised to be the adult of human history.

Yet, had Durkheim invented his definition of sociology just a decade later, after the publication of *Interpretation of Dreams* (1900), he still would not have been swayed. The sociology Durkheim invented could not have accounted for the unconscious life—not just because the unconscious was "psychological" but because it told the truth his sociology could not utter. Weber's comparably greater honesty about the irrational, against which modern reason calculated its way, was only slightly less an embarrassment to the original sociology. The greater embarrassment for Durkheim would have been the admission that society, the inferential correlate to his well-defined social facts, was real only as a figment of the collective unconsciousness of the modern, divided social world.

But it was Marx who best incorporated the moral and intellectual dilemmas of the first sociologies. Durkheim founded his science on the condition of a studied aversion to certain realities. Weber enriched the wider traditions of social thought through the oblique means of his studied ambivalences about the modern world. Freud, in his weak but important relation to the social, defined the condition of its limits. Freud and even Weber may have been more realistic in facing the unthought of modern life. But Marx, and Marx alone among these four, entered the fray of modern social thinking. He alone tried to think, and say, in so many words, the thinkable *and* the unthinkable; that is, to say everything about modern life, including the unspeakable hidden truths of capitalism. Marx tried to invent the pure science of the invisible structures of the capitalist mode of production.

Marx's sociology was nothing less than the attempt to demonstrate, explicitly and openly, that behind the visible play of market exchanges and labor values lay the secrets of production that could never be seen as such on the shop floor and never admitted by Mr. Moneybags, the capitalist. "We now know," Marx said at the crucial moment,

> how the value paid by the purchaser to the possessor of the peculiar commodity, labour-power, is determined. The use-value which the former gets in exchange, manifests itself only in the actual usufruct, in the consumption of labour-power. The money-owner buys everything necessary for this purpose, such as raw material, in the market, and pays for it at its full value. The consumption of labour is at one and the same time the production of commodities and of surplus-value. The consumption of labour-power is completed, as in the case of every other commodity, outside the limits of the market or of the sphere of circulation. Accompanied by Mr. Moneybags and by the possessor of labour-power, we therefore take leave for a time of this noisy sphere, where everything takes place on the surface and in view of all

men, and follow them both into the hidden abode of production, on whose threshold there stares us in the face "No admittance except on business." Here we shall see, not only how capital produces, but how capital is produced. We shall at last force the secret of profit making.[21]

Marx, here and in the remainder of *Capital,* projected the visible truth of social reality back into the hidden, contradictory secret of production. Between the marketplace and productive structures there was, for Marx, a logic that only historical materialism could decode. In this respect, Marx, of course, shared the intentions of Freud to explore and define the hidden regions of social life. But Marx, surprisingly, was more cautious. For Freud, the unconscious life was accessible only through a complicated series of decodings—of condensed, displaced, inverted meanings—none of which could ever finally be settled. Marx, more the modernist, took the more straightforward, though still radical, path. For Marx, the relation was inverted, but simply so. As in the camera obscura,[22] the hidden truths of production were straightforwardly an inversion of the visible truths of social life. For Marx, everything concerning modern social knowledge comes back to ideology, its nature and its critique.

The nature of ideology can be well illustrated by reference to one of the earliest important statements of the most global ideology of the twentieth century. Ambassador George Kennan's famous Long Telegram of February 22, 1946, alongside Winston Churchill's equally famous iron curtain speech of two weeks later, came to be a founding statement of post–World War II American foreign policy. Then began the ideology of containment, which gave portentous shape to the political culture in the United States and the West for most of what remained of the century.

At one memorable moment in the text, Kennan offered what today would be called a close reading of the Soviet national character. He said, in the language of telegrams:

> It was no coincidence that Marxism, which had smoldered ineffectively for half a century in Western Europe, caught hold and blazed for [the] first time in Russia. Only in this land which had never known a friendly neighbor or indeed any tolerant equilibrium of separate powers, either internal or international, could a doctrine thrive which viewed economic conflicts of society as insoluble by peaceful means. After [the] establishment of [the] Bolshevist regime, Marxist dogma, rendered even more truculent and intolerant by Lenin's interpretation, became a perfect vehicle for [the] sense of insecurity with which Bolsheviks, even more than previous Russian rulers, were afflicted.[23]

The logic here is plain: Russians by their nature are afflicted with a truculent and intolerant national character; by inference, Americans are peaceable, hence moral, by nature.

Against Kennan's text one might reconsider George Bush's statements on the same subject in 1992 when he had such difficulty telling the story of freedom in what had again become Russia. At the end of the Cold War, the predominant view of the character of the Russian people suddenly changed. They were, after all, less truculent, and capable of freedom. But, underlying this remarkable change of the American mind, there is the insistent fact that the idea was up against matters of fact. That there is a Russian people, affected dramatically by their Soviet period, there can be no doubt. Nor can it be doubted that the varying perceptions of them by the Americans affected those facts. Thus, the Kennan telegram, like George Bush's 1992 speech—one at the beginning, another at the apparent end of the Cold War—permits easy empirical reference to the nature of ideology's strange relation to reality.

Ideology, a subject of near endless definitions,[24] is commonly considered a cultural product in which the truth of things is simultaneously distorted and revealed. Stalin was indeed truculent. Marxism did in fact teach conflict as the proper theory of social change. Soviet foreign policy under Stalin was indeed aggressive. Yet, even so sophisticated a scholar-diplomat as George Kennan, a fine Princeton education notwithstanding, elaborated the truth of these things into a sweeping assessment of Russian national character, from which was constructed, in conjunction with the principle of American exceptionalism, the global ideology of the Cold War. Since then, many people have suffered and many died. Whatever ideologies do in relation to the facts they use, they are real in their effects. They have as much to do with power as they do with truth.

The history of the concept ideology has, until recently, tended to confuse, or positively disguise, the degree to which ideology is every bit as much a term in the vocabulary of political power as in a social theory of knowledge. In its latter aspect, as a diagnostic concept in the sociology of knowledge, ideology has been interpreted as a truth-distorting idea. In this form, which is properly associated with the writings of Karl Mannheim (1893–1947), ideology's relation to power has frequently been confused with references to an even more difficult concept, interests. Accordingly, sociology has struggled since Mannheim to justify its original Enlightenment belief in the accessible truth of the real world—an article of faith shaken by any admission of a systematic distortion of the human ability to see the truth.

In its other line of development, ideology has been the key term in the vocabulary of politically left, critical social theories. Beginning with Marx, ideology possessed at least two simultaneous theoretical values. On the one hand, it diagnosed the distortions of knowledge imposed by class and power relations; on the other, it defined that object the critique of which entailed the prospect of liberation. Thus Marx in *The German Ideology* remains indebted to the philosophy of the Enlightenment while making one of the early theoretical moves that would eventually call the ideas of truth, reality, and enlightenment itself into doubt. In the very same place, in this early text where surprisingly he affirms man's definite role in political history, Marx also, in one and the same move, affirms and inverts human consciousness: "In all ideology men and their circumstances appear upside-down."[25] Whatever united them, and much did, Marx and Mannheim are at considerable divorce over the relation of truth to power in the formation of ideologies. Written nearly a century after *The German Ideology*, Mannheim's essays in *Ideology and Utopia* (published from the late 1920s into the 1930s) were more deeply preoccupied with the epistemological problems attendant to a theory of ideology than with the terrible political events of those same years in his native land. By contrast, Marx (writing in 1845) defined ideology in relation to a theory of historical change and, quite memorably, concluded his eleven theses on Feuerbach in the same year with a startling emphasis on political truth: "The philosophers have only interpreted the world, in various ways; the point, however, is to *change* it."[26]

It is not that the two sociologists most classically identified with ideology differ and diverge but that Marx and Mannheim represent the inherent instability of the concept itself—an instability that owes to its importance as a sign of, but also a force in, the culture of modern life. Though it presents itself as a theory of knowledge and its limitations, ideology is in fact always, and unavoidably so, a theory of social change, hence of power relations. In this respect, ideology masquerades as a neat cultural icon of modern culture itself—that is, the culture that presents itself as freedom producing truth, when it is in reality a culture of historical progress.

Yet, as consequence and corollary of this principle, any social theory of ideas that moves from the assumption that social conditions (invariably also power relations) distort our ability to see the truth must call into question the idea of truth itself. This, then, is the dilemma of modern life, in which constant preoccupation with historical progress makes ideas and the culture in which they are embedded actual forces in social life, notwithstanding the evidence and occasional desire to complain that economic matters matter more. In particular, the very presence of ideology in the vocabulary of sociology must aggress received notions of knowledge, thus moving social thought far from science and near to politics. This worried Mannheim, perhaps for temperamental as well as historical reasons. It troubled Marx less deeply, even if the eleventh thesis on Feuerbach did not prevent him in later years from writing a science of capital. The truth of ideology, for Marx, was more a serious rhetorical gesture than a well-developed argument. It is possible, one imagines, that his failure to discover a political epistemology explains his even more telling failure to describe a political theory. It would seem that one must give up entirely on truth and science, or at least must change radically the foundations on which they rest, if one wishes to state a theory of political power that is at once true and political. Through the modern era, from its first use in 1797, the concept ideology has served as a flexibly coded cultural marker requiring, among other things, a theory of political change that in turn requires historical consideration of actual changes in social history.

Today, however, it is necessary to consider ideology differently because, now, there is reason to think the world *has* changed. Ideology, in other words, is a concept closely identified with the history of the modern era, which is why, so far as it is known, the concept did not appear before the French philosophes in the late eighteenth century and seems now, in the past generation, to be undergoing important transformations consistent with the belief, held confidently by some, that the modern era has come to an end of its own.

Modernity, many agree,[27] can be defined as that historical period in which, on the surface, everything appears as progressive change while, upon inspection, everything social struggles continuously with forces of creativity and of destruction. Hence, the preoccupation in theories of modernity with ideals of progress, metaphors of evolution, and dreams of utopia. Each of these is a definite political move—each attempting, since the eighteenth century, to formulate a thread of continuity amidst a plurality of contradictions. The nineteenth century, in which these contradictions played themselves out in a series of political and economic struggles, was one in which a new social world was created out of the destruction of the old. In Marx's words, "All that is solid melts into air."[28] In the modern era, everything new costs deeply.[29]

In nineteenth-century Europe political and economic change was believed to have been continuous and progressive. In fact, however, the forces of regression and destruction fought progress to a draw. By century's end, in continental Europe, the French Third and German Weimar Republics were feeble social contracts unable to hold the forces of destruction that soon won the day. In the twentieth century, Europe's Holocaust was, as many have argued, in some sense an overt expression of one of the deeper, secreted logics of modernity. In the United States in the nineteenth century, modernity's contradictions were sharper yet, though more faintly felt. The century of expansionism against the frontier played, on the surface, as progress. In fact, it was a nearly pure form of imperialism in which the new republic fought on several fronts at once—against a natural barrier (the celebrated frontier); against the bearers of difference, those who suffered the cost of expansion (slaves and Native Americans); and against the original culture (Europe) out of which the American empire was seeking to define itself.

Europe's universal moment of horror came in the twentieth century, America's came in the midst of the nineteenth. The Civil War was, in effect, an explosion of the destructive forces that could not be hidden behind the ideology of manifest destiny. As Henry Luce put it a century later in the 1940s, the twentieth century was the American century. If it was, it was because Americans, having already passed through a national nightmare, were spared at this later date the terrors of modernity, its raw destructiveness. America's holocaust—that is to say, its time for neighbor to kill neighbor, for society to attack itself—came earlier with the Civil War. In the twentieth century the United States enjoyed relatively free play for its noble experiments in social creativity. From the Panama Canal and the new industrial cities, to the great world wars up to (but not including) Vietnam, the American century was a reenactment of the earlier frontier experiment. This experiment could be called imperialism with a human face. In any case, it was a pure expression of modernity's dual character—change appearing as progress on the surface; destruction ever always just below.

Modernity, therefore, might be defined as that culture in which social change is so fundamental that ideologies of continuity are regularly created out of the necessity to suppress the evidence of destructiveness in favor of the myth of pure creativity. By contrast, one might propose that traditional societies are those in which, in the absence of myths of progress, the destructive forces are less acute for the reason that they are not excited by wild dreams of creative change. Likewise, to complete the historical scheme, a society is postmodern when it gives up on ideologies of progress, thus attenuating the contradictions of social life and, as a result, displacing both creative and destructive forces into peripheral, eccentric places and forms.[30] If the postmodern is thus understood by the improbable mixing and juxtaposition of past and present form, the modern would be an arrangement of those forms along the improbable axis of continuous progress. The postmodern, even if it is only the ideology of a possible social world, tells the truth of social change—that there is no singular truth behind which to hide the corrupting force of power. Correlatively, the modern is the lie that linear truth organizes the conflicting valences of power.

Ideology, therefore, is a concept caught up completely in the culture of modernity. Modernity being what it is, we can therefore say that ideology has always been a theory of political truth by way of its decisive place in modernity's self-understanding. It is surely not by accident that the crucial moments in the history of the concept ideology correspond to times of massive political turmoil, to moments in the modern West that tested modernity's ideology of itself:

- In the revolutionary aftermath of the French Revolution (Destutt de Tracy's first use of *ideologue*).
- In the revolutionary prologue to 1848 (Marx's *German Ideology*).
- On the eve of the Nazi terror (Mannheim's *Ideology and Utopia*).
- At the height of the Cold War and in the aftermath of the Red Scare (the end of ideology of debate).
- Following the revolutionary culture of the late 1960s (in the postideology ideologies of decentering).

The first appearance of the term *ideology* was at the end of the eighteenth century in France in the last years of the Directory on the eve of Napoleon's reign; that is, just as France's revolution was fading, or transforming itself. Antoine Destutt de Tracy, drawing on Condillac, coined the term *ideologue* to define those who were to build the science of ideas. Here, ideology was seen as the expression of the Enlightenment belief that free human reason could make the world. Ideologues would develop the foundational ideas of the new social order. Napoleon, however, gave the term its negative connotation. He had other ideas about the building of the new order. The imperial ruler was not about to encourage the intellectual freedom implied in a science of ideas.

Thus, the philosophes could be taken as the founders of the sociology of knowledge. Like Saint-Simon and Comte, who followed Destutt de Tracy's lead, the idea of a science of ideas freed of distortion was built on the Enlightenment conviction that, at last, human persons were free, in Kant's words, to "dare to know"—words that owed an indirect spiritual debt to the great French Enlightenment thinker Rousseau, whom Kant admired deeply. Thus, Destutt de Tracy, in defining his science of ideas, went back to Bacon's analysis of the four distorting idols in the *Novum Organon*.[31] Even in the idealism of early positivism, ideology was based on the principle that ideas could be socially useful only if freed from the distorting effect of social life.

But the expression of ideology most familiar today first appeared on the eve of the 1848 revolutions. *Ideology* was the crucial term in the younger Marx's attempt to come to terms with Hegel's philosophical idealism. Quite apart from Marx's having, or not having, turned Hegel on his head, Marx's *German*

Ideology did invert the Enlightenment's ocularcentric image. Here appears the single most famous, and justly so, literary reference to ideology, Marx's camera obscura metaphor. If, said Marx, "in all ideology men and their circumstances appear upside-down as in a *camera obscura*, this phenomenon arises just as much from their historical life-process as the inversion of objects in the retina does from their physical life-process."[32] The sentence immediately following is, "In direct contrast to German philosophy which descends from heaven to earth, here we ascend from earth to heaven"—from which followed the well-known line in the *Manifesto* in 1848: "The ruling ideas of each age have ever been the ideas of its ruling class." And, thereafter follows, twenty years later, the fetishism of commodities, which both completes the mature theory of value and unites *Capital* with the earlier, still Hegelian, writings in the *1844 Manuscripts*.

With Marx, the two sides of ideology are united—that of Destutt of Tracy, who undervalued its distortion of reality; that of Bonaparte, who overvalued that distortion. The camera obscura definition entails the more subtle principle of distortion: Yes, ideas in society are distorted, but they are *systematically* distorted. Inverted images, though distorted, can be read. Fifty years later, Freud would make the same claim about dreams. But Marx's idea of ideology was the first important theory of the coherent duplicity of modern knowledge. It was a subtle, double-edged idea. On its one side, as a rhetorical element in Marx's political vocabulary, ideology served to attack the foundations of economic exploitation. On the other, as a description of the interpretability of ideas, through and in spite of their distortions, ideology led to an advance in ideology as a concept in the sociology of knowledge.[33]

What moved subsequent interpreters of Marx's theory of ideology was his contribution to the creation of the moral space of modern man. With Marx's double-edged idea of ideology it became possible, even desirable, to think of knowledge in relation to power. That is, with Marx, man's double nature reappears in the double truths of ideology: Truth distorted by power meant truth's power lay in its own critique. For whatever reason, the prospect of truth's relation to power was never seriously broached prior to the modern age. When finally it was, Destutt de Tracy and the revolutionary ideologues posed it as a science in which the power relation was in the background, while Bonaparte in crushing them saw all too keenly the implications of the ideologues for his politics. Because he doubled these two perceptions into one, Marx's camera obscura is justifiably the locus classicus of ideology. The most important reappearances of ideology thereafter struggled somehow to explain, deny, or rethink the problem posed when one dares to think of truth as somehow conditioned by power. Mannheim tried to justify truth itself; the end-of-ideology ideologists denied the dilemma altogether; while Foucault and others pursued, and redefined, truth's links to politics.

Mannheim acknowledged, of course, the effects of political power on knowledge. But his interest was ultimately in saving knowledge from these effects, or at least justifying its possibility in spite of them. Thus, after the first essay on ideology in 1929, he turned increasingly to founding the sociology of knowledge. One need only read Mannheim's statement of the difference between them to appreciate his interests:

> The sociology of knowledge is closely related to, but increasingly distinguishable from, the theory of ideology, which has also emerged and developed in our time. The study of ideologies has made it its task to unmask the more or less conscious deceptions and disguises of human interest groups, particularly those of political parties. The sociology of knowledge is concerned not so much with distortions due to a deliberate effort to deceive as with the varying ways in which objects present themselves to the subject according to the differences in social settings.[34]

These ideas were taken up in the 1940s by Robert K. Merton, who was important to the early introduction of the sociology of knowledge in the United States and, not at all incidentally, the founder of the sociology of science. Thus, Mannheim's justification of the possibility of truth in spite of power led to new academic disciplines concerned largely with the production of knowledge.[35]

The claim that modernity had progressed sufficiently to be able to rid itself of ideology was asserted in the heat of the Cold War. The first public proclamation of the end of ideology is usually attributed to Edward Shils's 1955 *Encounter* article summarizing the proceedings of an international conference, earlier that year, in Milan, Italy. Thereafter, Edward Shils, Daniel Bell, Raymond Aron, and Seymour Martin Lipset (all participants in the Milan conference) became the leading proponents of the end of ideology, meaning, of course, the end of Marxist ideology. Lipset, for example, began his *Political Man* in 1960 with the following statement: "A basic premise of this book is that democracy is not only or even primarily a means through which different groups attain their ends or seek the good society; it is the good society itself in operation."[36] The ideology of the end of ideology was a preemptory strike in the Cold War in which certain Western intellectuals declared victory perhaps in order to avoid surrender. They attacked Marx's belief that capitalist doctrine distorted the true conditions of estrangement wrought by modernity. Those who shared the worldview of Bell, Shils, Aron, and Lipset saw the American standard of living as evidence of not only distortions in Marx's theory of modernity but also the supposed ideological confusion in the Marxist theory of political truth.

In the late 1950s the end of ideology was an intellectual's moral equivalent to Vice President Richard M. Nixon's famous kitchen debate with Soviet chairman Nikita Khrushchev in 1959 (the year before Lipset's book). Nixon faced Khrushchev in Moscow in an exposition display of a model American kitchen. He confronted Chairman Khrushchev with the argument that capitalism's lead in consumption capacity proved its superiority. "Would it not be better," argued Nixon, "to compete in the relative merits of washing machines than in the strength of rockets?"[37] It was a clever point, given that this was two years after Sputnik, which was then taken as suggestive evidence that the United States could not compete equally in rockets, or even in other fields of advanced technology. In simple terms, the end-of-ideology doctrine held strongly to the belief that modernism had discovered the incorruptible final truth of social life. No revolutionary social change was required because modernism driven by capital energy had already changed the world, truly.

Though, in retrospect, it is easy to view the end of ideology as the worst sort of ideological self-deception, it is also possible to see it as a purgative necessary to intellectual and political life in the United States after Senator Joseph McCarthy's reign of terror. The absurdity of its argument, its refusal to acknowledge its own implausible distortions, came to be one of many cases pointing to the need for a more self-critical sociology. C. Wright Mills, writing at the same time, prepared the way for the New Left by staking out a third-force strategy between Marxism and more familiar social ideas (particularly those of Weber and pragmatism). Mills inspired *The Port Huron Statement* in 1962—itself explicitly shorn of either Marxist or capitalist ideology. The New Left student movement of the early 1960s was, after all, new because it sought a new version of Marxism as much as a new social order in the United States. A decade later, Mills was somewhat the inspiration for Gouldner's *Coming Crisis in Western Sociology*—also a third-force strategy.

It is a bit shocking to look back at these early texts of the New Left and to find them quaint, almost old-fashioned, when compared to current discussions of ideology, truth, and power. *The Port Huron Statement* in 1962 defined its theoretical and political issues well within a social world understood as split between subjects and objects:

> The apathy here is, first, *subjective*—the felt powerlessness of ordinary people, the resignation before the enormity of events. But subjective apathy is encouraged by the *objective* American situation—the actual structural separation of people from power, from relevant knowledge, from the pinnacles of decision-making. Just as the university influences the student way of life, *so do major social institutions create the circumstances in which the isolated citizen will try hopelessly to understand his world and himself.*[38]

The Port Huron Statement, like Mills's sociological imagination (and, later, Gouldner's reflexive sociology), assumed a world of subjects hopelessly abused by objective structures, cut off from true understanding. Just the same, these rebellious sociologies on either side of the sixties pressed to its limits the old moral culture in which subjects sought power in objective truth. The failure of 1960s left politics to change the world contributed to the disorganizing and reframing of the questions subsumed in the concept ideology.

Thereafter, the original formula—ideology as truth distorted by power—gave way to a different set of controversies. In the past generation, the simplicity of those controversies has suddenly become more, even, than just complicated. The earlier theoretical culture in which they, and their formulae, thrived has collapsed—not utterly, but enough to change the terms in which these things are discussed. It is as though the levees protecting towns and villages alongside a swollen river have burst, flooding fields and homes. The plots and structures are still there, partly visible and perhaps recoverable. But all the talk is of what is left, or what will be when the waters recede, if they do. It is not so much that one knows the eventual truth of these things but that the disruption is real enough to change how people talk, and what they talk about. Power has so seeped into the foundations of truth that not even ideology, with all its uncertainties, can contain the difference. As a result, the once invincible barrier between practical and professional sociologies—between, that is, the moral concerns of daily life and the global imperatives of science—is ruptured. Sociologies have become the preoccupations of daily life, as the early New Left sociologies predicted, though in ways they could not have imagined. One hears of the postmodern as much on MTV as in the no less obscure writings of people whose views were once, but no more, thought to be "merely academic."

There are, currently, three broad positions in a complex debate in the theoretical space where once ideology stood. Each position now acknowledges that distortion can no longer explain what becomes of truth in the face of power. Increasingly, the conviction spreads that truth might no longer serve as a normative standard for thought or action. Each position seeks some comfort with this different set of theoretical circumstances.

- *Radical postmodernism* abandons the very idea of truth; accordingly, the problem of ideology is relieved. *critic about what is normative*
- *Radical modernism* seeks, by several means, to retain the idea of truth and thus retain ideology as at least a rhetorical cover for more complex riddles.
- *Strategic postmodernism* attempts the trick of destroying modernity's foundational quest for truth by revising without completely rejecting modernity's categories.

abandoning the very idea of truth
(nothing is real)

▼ ▼ ▼ ▼ ▼

The astonishing ubiquity of the term *postmodernism,* including the perverse varieties of its uses, signifies what has become of the moral concerns that were once reasonably well organized, even kept under control, by the concept ideology. From the French philosophes through Marx, then Mannheim, and the New Left critique of the end of ideology, the concept ideology served as a kind of battleground. In times of social upheaval, struggle over the meaning of ideology has served to redirect attention to the boundary terms of modern culture. Now, in the broad cultural and political anxiety represented by postmodernism, the prior formulations of the distorting truth of ideology are, respectively, rejected, defended, or revised.

Radical postmodernism, in its most extreme form, attacks directly the traditional relation between truth and reality by arguing that the social world has changed in ways that do not permit one to speak of reality as true. According to this view, the real has, in effect, outrun any possible standard by which it might be proven or measured. Hyperreality, thus, is the space in which the real and its imitations are not so much indistinguishable as virtual equivalents; or, in which imitations of reality are, for all social intents and purposes, the principal reality. Perhaps the most notorious of the radical postmodern theorists is Jean Baudrillard, who views the social as composed not of any concrete reality but of simulacra and simulations. He has said, for example, "To dissimulate is to feign not to have what one has. To simulate is to feign to have what one hasn't."[39] Disneyland, he adds, is the perfect example of society as simulation. One need not look beyond it for any truer reality of American life.[40] Thus, in collapsing the distinction between reality and its distortion, Baudrillard allows and requires every social thing to be ideology. If society is simulated spectacle, then truth is distortion.

A common criticism of such a position is that it is so extreme in its playfulness as to be unworthy of serious attention. But in fact, Baudrillard's and other radical postmodern theories can be traced back to the same social and political struggles as those of the American New Left. They both arose, in the late 1960s and early 1970s, in attempts to rethink classically left ideas of political change. In France the then new poststructuralist theories of language and political signs were related to the theatricality of May 1968. One of the historic reasons for thinking of the new society as spectacle or simulation was that failures of the 1968 revolutions in Paris reminded that the young and Marxist left were as much political play actors in an unreal social drama as were President Charles de Gaulle and his government. For example, Guy Debord's 1967 classic situationalist manifesto, *Society as Spectacle,* began:

> In societies where modern conditions of production prevail, all of life presents itself as an immense accumulation of *spectacles.* Everything that was directly lived has moved away into representations. . . . The spectacle presents itself simultaneously as all of society, as part of society, and as *instrument of unification.* As a part of society it is specifically the sector which concentrates all gazing and all consciousness. Due to the very fact that this sector is *separate,* it is common ground of the deceived gaze and of false consciousness, and the unification it achieves is not but an official language of generalized separation. . . . The spectacle is not a collection of images, but a social relation, mediated by images.[41]

Radical postmodernism, thus, is not necessarily a frivolity or, as it is sometimes said, an adventure in nihilism. Rather, it is the point to which modern thought arrives when pushed beyond its limits. Thus, for example, for Durkheim society was the reality sui generis represented by religious images. But, for the radical postmodern, these images (or, in Durkheim's terms, collective representations) of society are the reality sui generis and society becomes nothing more (or less) than one of its own spectacular representations.[42]

At the least, radical postmodernisms illustrate the power of ideology in modern thought—a power that serves to manage the uncertain relations of knowledge to power. In the earlier times of ideology's history, power was that which, in distorting true knowledge, became, when unmasked for what it is, the basis for an Enlightenment hope that true knowledge can become the final power. In the radical postmodern view, ideology has become all there is because power has forced knowledge beyond any plausible claims to be the judge of reality. In Debord's words,

> When ideology, the *abstract* will—and the illusion—of the universal, is legitimized by the universal abstraction and the effective dictatorship of illusion in modern society, it is no longer a voluntaristic struggle of the partial, but its victory. At this point, ideological pretention acquires a sort of flat positivistic exactitude: it is no longer a historical choice but a fact. In this type of assertion, the particular *names* of ideologies have disappeared. Even the role of specifically ideological labor in the service of the system comes to be considered as nothing more than the recognition of an "epistemological" base that pretends to be beyond all ideological phenomena. Materialized ideology itself has no name, just as it has no expressible historical program. This is another way of saying that the history of *ideologies* is over.[43]

In making everything ideology, radical postmodernisms disallow any normative point of leverage from which to critique the horrors visited upon human beings even, perhaps especially, in the spectacular society.[44] Disneyland probably is not emancipation. This worries those holding the second of the three positions in the current debate.

Radical modernism includes, of course, Jürgen Habermas and other critical theories in this important tradition[45]—that is, those who defend modernity if for no other reason than that it provides the only normatively powerful critique of power we know. The power of the radical modern position is demonstrated by writers like Habermas and Martin Jay who take an appreciative and serious reading of the postmodernisms still to defend the value of the modern. Jay, for example,

> The old metaphor of a camera obscura showing ideology as a reverse and inverted image of a truly existing world may . . . be difficult to sustain in our antiocular age, but another link between ideology and the visual may not. That is, what we are looking *for* when we criticize the distortions of ideology may be present in what we are looking *at* in certain manifestations of ideology itself. The images of specular reciprocity, transparent meaning, standing in the light of truth, and so on, may all be easy to deconstruct as chimeras, but they are perhaps also ciphers of that unattainable "Other" of ideology—this time with a capital "O"—on which all critique must ultimately rest.[46]

In this view, truth, whatever its illusions, is better than nothing at all.

It is not an accident that radical modernism prominently includes a number of feminist theorists, most especially those like Nancy Hartsock and Dorothy Smith in the standpoint tradition. From one point of view, this tradition could be considered the right wing of left modernism insofar as it seeks to substitute the truth of women's reality for modernity's patriarchal idea of truth. From another point of view, it is an aggressively radical assertion of women's truth as the foundation for feminist action. In Dorothy Smith's words, "The critical force of these methods is contained in . . . enlarging women's powers and capacities to organize and struggle against the oppression of women."[47] It is particularly instructive to take the standpoint feminists as illustrative of the radical modernist position because with them the precise political urgency of abandoning the ideal of truth as emancipation from the distortions and dehumanizing force of power is most palpable. If the seriousness of the political concerns expressed by Dorothy Smith makes the radical postmodernists look frivolous, so too they pose important questions of the strategic postmodernist position.

Strategic postmodernisms, all too often confused with radical postmodernisms, are neither so quick to abandon the power of knowledge as are the radical postmodernisms nor so steadfast in clinging to the modernist formulation of knowledge's power. Strategic postmodernisms are attempts more to redefine truth and power than to either dismiss or preserve their classic modern relations. This, therefore, is the name for those positions that attempt to make two moves at once—rejecting modernity's values while using its language. This strategy is evident in one form in deconstructionist literary studies, and in another in Foucault's history of the modern subject, as well as in numerous other related activities.[48] Foucault, however, is the crucial case because it is against Foucault that radical modernism, including its feminist expressions, has principally defined itself.

When Foucault first came to world attention in the late 1960s and early 1970s he was viewed much as Baudrillard is today. With the passage of time, however, Foucault has come to appear more moderate. True, he rejected the philosophies of modernity—linear history, teleological ends, progress, the original Subject, histories of consciousness, and so forth. Nonetheless, his entire effort (with several notable deviations[49]) can be characterized fairly as a critical history of modernity. Ambitious perhaps, but not exactly wild-eyed. Foucault argued that the social logic of modernity served to subjugate subjects gently. Herein lies, simply, the central problem and genius of his method. Foucault understood that one cannot write the history of modern subjecthood from any point within modernity.

But why must one leave the modern world in order to write its history? Because modernity was constituted with the support of the ideology of the historical Subject—from the enlightened consciousness to the free political thinker to economic man. If, he reasoned, modernity covered its own contradictions in the veil of subjectivity, then that veil can hardly also serve to expose the awful truth it hides. Critical analysis, Foucault believed, must work from the "forms of resistance" to modernity. Thus, he said of his method, "Rather than analyzing power from the point of view of its internal rationality, [my method] consists of analyzing power relations through the antagonism of strategies."[50] He began, therefore, with oppositions, strains, resistances, differences within and against the dominant ideology of modernity. In intentional distinction from Enlightenment practices (like those of Durkheim) in which the social is defined within the metaphysical couplets of double man, the oppositions Foucault identified were empirical and political. For example, "There are two meanings of the word *subject*: subject to someone else by control and dependence, and tied to his own identity by a conscience or self-knowledge. Both meanings suggest a form of power which subjugates and makes subject to."[51] Like the similar play he made on the historical concept *discipline* in reference to the history of the social sciences, this play on the double meaning of *subject* can be interpreted as a revision of the problems addressed by the concept ideology. If ideology was one of the terms by which modernity simultaneously confessed and denied its contradictory nature, then a duplicitous play on terms like *subject* and *discipline* intends to expose the failure of nerve within the critique of ideology.

The critique of ideology, Foucault might have said, was still too modernist to be sufficiently critical. It was, as such, too susceptible to the quest for truth found in Mannheim and the uneven attention to politics in Marx. Ideology must be broken apart, reshaped, and used—not as a master category but as an element in a politics of historical knowledge. Thus, the term *subject* is taken in its two parts—subjugation and subjecthood as identity—both of which must be kept in mind if one wants to understand modernity. In other words, Foucault destabilized yet held together the term *subject* in order to define the ideology whereby its one meaning, subjecthood, was used to mystify its political effect, subjugation. Likewise, just as the play on the term *discipline* identified the role of the new social sciences in the disciplining of laboring bodies, so the amalgamated expression *power/knowledge* brought into the open the role of the will to truth in the workings of power.

In Foucault's account, in the introduction to his *History of Sexuality,* of Jouy, the nineteenth-century farmworker, the peasant man's sexuality was disciplined, his desires subjugated—not by punishment but by the scrupulous investigation of the moral, medical, and psychological aspects of his subjecthood:

> One day in 1867, a farm hand from the village of Lapcourt, who was somewhat simple-minded, employed here then there, depending on the season, living hand-to-mouth from a little charity or in exchange for the worst sort of labor, sleeping in barns and stables, was turned into the authorities. At the border of a field, he had obtained a few caresses from a little girl, just as he had done before and seen done by the village urchins round about him; for, at the edge of the wood, or in the ditch by the road leading to Saint-Nicolas, they would play the familiar game called "curdled milk." So he was pointed out by the girl's parents to the mayor of the village, reported by the mayor to the gendarmes, led by the gendarmes to the judge, who indicted him and turned him over first to a doctor, then to two other experts who not only wrote their report but also had it published. What is the significant thing about this story? The pettiness of it all; the fact that this everyday occurrence in the life of village sexuality, these inconsequential bucolic pleasures, could become, from a certain time, the object not only of a collective intolerance but of a judicial action, a medical intervention, a careful clinical examination, and an entire theoretical elaboration. The thing to note is that they went so far as to measure the brainpan, study the facial bone structure, and inspect for possible signs of degenerescence the anatomy of this per-

sonage who up to that moment had been an integral part of village life; that they made him talk; that they questioned him concerning his thoughts, inclinations, habits, sensations, and opinions. And then, acquitting him of any crime, they decided finally to make him into a pure object of medicine and knowledge—an object to be shut away till the end of his life in the hospital at Mareville, but also one to be made known to the world of learning through a detailed analysis. . . . So it was that our society—and it was doubtless the first in history to take such measures—assembled around these timeless gestures, these barely furtive pleasures between simple-minded adults and alert children, a whole machinery of speechifying, analyzing, and investigating.[52]

Thus arose modern knowledge with its power to treat, confine, and reduce by analysis any subject of whom it has need and interest. Power turned the simple-minded farmhand, Juoy, into an object of knowledge.

Power/knowledge, thus, is a strategic reinterpretation of *ideology.* The method heightens attention to the discursive term in order to engage a political practice. Foucault, thus, departs from the Enlightenment conviction that knowledge distinct from power *is* the final power. This, of course, is what unnerves some radical modernists. Here, Foucault seems all too close to the extremes of the radical postmodernisms in which there is no reality other than discourse, signs, and spectacle. Foucault does intend to disturb the modernist ideal of language as the representation of reality. Yet, he remains a strategic postmodernist. Even where it seems he takes discourse as the only reality there is, Foucault still believes in knowledge. True, Foucault's knowledge is not that to which we are accustomed. It rests on no foundation; it mirrors no ulterior world. Yet, neither is power/knowledge a trick.

The seriousness of Foucault's critical analysis of modernity is most evident in his strategic effort somehow to get around the foremost barrier to social knowledge, to get around the fact that in modernity the surest way to limit what is known is to take modernity at face value. If one is to believe modernity's ideology—that terms and concepts can capture reality—then it will never be possible to criticize modernity's self-deception. Modernity is cleverer than we are; cleverer even than the political radicals, those in the tradition of Marx. It can never be enough to clarify our concepts or inflate our critical consciousness or make more exact our terms. These are procedures bound to the traditions and values of modernity itself, caught in the recesses of the double hermeneutic.

The most striking example is Foucault's critique of the repressive hypothesis at the beginning of the first volume of *The History of Sexuality.* He has in mind both the specific assumption that, in the Victorian era, power repressed sexuality and the broader theoretical axiom that power works negatively, explicitly, and from the top down. What he aims to show is that power worked on, and through, sexuality not by repressing it but by stimulating talk about it. This would sound, as many have pointed out, very much like Herbert Marcuse's critical theory of repressive desublimation were it not that Foucault makes one more twist than does any critical theory. He argues that even the language of social criticism participates in the play of power on sexuality. "Did the critical discourse," he asks, "that addresses itself to repression come to act as a roadblock to a power mechanism that had operated unchallenged up to that point, or is it not in fact part of the same historical network as the thing it denounces (and doubtless misrepresents) by calling it 'repression'?"[53] In other words, notwithstanding his debts to Marx and his cultural left politics, Foucault requires a ruthless attack on modernity even where its political ambitions are sympathetic to his.

Thus, Foucault would have argued, had he addressed himself straightforwardly to a history of the concept ideology, that ideology (no less than repression and, certainly, no less than truth) was part of the complex process whereby modernity subjugated gently. Ideology's intention to criticize itself, to critique the distortions of the dominant culture, to point out the repressions it justifies, could not save ideology from its own duplicity. This, precisely, is the crucial difference between Foucault and his teacher Louis Althusser. Althusser's famous notion of ideology as the representation of "the imaginary relationship of individuals to their real conditions of existence"[54] serves to maintain the tensions inherent in Marx's classic view by defining ideology as the interpretive index to state and, by implication, social reality. By contrast, Foucault ignores ideology as if to say it no longer accounts for the more complicated play of power and truth in modern culture.

Ideology, one would say from Foucault's perspective, is a particularly troubling roadblock to social analysis. Like the top-down, repressive theory of power, it deflects analysis from the most stunning, and ubiquitous, fact of the modern age. Ideology in its two senses—as the distortion of truth and as the critique of this distortion—is an instrument of power because it is part of a culture wherein calling attention to the distortion of truth serves to reinforce the will to truth. Thus, for ideology he substitutes the expression *power/knowledge* as a continuous reminder that the only truth is that truth is a function of power. From this ensues a method and program that guides all of his empirical studies. It is accurate to consider Foucault's program strategic (hence moderate relative to the radical postmodernists) because, though he abandons the ideals of reality, he pursues a systematic, and balanced, analysis of the modern age. "I would like," he has said,

> to search instead for instances of discursive production (which also administer silences, to be sure), of the production of power (which sometimes have the function

of prohibiting), of the propagation of knowledge (which often cause mistaken beliefs or systematic misconceptions to circulate); I would like to write the history of these instances and their transformations.[55]

Among the more telling criticisms of Foucault are those by feminist theorists. Nancy Hartsock, for example, asks: "Why is it that just at the moment when so many of us who have been silenced begin to demand the right to name ourselves, to act as subjects rather than objects of history, that just then the concept of subjecthood becomes problematic?"[56] The severity of Hartsock's criticisms comes in large part from her allegiance, as a standpoint theorist, to radical modernism.

Is Foucault really a conservative voice, as Habermas and Nancy Fraser have asked?[57] Fraser's critique, though more subtle than Hartsock's, still attacks the same point. "The problem is," Fraser states, "that Foucault calls too many different sorts of things power and simply leaves it at that." And she adds, "What Foucault needs, and needs desperately, are normative criteria for distinguishing acceptable from unacceptable forms of power." Just as Hartsock thinks Foucault eliminates the critical power of subjecthood, Fraser fears that his theory of power is so diffuse as to lack any normative dimension.

These concerns deserve a different, higher, order of respect when expressed by those engaged in a political struggle. Yet, their attacks on Foucault are somewhat ironic. He, and the feminist theories opposing him, share the view that politics must be brought into the open, out from behind falsely dialectic concepts, like ideology, in which the raw effects of power are tenderized by gentle worries over the distortion of truth. Foucault and his feminist critics agree: If there is any possible foundation for knowledge, it must be frankly political. Where they differ is in the demand for a normative basis to distinguish good from bad power, which is, in the end, a demand still to found a political critique on some principle within, even precious to, modernity itself. In Fraser's case, normativeness is left unexamined. Perhaps it must be, like Martin Jay's suggestion that ideology's signification of its Other is power, if not power enough.

But wherever one takes a stand, this is the issue between radical modernism and strategic postmodernism. In many ways it is a remarkably familiar issue. Can any social world generate the principle of its own critique? Can modernity generate any truth, any norm, sufficiently powerful to criticize itself? From Hartsock's and Fraser's points of view the political objective is too dear to risk giving up the most emancipatory features of the world we know.

From Foucault's point of view the world we know knows us too well. Having made us, it will not ever allow us to outwit it. For the radical modernists, the idea of a postmodern world seems to demand too much that seems familiar: giving up the gains in the world one knows to begin again the struggle. For the strategic postmodernists, the idea of a postmodern world is less an historical reality than a critical necessity for transgressing the limits of the world we know in order to expose its deeper structures.

To each her own does not apply here. The issues are real, and yet to be resolved. Where there is reasonable clarity, and some agreement between Foucault and his critics, is over the importance of bringing power out of the closet of truth. This, in turn, affects even the most dynamic of categories we have traditionally used, including ideology.

Kennan's ideology of containment helped establish Cold War knowledge of the world, on the basis of which world power was organized. In light of the debate over the postmodernisms, this is now entirely evident. But did the critiques of Cold War ideology that led to its collapse in the last months of Bush's presidency emerge from within? Probably not. In the Soviet bloc itself, there is no historical evidence that the prevailing Marxisms were able, and they were certainly not willing, to criticize themselves. In the West in the 1950s, when the desire to criticize the culture of the Cold War was most urgently felt, liberal intellectuals and politicians were busy declaring the end of ideology in terms that had no detectable effect on either the Marxism they thought dead or the liberal culture they considered ideology-free. The New Left critics who followed, try as they did, did little more than force the hand of Marxism to show it held no wild card after all.[58] Nor is there, in retrospect, now that the one big ideology is really at its end and the other in a quandary, reason to suppose that the Cold War ideologies asserted themselves in the last half of the twentieth century in a top-down fashion that would allow us to explain the current world disruptions in terms like exhaustion or contradiction or merely the failure of those in power to assert its truth more vigorously.

Elaine Tyler May's *Homeward Bound*, a study of family life in the 1950s, explains how this same Cold War ideology was so diffused throughout American culture that it instructed in the most exacting detail the lives of ordinary people.[59] In particular, May describes the general moral instruction that in the 1950s taught that female sexuality was an explosive force to be contained. Sexualized women were described as bombshells. The bikini was named four days after the explosion of a nuclear bomb in the Bikini Islands. Family life in the suburbs was understood to be not only the necessary containment of these explosive forces but also the best American response to the communist threat. Family life, a good marriage, and fine children made Americans mature, responsible, strong. The consumption of appliances for cleaning and cooking was a manifestation of America's exceptional destiny. What Nixon argued with Khrushchev was believed and acted out in daily lives. In effect, *Homeward Bound* constructs the cultural means whereby in post–World War II America the female subject was subjected within a global ideology.

The ideology of containment was everywhere, with powerful effect. It appeared, for example, in the life of Nora Grey, the fictionalized name of a respondent in the Kelly Longitudinal Study of 1950s adults. Nora Grey lived the principles of domestic containment. She bore four children who exhausted her. She repaired the house, shopped, mowed the lawn, paid the bills with no help from her husband, Chester. She lost interest in sex, but, as she said, "feigned it." When she thought of seeking psychiatric help to deal with her feelings of inadequacy, her husband said, "Your trouble is in your head and you don't have to feel this way if you don't want to." She endured and, after some years, came to believe and state that it was all worth it. She felt she had a "nice home I can run the way I want to," "a husband to be a life-time companion and protector," and "a fine group of children to keep life from being monotonous."[60] Nora Grey pursued so faithfully the good American life that her own personal needs were contained by the domestic arrangement that Nixon claimed to be the proof of American superiority and others at the time considered the sign of the end of ideology.

Is Elaine Tyler May correct that Nora Grey's life in the suburbs was directly linked to George Kennan's telegram, Nixon's debate, McCarthy's speech in Wheeling, West Virginia, in 1950? How does the distortion of truth by power work? From an elite down through the body? Or from the subtler paths of day-to-day gossip and instruction throughout the body? And how are such ideologies critiqued? By the generation of their principles of internal contradiction? Or by the slow, mundane altering of practices and beliefs? Nora Grey one day, finally, finding herself no longer containing, or willing to contain, her feelings?

Though they are not yet evident, the final answers to questions like these may also yield an answer to the original question of the modern world, Who was that man?

Alex Supertramp, like millions of moderns since and including Durkheim and the other early social theorists, believed he was the man who would find himself, and his humanity, off alone in the wilderness. He was the doubled man who, in the extremity of his moral actions, knew there was a limit to the human but believed the powerful truth of his identity was to be found just this side of death. Whatever he believed, it seems he was wrong—not because he was finite but because he believed somewhere he could find his truth.

Nora Grey is no less mysterious. Yet, she represents millions of those, and not just women in the American suburbs, who in their youth in the 1950s felt they were the problem. There is no current theory of truth and power that can account for the fact that individuals more or less in the same circumstance as Nora Grey in the 1950s rebelled as they grew older. If power, whether top-down or diffused throughout the body cultural, explains her false belief that she was at fault for the failure in her family, then what explains her astonishing ability to become something other in so short a time? It seems unlikely that it was either, simply, a sudden beautiful enlightenment or a dramatic new capacity for resistance. Rather, it seems simply to have happened somewhere in a cultural and political fault between truth and power.

Between the extreme fantasies of Alex Supertramp and the practical necessities of the Nora Greys is a striking contrast. The one seems to have searched for his difference in order to find his humanity; the other, perhaps without searching, found herself in her difference. Nora Grey, if she can be taken to represent the feminisms and others that came after her, did not become any one thing. She, and they, became, simply, different in all the senses of the word. It is, therefore, worth exploring the idea that somewhere in a possible failure of modern culture, in its seeming inability to maintain any sort of true relation to its own power, modernity's riddle has found its answer.

Who am I if things social are different? It is possible that in a world where there is no one commanding truth, difference is what is, and what one can be. This would be, of course, a totally unsatisfying answer to any sort of modernist. For him difference itself is the puzzle. It may not be any more satisfying for the varieties of postmodernisms that still, one way or another, seek the general, if not the essential, in social things. As it turns out, Foucault, and all he represents, was not utterly at odds with Durkheim, and all he represents. In the end, even the strategic postmodernists are tempted by the belief that there are such realities as power diffused through modern knowledge. It is not particularly likely that Nora Grey was shaped by just one power, or one ideology. In any case, she came to be someone other to the then dominant powers—modernity itself, the Cold War, whichever. It may be that there are only powers.

Thus, the question now may be, What happens to social hope if differences have no salient structure?

Weak world

Chapter 5

Measured Selves in Weak Worlds

Aт about the time Alex Supertramp set out to his end, when also George Bush had trouble telling the story of the Cold War's end, residents in an Upper West Side neighborhood of New York City were having troubles of their own.

The trouble was Larry Hogue. Though the neighborhood at West 96th Street is not one of New York's fanciest, it is a relatively safe and secure corner of the city for many middle- and upper-middle-class families and elderly people for whom Hogue was a menace. A man of imposing physical stature, Larry Hogue considers West 96th Street as much his neighborhood as theirs. Their complaint was that he threatened passersby (once hoisting a sidewalk bench above his head in a menacing fashion), disrupted traffic and local businesses, and generally struck fear in the hearts of local residents. In the many accounts of Hogue's troubled relations with the neighborhood, various explanations for his behavior are suggested, though none is ever finally argued.

Captions used by the *New York Times* through spring 1993 suggest its interpretation of this story of troubles: "West Side Homeless Man Is Tentatively Ruled Ill; He Should Be Committed, Psychiatrists Say" (August 29, 1992); "Mentally Ill Man Committed Against His Will by Judge" (December 23, 1992); "Man Accused of Harassment Ordered Freed from Hospital" (February 3, 1993); "Man Who Attacked Pedestrians to Stay in Hospital Until Hearing"

(February 9, 1993); "Forced Confining Is Upheld for Mentally Ill Drug Addict" (March 2, 1993). The stories themselves more or less point to Hogue's state of mind as the problem. It is also implied that he is poor and addicted to crack cocaine. His attacks are, it seems, most often social insults of a severe kind rather than actionable assaults.[1]

The real problem for the locals in his Upper West Side neighborhood is that when Hogue is drug-clean and under treatment he is perfectly lucid and decidedly competent with respect to his civil rights. As the *New York Times* captions indicate, those who took official interest in the matter risked rebuke by the courts. Like many in similar situations, Hogue does not desire the gentle ministrations of the state. To make it worse for those he menaced, Hogue knows his civil rights and is often able to persuade the courts that he cannot be forcibly confined for the purpose of "care." Once, he won release outright, then lost it in March 1993. Later that summer, he rewon his freedom, only to lose it again.

Though the *New York Times* predictably took a high reportorial road by framing the story in medical, social welfare, or legal terms, other media saw it differently, more in keeping with the basic instinct of Western thought. A *New York Post* caption read: "'Wild Man' to Get Taste of Freedom: Granted Two Furloughs from Mental Hospital" (August 11, 1993). Another put it simply: "Step Toward Freedom for 'Wild Man'" (*New York Daily News,* August 11, 1993).[2] Deep in Western culture lies this struggle with the primitive, the wild savage—from whom freed men are descended, from whom they must distinguish themselves. The wild man is always linked to human freedom—whether Larry Hogue's or Supertramp's. It is not by accident that the wild man theme entered the story just at the point when Hogue seemed to have secured his freedom—based equally as much on his access to reasonable means of support as to the insistence upon his civil right to refuse confinement for care he does not want.[3]

It is not, therefore, entirely clear just who Larry Hogue is, or how, exactly, to figure him. The story of Larry Hogue is never what it seems from a particular point of view. None of the media accounts can quite determine what his line is—homeless? addict? mentally ill? wild man? Vietnam vet? trouble? free man? or, even, the one they dare suggest only in photos accompanying stories, Black? No less, the courts and other officers of state protection regularly come up against his deep capacity for insistence on his rights, his lucidity when drug-free, his material resources that promise independent living. And Hogue himself seems to live in different worlds, though always drawn back, for some reason, to West 96th Street. Nothing in his story is ever simply a case of mistaken identity, of honest (or dishonest) errors in perception, presentation, or interpretation of the man's true nature. Hogue's true nature is somehow beyond traditional wisdom.

Put differently, it is hard to take the measure of Larry Hogue, harder even than to figure the nature of Alex Supertramp. Chris McCandless, in assuming another name, claimed an identity for himself, however inscrutable. There is no reason to suppose that Larry Hogue chose to be the "Wild Man of 96th Street." On the contrary, according to reports, everything he has been able to do on his own behalf serves to prove and assert his rights of free citizenship. In the one case, McCandless's, a free man gave them up to seek his truth in the wilderness. But the other case is not an obverse. Hogue is not, by contrast to Supertramp, the wild man seeking his civilization. More evidently, he is a man of uncertain identity caught, though not passively, between the fears and revulsions of a local neighborhood, the gratuitous services of well-intended officers of the state, and his hard-to-deny rights to liberty under the law.

Nor is it that Hogue can be presumed to lack any sense of himself. So far as one can tell from the stories told about him, Hogue seems to possess a definite idea of who he is, even if it may at times be dislodged by the effects of a brain injury or crack. Nor can the differences between Supertramp and Mr. Hogue be attributed to any standard sociological variable like class or race. The one renounced his class origins, the other insisted on his class rights. Both were men with access to sufficient means. One, being white, sought the darkest corner of the North American continent; the other, being Black, brought the light of his reasonable rights into a corner of social life darkened by the reluctance of local needs, state generosity, and civil law to fall into clarifying harmony. In the West, light and dark oscillate oddly, often just out of the normal range of human sensibility. Race may be one of the ultrasounds of culture and politics, but it is not one that can produce its barely audible but terrifying effects without setting in motion the less abstract structures of social life.

The stories of both men resist reasonable interpretation. Yet, the barrier to truth in each is different. Alex Supertramp died without giving up a clear and distinct meaning to his purposes. Yet, even allowing for the possibility that madness had crept into those purposes, he was acting out an entirely normal pilgrimage of young men in the West. Throughout the modern age, beginning with the great explorations half a millennium ago, men not much older than Chris McCandless set out to find and test the limits of civilization. It is not by chance that McCandless followed nearly exactly the legendary trail of two young men—Meriwether Lewis and William Clark—out from the South, across the Mississippi, through the Missouri and its tributaries, to the Northwest. Still, today, that journey is a quest for the last frontier.[4]

The story of Larry Hogue is vastly more complicated. It cannot be shaped by any of the staples of Western literature. There is no moral journey. We are not told from whence or where he came, only that his troubles *may* have begun with an accidental head injury in 1968. He wants, simply, his right to freedom. Even the presumption of madness cannot erase the good sense of this desire. Yet, this right is not wanted for some grand moral purpose. At one moment all Hogue wanted was to settle down in Bridgeport, Connecticut—the only city of any scale in America ever to file for bankruptcy. Bridgeport in 1993 is not what Thomas Jefferson had in mind for America when he sent Lewis and Clark on their adventure nearly two centuries before. It is hard today to take the measure of individuals in Larry Hogue's social world because the larger world is, today, so weak.

On June 20, 1803, President Thomas Jefferson wrote his extraordinarily detailed letter of instruction to Captain Meriwether Lewis. The letter was mostly filled with precise instructions for the route and the mapping, which Jefferson knew to be crucial to his ambition of extracting wealth and power from the great Northwest. But the president also included instructions for the ultimate safety of Lewis and his party. Though cut through with Enlightenment calculations, Jefferson's words to Lewis reflected the considerable strength of his world in contrast to Larry Hogue's weak world of today. Jefferson wrote:

> As it is impossible for us to foresee in what manner you will be received by those people, whether with hospitality or hostility, so is it impossible to describe the exact degree of perseverance with which you are to pursue your journey. We value too much the lives of citizens to offer them to probable destruction. Your numbers will be sufficient to secure you against the unauthorized opposition of individuals, or of small parties: but if a superior force, authorized or not authorized, by a nation, should be arrayed against your further passage, & inflexibly determined to arrest it, you must decline it's further pursuit, & return. In the loss of yourselves, we should lose also the information you will have acquired. By returning safely with that, you may enable us to renew the essay with better calculated means.[5]

Then, when America and the West were still young and shaping themselves, the others ("these people") were in fact discernibly Other. Lewis and Clark knew they should expect hostility from those native to the wilderness they would breech, or from Spanish and other European competitors in the new republic who wanted the Northwest Passage as much as Jefferson.

Then, one knew one's rivals and enemies. In Larry Hogue's world, the startling fact is that "these people" are not so much Other as "us." The social world on the Upper West Side in which he aims to live and move, for whatever reasons, is not after all any longer a wilderness, and its residents and their official state authorities are not foreign in any way. The remarkable nature of Larry Hogue's social world is that he, whatever his state of mind, faces others who face him in much the same way. Neither for Hogue nor for the residents of West 96th Street is there any way out, and no enlightened Jefferson to guide them. The law, like the doctors and caseworkers who treated Hogue, have no more way to be clear on what to do than did the protesting neighbors. If anyone in all that knows what he wants exactly, it is the so-called Wild Man, who, by insisting on the most elemental principle of law, may yet win his right to live in Bridgeport, of all places.

In the absence of a strongly structured world, these things are hard to figure.

The idea that any individual lives in a social *world* is a figure of sociological speech. In English, the word "world" has many meanings. But to speak of Larry Hogue's "world" in relation to Alex Supertramp's is to speak of the two different modern senses of the word, neither quite literal, neither quite divorced from the other, neither quite in harmony with the other as it once was. In modern language "world" means (1) "the order of things as such," and (2) "the sphere of interests that explain who one is."[6] The familiar sociological locution "social world" subtly combines these two meanings, but in a way that leaves open the relation of the parts. Alex Supertramp's social world was well (if bizarrely) ordered within the normal worldly terms of the West. It was weakly structured only as a sphere describing and explaining his interests and, thus, his identity. Larry Hogue's world of social things is, again, not quite an obverse of this, but a distortion of it in which the two defining elements are evident but in a relation that seems to change everything. For Hogue, the world as the ordered system of things is so utterly out of kilter because its kilter is convenient neither to him nor to those who would remove him. Though perhaps not quite as a result of this, his sphere of personal interests gives the appearance of being thoroughly coherent either in spite of or because of the alleged effects of his mental illness.

Neither man represents a social world that makes strong claim on the interpretive senses. Both are wild but in utterly different ways—Chris McCandless because he went too far out; Larry Hogue because, holding defiantly to the center, he furiously insists on his rights. But the difference that ought to capture the imagination is the one that puts the Supertramp in perspective. If he was a perversely clear representation of the extremes of modern ethics, then Hogue may be the similar in relation to what comes after. One might hesitate to call him postmodern, yet it is certainly evident that he is not a "Wild Man" as, under the earlier influence of modern culture, he would have been. He, possibly, represents the social world that today no longer sustains collective representations, as once so many, especially Durkheim, thought it ought.

It is difficult today to take the measure of persons like Larry Hogue because they live strongly in weakly structured social worlds. As enigmatic as this may sound, this may well be a sufficient way to describe the current situation for social theory and sociologies of all sorts.

▼ ▼ ▼ ▼ ▼

Since Marx, Durkheim, Weber, and Freud—and all those they represented, those for whom their representations of the social world made passable sense—sociologies have struggled inconclusively with a fixed set of moral and theoretical riddles. Each, as I have said, is contained in the one Durkheim stumbled on: *Who am I if things social are different?* Early sociology, thus, expressed in this one question a series of questions that now are asked differently. In that day the most salient social facts were those of the new social division of labor. Experiencing the world as irrevocably structured along lines of salient differences, moderns of all kinds had to think freshly about themselves and their world—that is, about the social world that defined their sphere of interests and was structured through material systems of social order.

For which the concept of double man, whether voiced or not, served as the provisional answer. For Durkheim, double man was exhaustively social, hence moral, hence generic. There was no socially viable Other within the social division of labor—not woman, not children, not his Jewish past, not even the true differences of the elemental primitive. This was the duty excised by Durkheim's need to keep the primitive collective conscience as the primal source and ultimate moral standard for modern moral life. But Durkheim was, in this respect, an exception among the classic social theorists only in the constraining effects produced by his desire to establish a sociology. The others among the four worked with much the same riddle—each in his way adding dimension that Durkheim could not quite allow himself.

Marx insisted on pursuing the unthought, defined as the hidden structural contradiction of modern life. He was wise to do so but, it turn outs, foolish to believe it could be done entirely within the language and methods of any modern sociology, even one so doggedly and brilliantly elaborated as his. He too relied on the defining culture of the double man. Marx's modern man was, like Durkheim's, a doublet: drugged and alienated by the structures of things modern, yet possessor of the capacity for emancipatory knowledge. Marx courageously pursued the hidden secrets of productive life behind the visible accords of the marketplace, believing that if those truths were told, power would right itself. It would be wrong to judge Marx too harshly for his failure, if only because his purposes were decent, even noble.

Freud pursued a goal similar to Marx's, to uncover the secrets of the invisible aspects of the modern mind, but, oddly, he did so in a fashion similar to Durkheim's. If Durkheim fixed the moral terms of modern life in a primitive original state, then Freud did much the same in fixing it in the primitive original instincts that continued to struggle with the modern soul. Their differences lay only in their reversal of fortunes. Durkheim assumed the modern soul was sufficient to the moral origins of man and thus would always win the battle with the passions. Freud doubted this until the end, when it seemed that there was no other course but to affirm even a discontented civilization over the forces of destruction.[7] But, in his youthful and mature theories of the psyche, Freud, like Durkheim, saw modern man doubled—for Freud between the priestly demands of the superego and the deep urges for death and life of the id.[8] To the extent that the social element in Freud's moral theory was more priestly than pastoral—a stern, demanding insistence on repression—he was simultaneously true to the empirical conditions of modern life and false to its naive belief that the truth would always out.

Weber, though he did not use the expression prominently, as did Durkheim, was in some respects the most forthright classic theorist of the double man. More than any of the four, Weber defined the formal terms of the riddle. He alone explicitly deployed the classic formulation of modern social thought that first took shape in 1639 in Réne Descartes's *Discourse on Method,* thereafter to be debated and reshaped (for Weber most prominently by Immanuel Kant). Weber, among the four nineteenth-century social theorists, put the riddle most clearly: What is the moral fate of the subject's inner truth when the outer social world, with all its superficial straining for rational order, is so thoroughly structured along lines of division?[9] Against his deeper wishes, Weber was the sociological ironist. In *Protestant Ethic and the Spirit of Capitalism,* his early application of a new method, Weber so powerfully defined and documented, page after page, the rationalizing effects of the modern ethic that, in the end, it is surprising to the reader that he retained the capacity for self-reflection, with which he looked not just at what he had wrought but at the modern world itself to see that all the alleged benefits of rational culture were at some odds with the human spirit. Durkheim lacked this courage. The modern world, Durkheim insisted, was at perfect, if deferred, accord with the true human spirit. Marx, in consigning the promise of human reason to the netherworld of alienated social being, put himself into the complex dilemma of being the *only* possible individual sufficiently free of false consciousness to be able to diagnose the nature of things in order to save the world. As Gouldner once remarked, Marx could not explain himself. Either that, or he could not explain how the emancipatory revolution would derive from the ignorance of the working man.[10] And Freud, at once the most perverse in his conclusion about modern man and the most naively optimistic adherent of a method of enlightenment, simply held, in his clinical theories, that the talking cure could work in the free environment of the analyst's couch against the terrible odds of the ego's attempt to mediate the insane battle between the irrational secrets of the id and the demanding conscience of the superego.[11]

Among these four, there is no clear resolution. It remains, in hindsight, only to see in their respective, related struggles to solve the moral dilemma of their day the terms of the modernist riddle, now more formally stated:

1. It is subjective meaning (in all the senses of the term) that distinguishes modern man from the original essence of the Human.
2. Yet, this Subject never was known to have been thought outside a social world oriented not to the supernatural but to human history.
3. As a matter of historical fact, History as a sphere of uniquely human interests did not exist prior to, or outside the time of, the era of human explorations of the world, beginning roughly around 1500.
4. The Human, therefore, is more or less coterminous with modernity itself, which, in turn, is more or less equivalent to a moral culture that believes (even when it cannot explain it) that the primitive nature of social things will progressively fulfill itself in some uncertain future.

To which principles it is necessary to add the usually unacknowledged and baffling corollary:

5. For such a set of principles to describe a social world, in the sense of an ordered system, there must always be against or behind it a set of limiting terms.

This is what has been called the unthought,[12] which, as we have seen, stands for the fact that the culture of modern life always is confounded by the Other it cannot explain.

If nothing else, that unthought Other is there to account for the queaziness one feels in the face of principle 4. If the truth is always ultimately yet to be discovered, then how long must some suffer the injuries of present frustrations and pains? The unthought is a name for the circumstance in which deferred progress is implied to be a natural condition.

What makes the story of Larry Hogue so disturbing, however, is that it seems to represent a condition in which everything truly has been thought of. Still it does not make sense. This is why sociologies, always a part of the moral culture of modern life, their importance not lesser in this time of crisis, need to meet the moral and intellectual challenges posed by worlds such as those inhabited by men and women like Larry Hogue—persons difficult to figure who live in and seem to be encouraged by an overall weakness of the world's structures.

When the world is considered strong and powerful, as it was in Europe and America through much of the nineteenth and twentieth centuries, modernity's riddle worked its ways quietly, secretly—in the form of grave, but understated, doubts like those of the classic sociologists. But when, as in the years following the late 1960s, the strength of world order is shaken, the riddle breaks into the open, disrupting the superficial calm whereby the more comfortable think they know who they are in the world. Weak worlds weaken the normal measure of self-worth. Hogue is not alone in thinking of such a world circumstance as a mess.

Though at different times, and in different ways, sociologies have used a variety of languages to describe their activities, sociologies have but three fundamental problems to solve. Each is related in a unique way to the riddle Durkheim could not solve, and none can be done away with. In the simplest of terms those problems are those already evident in the preceding, namely:

1. What does the structured world demand or allow?
2. What am I, in and of my-self, to do and be in relation to those demands and permissions?
3. How is such a self in such a world to measure the social and moral space between and within the relation of self to structure?

Simpler still, sociologies involve considerations entailed in the relations among (1) *structures,* (2) *selves,* (3) *measures.*

Everything necessary for a sociology is in the relations among these three; accordingly, the relations among them define and determine the necessity of all sociologies, both moral and professional. Though the terms used tend, as here, to imply a privilege for the language of the professional social sciences and philosophies over those of less technically schooled moral individuals, the appearance is deceptive. The deception is created by the attempt to use language to describe the most fundamental moral dilemma of life in the modern world. Were it not for the obligation, made all the more serious by the discipline sociologists accept to describe the dilemma in the clearest, most precise terms, it is at least possible that the appearance of an excessive formality in the terms merely distracts attention from the ubiquity of the dilemmas to which they refer.

When the terms *structure* and *self* are used in the first two instances, one is right to suppose that the individual encounters a straightforward matter of resolving the balance between two differing, yet related, social things, much like those upon which Durkheim sought to found his sociology. When one views the terms in this way, one finds topics of compelling interest to philosophers and other professional social thinkers and scientists, but not of their relation, which is of greater interest to the moral individual, whether tutored or not. Persons in a social world they consider real enough to take seriously face the issue posed by the connection of the terms: *How does the structure of this world affect my sphere of interests and activities?* This is the classic question of selfhood. Who am I? is, at least in modern life, always a morally interesting question in its relation to the structured social environment that creates the conditions, material and moral, which allow an answer. This, of course, is the basic fact of sociological reflection on moral life that Durkheim understood perfectly. Whatever one is, he is, always, in relation to the effects of structured social things.[13]

But what is easily overlooked (and not just by Durkheim) is that in actual moral life the relation between selves and structures is never fixed. Certainly not in the modern world. More accurately, the relation can never be presumed to be fixed, for it is certain that prior to modern times the structured world changed more than theory would suggest. What did not change in premodern cultures was the cultural *expectation* that the changes were real, final, and necessary. It was, by contrast, only in modern times that the essential moral dilemma became that of measuring the possible relations between structures and selves in order, to put it simply, "to know where one stands." If it is widely believed that the world (that is, the ordered system of things) is fixed, immutable, and not susceptible to arbitrary or surprising change, then, between individuals and their worlds, there is nothing to be measured. In, for example, the medieval West, which was such a cultural environment, what one measured was one's relation not to this world but to the other, the supernatural.[14] By contrast, when Georg Simmel observed that "the modern mind has become a more and more calculating one," he meant nothing less than that the moral task of modern subjects is measurement.[15]

The self, therefore, whatever else it is, is the moral element of the modern individual; as has been observed,[16] the soul is its equivalent in premodern moral cultures. If, thereby, the soul is the moral heart of the subject's orientation to another, supernatural world, then the self is the subject's moral orientation to the demands of this world. Of the three categorical terms, *self* is the one used more commonly in practical as well as professional sociologies. But even when the term *self* is not used in explicit relation to the other two, *measurement* and *structure* are its reasons for moral being. In modern times, the self is moral by virtue of its attempts to measure its relations between whatever it is and the structured worlds against and in which it does this work. Though abstract when stated this way, the relations can be neatly illustrated from almost anywhere in the literature of modern culture.

Near the very beginning of that literature, it is possible to refer to Descartes's 1639 *Discourse on Method.* Though there have always been controversies over his method, there is wide agreement that René Descartes (1595–1650) enunciated the foundational terms of modern thought. In this, he was even more influential than Francis Bacon (1561–1626), who preceded him by a generation, and his somewhat elder contemporary, Thomas Hobbes (1588–1679).[17] Descartes's importance was great because he so succinctly defined modern culture in relation to a philosophy of modern knowledge and science. The certitude he claimed in relation to his foundational principle—*I think, therefore I am*—is obviously also the first clear and distinct certitude associated rigorously with self-reflection. This fundamental precept led, thereafter, in many different directions—toward a formal science of the objective world, at one extreme; toward a systematic examination of consciousness itself, at another. But, regardless of the direction, any theory of modern knowledge pursued thereafter was poised in relation to the question of personal identity. Thereafter, until very recent times in the late twentieth century, "Who am I?" and "What do I know?" entailed each other, however implicitly. Modern knowledge, including the moral concerns of daily life, as much as the principles of science, was from the beginning considered an act of self-knowledge—a reflection that begins with the assurance, whether conscious or not, that the individual self, in being conscious of itself, possesses the capacity to think the world. Everything known in this moral culture is measured against this founding standard. Though Descartes himself continued in *Discourse* to use the term *soul,* this was the first systematic articulation of the moral properties of self.[18]

What is overlooked in attempts to discover the origin of such things as the concept self are the details of the thinker's discursive concerns—that is, those audible (and readable) asides someone like Descartes may utter to clear the way to the central notion. Such discourses as these are likely to be of particular significance with Descartes, whose expressed purpose in *Discourse* was to clear away all prior thinking, and its habits, in order to discover the one most elemental principle of modern thought itself.[19] But one can hardly expect such a clearing away to proceed without leaving behind some debris that, upon inspection, might leave clues to what the thinker found most resistant to his efforts. In the case of Descartes, one such piece of uncleared brush was, curiously, dreams. In the paragraph in which he first announced his famous *cogito, ergo sum,* Descartes talked on about dreams:

> When I considered that the very same thoughts (presentations) which we experience when awake may also be experienced when we are asleep, while there is at that time not one of them true, I supposed that all the objects (presentations) that had ever entered into my mind when awake, had in them no more truth than the illusions of my dreams. But immediately upon this I observed that, whilst I thus wished to think that all was false, it was absolutely necessary that I, who thus thought, should be somewhat; and as I observed that this truth, *I think, therefore I am,* was so certain and of such evidence, that no ground of doubt, however extravagant, could be alleged by the Sceptics capable of shaking it, I concluded that I might, without scruple, accept it as the first principle of the Philosophy of which I was in search.[20]

What might it mean, if anything, that Descartes, upon reflection, believed he came to the first principle of modern knowledge immediately after, and because of, a meditation on dreams? On the surface, the words clearly are meant to suggest a rigorous philosophical procedure. He meant to say (in an oblique attack on the Scholasticisms to which the modernizing seventeenth-century philosophies objected) that knowledge is not to be found in the form of articulated thought, of its "presentation" or, we might say, "representations." Since a thought can appear equally in dreams as in a wakened state, it is not the thought that accounts for knowledge but the prior consciousness from which the thought proceeds. But Descartes's assumption is crucial, for, obviously, he believed (quite reasonably in his day) that dream language was, to use his word, "false." Hence the cleverness of his rhetorical gesture. He played on the unquestionable assumption, then widely shared, that dreams are not true, from which he extracted the notion that, since the language of dreams is also the language of waking thought, the truth of thoughts must be prior to their representation in language. From this rhetorical move came not just his philosophy but, in large measure, the basic dilemma (or as it is sometimes said today, "the project") of modern thinking. But it should be noted for future reference that not only did Descartes make certain unwarranted assumptions about dream language, he also came to his clearest and most distinct first principle of modern thought in exact response to reflection upon that which he considered the unthought. Dreams, in being self-evidently false, were for Descartes the final debris in the way of perfect clarity of knowledge.

Descartes was, thus, the first to define the terms of modern moral thought. In his first principle of thought and being, he defined the standard against which all else known and knowable would be measured. That standard, remarkably, is also the standard whereby the very idea of the moral self was fixed in its modern form as the act of discovering true knowledge by means of a moral journey through the wilderness of all prior thought, cluttered though it may be with wild, meaningless thickets. This is the sense in which it is possible to say that the imagined relation among objects and subjects, structures and selves, is a moral measure—a sizing up of the exact enough degree of the good in real worlds comprising selves structured by social things.

More than two centuries after Descartes and the other seventeenth-century inventors of modern thought such as Hobbes, Bacon, and John Locke (1632–1704), the classic sociologists reformulated their concerns with reference to the by then undeniable structure of Western urban societies. Durkheim was most faithful to the general terms of the original formula. He alone among the classic thinkers sought precisely to measure the moral fate of the modern individual against the exact and factual evidence of socially structured things. He erred, however, in trying so earnestly to make a science distinct from philosophy and psychology that his ill-conceived neglect of the identities of selves forced his thinking into excessively rigid forms, which, in turn, had the effect of disrupting his empirical arguments. Durkheim was too preoccupied with society. In making it the standard of moral life, he thought he had invented the key to exact sociological measurement of moral facts. Instead, he produced a straightjacket for himself and, by consequence, much of subsequent professional sociology. Even those who could not be said to have followed Durkheim directly fell more or less under the same spell he did. In his, and their, enthusiasm to defend and define a pure science of the social—that is, a professionally explicit sociology—he and they committed themselves to a false universal. The "structured society" may well be an analytically useful category, but to the degree it may be, it costs itself the wider utility of describing the more subtle realities of ordinary moral life. At the least, structured societies are nothing apart from the moral concerns of selves who inhabit them. To think they are (that is, to think too earnestly of a sociological science) is to trap oneself not so much in abstractions as in a cramped corner of the moral logic of modern life. Durkheim serves well to remind us of this temptation and its limitations.

But he was not a fool. Far from it. Others made essentially the same error by different, possibly more complicated, routes. That they did suggests just how likely it is that the error itself is a necessary feature of modern social logic—an error that is implied at least by its resistance to thinking the unthought. Consider, in sharp contrast to Durkheim, Weber's difficulties in the same area.

Weber, more than Durkheim or Freud, and just as well as Marx, was a master sociologist of modern life. Like Weber, Marx set out to explain the true nature of modern social and economic life. Unlike Weber, Marx did so from a set of prior judgments, already fixed in his youth, and not from any attempt to measure exactly how the structures of modern life might have evolved in some evident relation to changes in nature of the modern self. It could even be said that only by dismissing the subjective self in his most early writings could Marx have concentrated his efforts on the secreted structures of the capitalist mode of production.[21] It was, of course, this omission every bit as much as his materialism that made Marx the necessary foil for Weber's investigations into the moral origins of capitalism. Weber had only to grant, as he readily did, the truth of capitalism's overdetermined class structures in order to set the groundwork for his sociological interests. Weber intended to do what, unbeknownst to him, Durkheim had failed to do—the very same that Marx had neglected. Weber, more than they (and certainly more than Freud), intended to provide the first complete sociological description of the real historical relations among the three constituent elements of modern life: selves in measured relation to structures.

▼ ▼ ▼▼ ▼

Weber's *Protestant Ethic and the Spirit of Capitalism*, though the best known and most influential of his works outside the circle of professional sociologists, was not the only instance of its author's preoccupation with selves, structures, and measures. With scant exception, most parts of Weber's sociology as it developed over years of empirical work were designed to answer the question he asked with special poignancy late in life. In the famous lecture in Munich in 1918, "Politics as a Vocation," he put it simply: "When and why do men obey?" It was a question he posed in the lecture after conceding, in understated fashion, one of the most counterintuitive moral dilemmas of modern life—that state politics, far from being liberatory, were nothing more than legitimate *domination.*[22] In general terms, here as in his discussions of bu-reaucracy (no less in the famous lines at the end of *Protestant Ethic*), Weber posed the troubling question: If modern life is an advancement over the tradi-tional, then why does it not more immediately provide the promised rewards of a good and free society?

Why do men obey? The very question is ironic when set against the moral expectations of modern life. If the modern was to have been the time in which democratic politics would resolve by peaceable means the conflicts of social life, then why is the legitimacy of political authority still so uncertain? To ask "Why do men obey?" so late in the history of the modern world is to ask a very particular moral question: What has happened to the promise of the lev-eling of social differences that we have political and bureaucratic forms that have the same stultifying, even evil, consequences as those associated with tra-ditional life in the West?[23]

The question, its irony notwithstanding, was posed in the 1918 lecture at Munich, as it had been earlier in *Protestant Ethic,* in order to define the terms of the sociological question Weber put to modern life. To ask "Why do men obey?" is also to ask a question of the structured nature of political life, which could not but have been a question of modern life itself. Here, again, is the question with its full context:

> Like the political institutions historically preceding it, the state is a relation of men, a relation supported by means of legitimate (i.e. considered to be legitimate) violence. If the state is to exist, then the dominated must obey the authority claimed by the powers that be. When and why do men obey? Upon what inner justifications and upon what external means does this domination rest?[24]

In *Protestant Ethic,* and elsewhere in Weber's many studies of the modern world,[25] the question took an analogous form: Which is the ethical disposi-tion that accounts for the elective affinity between certain parts of the Western cultural world and the rise of capitalism? Or, which kind of self is the necessary cause, and natural effect, of modern social structures? The purposes of the studies that were collected to form *Protestant Ethic* were many, but chief among them was that of measuring the nature and origins of the modern, ra-tional, calculating man in his two relations: on the one hand, to the estab-lished fact of capitalism's uneven world distribution; on the other, to the dis-covered facts suggesting a corresponding overdistribution of Calvinist religious teachings in the capitalized regions. These facts were the principal concerns of the "Author's Introduction" and the first chapter, "Religious Affiliation and Social Stratification," which together formed the empirical basis for the book's question. Weber's account of these striking measures of the modern world against its Other is the purpose of the remainder of the book, in which he answers his own question. Which kind of self is necessary, if not sufficient, to the structures of capitalism? That self which arose from the rational elements hidden within the irrational features of Calvin's doctrine of *certitudo salutis*, a doctrine that led, over time, to the spread of a utilitarian moral attitude and that, in more time, provided the moral basis for the entrepreneur without whom, necessarily, capitalism would not have been.

At almost every turn of the page, Weber teases the reader with references to the irrational nature of the modern social world. The book, as it came to be composed,[26] begins with the major theme, which goes far beyond the more limited inquiry into the origins of Western capitalism. In the opening lines of his introduction, Weber asks a sweeping question of the origins of practical reason, of rationality itself, which he does not hesitate to locate unequivocally in the West itself. In fact, this equation is the first hint of his theoretical nod toward the irrational. In the opening pages (including the first chapter) Weber puts the irrational squarely near, if not at, the center of his concerns.[27] He begins by asking why the rational method in science and culture appears so strikingly in the West but not in the East. Though he is careful not to suggest that the cultures of the East lack their own kinds of reasonable activities and conventions (musics, administrative rules, arithmetics, sciences, and so forth), he is clear that the West is greater because it developed the rational ethic. Weber presents his initial question tactfully, always careful to be circumspect, as much in his literary manners as in his science. But, there can be no question—strictly speaking, there would be no question for the book to answer—that Weber wants his reader to understand not only that the West is measurably superior to the East but that the measure of its superiority is reason itself. In suggesting this advancement of the Occident over the Orient, he makes it clear both that the former has discovered the better rational method and that the latter must be thought of not just as *less* rational but as at some risk of being irrational.[28]

In the crucial second chapter, "The Spirit of Capitalism," the book seems to shift to a discussion of the development of modern rationality out of medieval traditionalism—a discussion that would seem to make no further reference to the lesser reason of the East. But, as in Durkheim's casual equation of the Australian and North American aboriginals with Ancient Israel, it is hard to get around the idea that Weber thought the premodern traditionals in the West suffered the same developmental limitations as did even the most sophisticated scientists of the East.[29] One of the effects of the unthought is to assimilate differences, sometimes into what today is called simply "the Other."

In any case, the "Spirit of Capitalism" chapter is crucial to what follows because here Weber introduces, again in understated terms, each of the essential elements out of which he will eventually build his argument. First, he presents his method of the historical individual (more commonly known as the "ideal type"), which he illustrates with the memorable practical aphorisms from Ben Franklin's *Necessary Hints to Those That Would Be Rich* and other of Franklin's popular writings. For example, "He that loses five schillings, not only loses that sum but all the advantage that might be made turning it in dealing, which by the time a young man becomes old, will amount to a considerable sum of money." Or, "Remember, time is money." Illustrations like these have a powerful effect on all that follows. Without them, readers not schooled in the history of the religious doctrines to which Weber devotes the bulk of the remainder of the book would likely be at some loss to follow him. But, the utilitarian calculations made perfectly sensible in Ben Franklin's aphorisms define Weber's principal idea clearly. Reading the Franklin passages, one understands upon reflection that Weber is using a method whereby a striking historical individual (Ben Franklin in this case) serves both to illustrate and to embody the truths associated with a more general, perhaps universal, concept (here, the spirit of capitalism).

But, by this simple literary gesture, Weber explains that, in addition to a method, he is defining a theoretical position. One may at first be distracted by the informality of the locution "spirit of capitalism." Yet, the innocent phrase actually contains the discernible elements of a complete theory of modern society, as is evident in his summary justification of his method in this second chapter:

> The capitalistic economy of the present-day is an immense cosmos into which the individual is born, and which presents itself to him, at least as an individual, as an unalterable order of things in which he must live. . . . Thus the capitalism of to-day, which has come to dominate economic life, educates and selects economic subjects which it needs through a process of economic survival of the fittest. But here one can easily see the limits of the concept of selection as a means of historical explanation. In order that a manner of life so well adapted should be selected at all, i.e., should come to dominate others, it had to originate somewhere, and not in isolated individuals alone, but as a way of life common to whole groups of men. *This origin is what needs explanation.*[30]

There could hardly be a more explicit statement of the theoretical demands on a sociology of modern society. How is one to measure the selective effects of this "immense cosmos," which, though it appears to the individual as "an unalterable order of things," would not be what it is if some number of those individuals did not themselves select an ethic, "a manner of life," capable of shaping a common life supporting the cosmic effect? In asking the question, Weber decomposes the elemental features of modern life and sociology itself with elegant simplicity. The most immense structures depend on the ways in which people orient themselves ethically in daily life. Yet it is not the "isolated individual" who counts, but some feature of the individual's social nature that is shared with others. In *Protestant Ethic,* Weber calls this feature, simply, an ethic or "manner of life." More recently, it has been called a disposition, or *habitus.* Weber's ethic refers, with evident subtlety, to that moral and social space which defines the modern subject. Though an individual, the subject is also an ethical member of structured societies—a social being who possesses this hard-to-define capacity for social orientation that is neither rigidly structured by society nor irrationally idiosyncratic.[31]

Weber's genius lay in his unwillingness to press the analytic case too far. The space of this social ethic is, in a certain sense, beyond definition. Rather than define the inner workings of the ethic, Weber let the matter stand on historical logic. Without capitalism, subjects are not selected for enterprise; without ethically rational subjects, there is no capitalism. It can never be simply a matter of subjective selves or social structures, but both at once, somehow.[32] What is hidden and revealed in the many moves Weber makes in the second chapter of *Protestant Ethic* is what is also revealed and concealed in the first chapter. In both places, as throughout his sociology, there is an irrational lurking behind, before, within, and alongside even the rational habits of modern ethical life:

> Rationalism is an historical concept which covers a whole world of different things. It will be our task to find out whose intellectual child the particular concrete form of rational thought was, from which the idea of a calling and the devotion to labour in the calling has grown, which is, as we have seen, *so irrational from the standpoint of purely eudaemonistic self-interest, but which has been and still is one of the most characteristic elements of our capitalistic culture.*[33]

The rational ethic fundamental to modern life arose from the irrational features—not just of traditionalism, nor of the religious life, but of the most straightforwardly irrational elements of the moral teachings of, first, Martin Luther's idea of the calling (which Weber discusses in chapter 3); and, more exactly, Calvin's and latter Calvinism's doctrines with their pure rational orientation to the individual's irrational need to calculate the odds of salvation by an inscrutable God who saves according to his own unknowable reasons (which are discussed in Weber's chapter 4). In this sense the book is about the irrational origins of the modern world.

Thus, much as Durkheim found the moral principle of modern society in the primitive forms of the most elementary religious cultures, so Weber found the pure reason of modern ethics in the irrational divine logic of a traditional God. With Weber the scope of his historical and cultural claims is more explicit and, therefore, more ambitious. But both found the principle of modernity in a primitive. Both were, thus, required to collapse much of the world into foundational principles that could not, and did not, make room for the real differences before their very eyes. With Durkheim, the Woman, the Jew, and (by implication) all those not of the European races were made to seem as one. For Weber, the equivalent was his careful move around the irrational as though not to disturb its necessary place. God and the Orient were, for Weber, theoretical equivalents, and both were part of the unthought of modern culture. Each possessed a common attribute. Each in its own way was rational, though irrationally so. It was not that Calvin's God was lacking reason to a greater degree than, say, the East Indian natural sciences or musical scales. Their crucial difference from the rational culture of the West was that their reasons were, in effect, of the wrong kind. God had his reasons, Calvin taught. But they were not reasons knowable to the petitioning human soul, who, lacking any promise of divining God's intentions for him, was required, in order to certify his salvation, to act rationally in the world.

Similarly, what prevented the sciences of the East from becoming true and universal sciences was that they too prevented others from knowing their reasons. The Oriental methods were, thus, expressive, hence in their way unthinkable, not truly methodical. For example, Weber says in his assessment of literacy in China: "There was printing in China. But printed literature, designed *only* for print and only possible through it, and above all, the Press and periodicals, have appeared only in the Occident."[34] To use the stigmatizing term still current today, literacy in ancient China was, in effect, inscrutable, like Calvin's God. Calvinism was, thereby, the irrational East in the West. More generally, the contrast so essential to Weber's political and legal theory—that between traditional and modern rational authority—was, in strange effect, a contrast significantly parallel to that between the East and the West. Weber's sociology was very considerably affected, as was Durkheim's, by such a deep embeddedness in modern Western culture that evidently different social things were brought into what today would be recognized as actually quite impossible harmonies.

Thus, Weber's attempt to construct a sociology as sensitive to the inner meanings of subjects as to the external structures of societies was indebted to a prior historical judgment. There would have been no sociologically interesting question were it not for the presumption that, at the end of the nineteenth century and the beginning of the twentieth, modernity had as yet failed to keep its promises. Had modern political and economic life actually spread the benefits of rational democracy and capitalist enterprise across, if not the globe, the whole of the West, then there might have been less reason to wonder why men obey. Had modernity progressed as Ben Franklin, Thomas Jefferson, and the eighteenth-century followers of Calvin believed it would, then Weber might not have asked, "Why do men obey?" and Durkheim might not have asked, "Why do they kill themselves when left too much to their own moral devices?" The questions, however, were necessary for evident historical reasons. Durkheim's hope for modern society lay in the belief that, though modernity may have strayed too far from the collective morality of the primitive, the primitive conditions of knowledge and social order were still viable. They still offered a new moral order beyond the division of social labor.

For both, sociology was the solution—for Durkheim explicitly, for Weber implicitly. Weber's theory, when taken in general terms, is remarkably parallel to Durkheim's. For Weber the modern had similarly divorced itself from traditional ways. While Durkheim viewed this, initially, as a tragic loss, Weber viewed it initially (that is in the initial moments of *Protestant Ethic*) as not a loss but a gain. The reader of *Protestant Ethic* would be fully justified to wonder if its concluding pages had been written by some other person. Yet, we know from other of Weber's writings that though all parts were written by the hand of the same man, they were composed out of the separate parts of Weber's evidently split social consciousness. Even by the time of the *Protestant Ethic* (1904–1905) in the first years after his sudden recovery in 1903 from a long mental illness, Weber held the mixed opinions that as his work went on it became unbalanced in favor of pessimism. The pessimism of the book's concluding pages, however, was the product of moral confusion with respect to what he saw in the world about him. In the beginning chapters of *Protestant Ethic*, Weber succeeded in capturing the spirit of early capitalism—its wide-eyed enthusiasms and self-confidences. No less, in the book's closing paragraphs, he captured the justifiable doubts many had of capitalism's later history in the early years of the twentieth century in Europe. Both aspects of his literary and sociological sensibility were, however, indebted to his struggle to figure just what to do with the irrational in modern life. And this struggle was an entailment of the theory itself, an entailment apparent already in the odd way he quietly equated the East and Calvin's God. Neither was so completely Other to the modern West as Weber made them seem. Neither was utterly irrational, any more than traditionalism in the West was. But traditionalism's insufficient rationality was, for Weber, easier to calculate. Traditional political and economic life were, after all, orderly—even if their order was not fully reasonable. The ethical and practical irony of Weber's history of modern economic life lay not in its lack of coherence but rather in a coherence that thwarted future-oriented, goal-directed, profit-motivated ethical behavior.

Thus, rationality, as he defined it, was that reasonable order which, in uniting the individual self and the objective structures of social life, did so in a way that struck decent accord between the risks of freedom and the requirements of order. Thus, Weber viewed God and the East much as he viewed traditionalism. They were the flawed rationalities of an earlier time, those ethical orders the world left at the risk of losing its human soul. This Weber saw differently than did Durkheim. Where Durkheim trusted in the progress of modern culture, Weber was less naive, and more vexed. Weber doubted what Durkheim trusted—that the modern could produce the solution to its own problems.

For modern reason to hold its own—as both an ethical principle and the axiom of modern science—it had always to give account of itself. It required, as Descartes saw in his search for foundational principles, some point of beginning in relation to which everything else was measured. If, for Durkheim, that rule of moral measure was the elementary form of collective consciousness, then, for Weber, it was the oddly spoiled superiority of the West. The very first words of *Protestant Ethic* define his rule of historical and sociological measurement:

> A product of modern European civilization, studying any problem of universal history, is bound to ask himself to what combination of circumstances the fact should be attributed that in Western civilization, and in Western civilization only, cultural phenomena have appeared which (as we like to think) lie in a line of development having *universal* significance and value.[35]

While it would be strange to characterize Weber as a direct heir to Descartes, still in this passage one sees the continuing influence of even the earliest of modern axioms. Weber begins with a gesture of self-criticism. He astutely acknowledges that a European thinker must consider the fact of his European origins before reflecting on the nature of universal truth. But, having thus acknowledged his limits, Weber proceeds without regard to them, to assert, as if it were self-evident, that "in Western Civilization only" has there appeared cultural phenomena with *universal significance!* This was Weber's ultimate measure of modern social life.

No other of the great classic theorists took the pains Weber took to understand the non-Western world. Marx treated all prior and other modes of production schematically at best.[36] And, Durkheim knew what he knew, even of the totemic societies, through secondary readings of others' observations. He was, thus, among the first of the armchair anthropologists.[37] And, Freud derived his knowledge of the primitive horde from freely imaginative readings of secondary sources, including, curiously, the classics of Western literature.[38]

But Weber, and Weber alone among the four, mastered the non-Western languages in order to study others as close to firsthand as he could. Just the same, this scholarly care had little effect on his cultural attitude toward the Other. Durkheim was forced by the elementary standard to which he held all men to think as he did about women, the Jewish people, and primitive society; Weber defined the modern against a comparable standard—the universal truth of Western civilization. It is not just that he was, in this regard, time-bound. It is more that Weber, being bound to the culture he tried to study, obeyed its foundational social and epistemological laws.

In the modern world, the practical question *Who am I if things social are different?* does its best to conceal the three elementary parts of modern social logic: the self, the structured world, and the moral demand that the relations and differences between them be measured. Sociology began as the science set upon measuring those relations. Even when a genius like Weber attempted to get around the difficulties entailed in the unstable balance among them, he could not avoid the necessity of searching for and finding a first principle. With Weber, as with Durkheim, that final measure was the awkward, hard-to-defend assumption of the West's universal significance.

▼ ▼ ▼ ▼ ▼

The crisis after which sociologies seek today to reconstruct themselves could well be defined simply as the public crisis of accord over the universal significance of the West.

The West was invented and enriched as an object of cultural value mostly in the nineteenth century, and mostly on the basis of the success of the Western colonial achievements in that century. This historically contingent "West" began to decompose as a pure object of truth when its world system of colonial interests began not so much to rebel as to withdraw from the universal accord. It was not that the colonial subjects had believed the West's claims to superiority[39] but that the West believed in itself so mightily that it could not, and would not, hear the signals of discontent.[40] Today, very few are seriously deaf to those signals. This, surely, is why George Bush could not quite tell the story of the end of the Cold War. It is not that he lacked the proper skill in language but that the world had not, and still has not, provided those who want to believe in the West a proper way to think about it after the crisis. In this one small respect, Descartes is still right. What counts in political communication is not so much the words but the consciousness from which thoughts arise. Those, today, who insist against all evidence that the world is meant to be ordered by a West will necessarily see things through a mirror. The world for them will have the appearance of being whole, yet the appearance will surely be at odds with what any one of them feels.[41]

This, in the end, is the crucial difference between modern man and whoever comes after—between the stories of Alex Supertramp and those of Larry Hogue. Alex (his story, that is) belonged to the last days of President Bush's world. Whatever may have confused him, he seems to have felt that he could change his identity and thus rediscover the deep structures of a free world. It may be inferred that this lost man believed that the world in its nature was orderly, even far beyond the limits of civilization. As the stories of his end suggest, Alex Supertramp thought as did George Bush, who believed, in his last official days, that America was still the world's last best hope, even though he could not infer from this principle an accurate account of the proudest achievement of his presidency—the so-called defeat of communism.

Larry Hogue's is quite another story. His is a world where rights and good intentions are without any self-evident principle. The stories of this so-called wild man and his struggles with the police, the courts, the doctors, and his neighbors are striking because no one, on any side, knows what to do with him or his insistence on his rights. In an August 1993 rebroadcast of an earlier story by CBS News, the *60 Minutes* investigative reporter, a well-groomed and confident news professional, challenged Hogue's right to return to 96th Street. She confronted him with visual evidence of his irresponsibility. She said: "We have pictures of you throwing garbage." He said: "What about the garbage, lady? The world is garbage." The correspondent was silent, so unsure that not even the film editors could reframe her composure. Even on 96th Street there might be those who would be similarly nonplused, however they feel about Hogue himself. In refusing to treat himself as though he were their garbage, Hogue poses a hard-to-answer question.

How do we take the measure of the world, or of ourselves in it, when so few of its most precious properties seem capable of putting the world in order? What are we to say to Hogue when he clearly and distinctly insists on his right to live in whatever neighborhood he chooses while describing the world as it very often is? How can the modern world hold its order if it sacrifices this right of an individual to determine for himself how he lives his life and views his world? So far, it seems that simple recourse to the prior rights of a community has not demonstrated their superior logic. But this is not a question of legal rights so much as of the disjointed relations among the parts of the social world in which structured things like health systems, legal procedures, neighborhood cultures, and police practices encounter an individual like Larry Hogue. Though (by some measures) he may at times be mad and otherwise ill, Hogue clearly knows and insists on the right to be whoever he wishes to be. And few can convincingly refute his insistence that the world is garbage.

Hogue's is a world in which one is without reliable ways to measure the uncertain relations among structured worlds and a bewildering variety of identities. Hogue is not simply different. He is not, that is, the difference behind the modernist riddle. It is more that he seems to know who he is and who that is in his own mind is right enough and should require no adjustment to those who fear him.

Today, there is much to be feared in most social worlds, and very little evident reason with which to measure the way out. This is the full manifestation of the crisis.

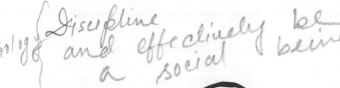

sociology { Discipline and effectively being a social being

Chapter 6

Structuring Differences

I N A W E A K W O R L D, it is difficult to know where to turn for clean, strong explanations. Under such conditions, there is an understandable lack of trust, especially toward those whose job it is to describe and account for that weakened world. This may be one of the reasons, to the world outside their own circles, professional sociologists are not well understood, nor particularly well appreciated.

In his novel *Angle of Repose,* Wallace Stegner puts the following words to his storyteller, an aging father who speaks of his son, Rodman, a former sixties radical turned sociologist:

> Rodman, like most sociologists and most of his generation, was born without the sense of history. To him it is only an aborted social science. The world has changed, Pop, he tells me. The past is not going to teach us anything about what we've got ahead of us.

Later, Stegner embellishes:

> Rodman is a great measurer. He is interested in change, all right, but only as a process; and he is interested in values, but only as data. X people believed one way, Y people another, whereas ten years ago Y people believed the first way and X the second. The rate of change is therefore. He never goes back more than ten years.[1]

Though Stegner is wrong in the degree to which he portrays sociology as ahistorical (historical sociology being one of the field's proudest accomplishments in recent years), he is right enough in other ways.

Professional sociology is sometimes tainted by its association with the politics of the 1960s. To some this is not good. To others it may have been good then but today makes the field's occasional preoccupation with formalities, like Rodman's Xs and Ys, just as irritating as Rodman is to his father.[2] It is apparent from even the most sympathetic interpretations of Durkheim and Weber that when sociologists do attempt to render account of the past, they are sometimes inclined to torture it into conformity with abstract measures ill suited to historical differences.

To make matters worse, in recent years professional sociology has been subjected to bad press. To the amusement of some, there have been reports of the closing of a department at a school in the Midwest, several announcements of possible cutbacks in departments, and confusing accounts of apparently bad behavior among members of a department at an elite school in Massachusetts. In one fairly typical instance, a prestigious school in Connecticut threatened to cutback several programs, including sociology. Quickly, however, the faculty forced a reversal of the decision, after which the school's administrators departed one by one (though not entirely for this reason alone). As it turns out, when they are given time to explain themselves, sociologists can be quite convincing.[3]

Ironically, professional sociologists frequently are held in disfavor by some for the same reason they are able to persuade others. Again, Wallace Stegner's reference is apt. In the schools, sociology courses attract large enrollments. Normally this would be good. But, very often, students trained in sociology courses put sociological knowledge to disruptive political effect in campus life. Before radical feminists, Afrocentrists, and queer theorists became the vanguard of campus politics, sociologists were often alone in the leadership of faculty and student protests.[4] It is in the nature of the subject matter—both as it is taught and as it is written into published research. Though it may seem strange to say it today, Weber and Durkheim, like Charlotte Perkins Gilman and W.E.B. Du Bois, were effective sociologists at least partly because they were in their times controversial public figures. Perhaps because it is controversial, sociology bothers some people.

I was once invited by a local chapter of the American Heart Association to address a workshop for health-care deliverers on the subject of stress. Since the medical effects of psychological stress was not an unlikely topic for a sociologist, I accepted and prepared a good talk of some twenty minutes in which, among other things, I made general reference to Durkheim's ideas on anomie. It was not a bad talk at all. It was, however, quite different from the talks of the other featured speakers, two of whom were distinguished cardiologists. A

fourth presenter was a nice person of unannounced qualifications who myste-
riously led the large audience of nurses, physicians, and other deliverers of
health in thirty minutes of relaxation exercises that involved quite a lot of
deep-breathing and other closed-eye activities, during which I realized I could
no longer remember my mantra. After, I was not surprised when the written
evaluations of the presentations ranked the deep-breathing presentation first
(by a mile), the talks of the two physicians second and third, and mine dead
last (by another mile). One anonymous comment, politely translated, was,
"He sounded too much like a sociologist." Sociologists have grown wearily accustomed to such remarks. They go with the territory.

Though impatient, perhaps, this public opinion of sociology is not without
its reasons. The surprising fact is that, whatever its reasons, that same public
tends to attend, and causes its children to attend, courses in sociology, and to
read the works of authors associated with sociology—evident witness to the
reading and thinking public's reluctance to act on its prejudices.

Sociology, as I have said, is two things at once: a natural, if not always well-articu-
lated, moral strength of real members of societies; and a professionally organized
academic field. If the close relation between the two contributes to the field's capacity to aggravate some members, it is equally so that nonprofessional members
of real societies cannot help but draw on the organized professional knowledge.
It could be said that Weber's theory of capitalism's rational ethic was a secondary,
professional theory of the new practical theory early moderns had of how to orient their behavior rationally. At the same time, it would be hard indeed to read
the newspapers for any stretch of time without encountering phrases like "the
work ethic" or "bureaucratic machines," which were introduced into popular
culture through Weber's own theories of modern life. The public, therefore, has
not been wrong to listen to and read certain professional sociologists. Sensible
individuals in the general public can hardly be blamed for their curiosity about
how the professionals discuss what they think about their worlds. For the same
reason, the public's occasional annoyance, like that of Wallace Stegner's old man,
may arise from a not unjustified interest in how the professionals may overstate
the Xs and Ys of what publics understand. At the least, sociologies of both basic
kinds are fundamental aspects of modern cultures.

If it were required, it might be possible to name sociology's most enduring
general contribution to modern culture's self-understanding. For myself, I

would nominate sociology's work in forcing moderns to think about the structural nature of the modern world. Though there are other possible contributions to consider (including the development of theories of the self and techniques of social measurement),[5] the study of the peculiar, powerful features of the modern world's structures is mostly the work of sociologies.

Yet, from the days of the classic nineteenth-century sociologists, the work of defining and explaining the structured nature of modern social life was done against the obstacle of modern culture's resolute denial of the evident corollary of any historically based social theory of structures: *the unyielding definiteness of differences.* The structures of the modern world were experienced, in Weber's phrase, as "an immense cosmos into which the individual is born, and which presents itself to him . . . as an unalterable order of things in which he must live." Weber's words in *Protestant Ethic* conveyed essentially the same experience as Durkheim's sense in *Suicide* of the modern division of labor that constrains individuals toward fatal anomie. The universalizing force of structures was acknowledged, while the force of the dividing and differentiating effects of structures was denied. It was the trusting nature of modern hope to believe in the ultimate disappearance of those divisions. This belief encouraged, indeed it entailed, denial of the prior fact of social differences. Modernity's foundations were laid on weak rock. Structured social differences were the very fundamentals that neither Durkheim nor Weber could figure into their measures of the modern world—women, the Jewish, the aboriginals, the East, even the traditional ways of life in the West. The effect of their denials becomes apparent when comparison is made to other sociologists writing at the same time who looked the structured world straight in the eye.

Writing just a year after Durkheim's *Suicide,* Charlotte Perkins Gilman, one of the leading feminist sociologists of her day, wrote: "In studying the economic position of the sexes collectively, the difference is most marked. . . . Economic progress, however, is almost exclusively masculine. Such economic progress as women have been allowed to exercise are of the earliest and most primitive kind."[6] Like Durkheim, Gilman understood the modern division of labor; unlike him, she did not believe in universal double man. Instead, the economic differences between the sexes were real as such. Similarly, in a book published just two years before *Protestant Ethic,* W.E.B. Du Bois, a young sociologist who enjoyed a mutually respectful acquaintance with Weber,[7] wrote:

> After the Egyptian and Indian, the Greek and Roman, the Teuton and Mongolian, the Negro is a sort of seventh son, born with a veil, and gifted with second-sight in this American world—a world which yields him no true self-consciousness, but only lets him see himself through the revelation of the other world. It is a peculiar sensation,

this double-consciousness, this sense of always looking at one's self through the eyes of others, of measuring one's soul by the tape of a world that looks on in contempt and pity. One ever feels his twoness,—an American, a Negro; two souls, two thoughts, two unreconciled strivings; two warring ideals in one dark body, whose dogged strength alone keeps it from being torn asunder.[8]

Though Du Bois understood Weber's sociology quite well, and may have been somewhat influenced by him,[9] he is highly skeptical of Weber's idea of the "universal significance" of the West's rational man. Difference is the prior and fundamental experience of the African American.

Writers like Gilman and Du Bois saw the world with special clarity. What they saw were the true differences of those who shared their social experiences. They were, thus, able to put themselves outside, to borrow Du Bois's word, the veil of modern culture, which was, after all, a veil affecting the lives of many of those, in addition to Black Americans, who were not visible from the point of view of universal man.

Thus the irony that even though sociologists like Weber and Durkheim, even Marx, were among the first to see clearly the moral and social evils brought by the structured nature of modern society, they could see but dimly. They, in effect, knew little or nothing of what was plain, if painful, to other sociologists. Gilman and Du Bois saw what they saw because they had been forced into a position where their lives depended, in a serious moral sense, on their willingness to affirm what the modern West denied. They understood that social difference is the first consequence of modern society and, thus, the more reasonable first principle of sociology. From any other principle within modern culture, differences cannot be thought through, critically and scientifically. This very likely is why Weber's and Durkheim's visions of modern society were so shockingly indefinite, uncertain, wispy, even imaginary.

From the point of view of those (like Durkheim) who believed in progress, or those (like Weber) who regretted its failures, the modern social world disturbed the normal expectation that the benefits of the good society were a universally significant property of the modern West. As a result, the canonical classical thinkers could only vaguely stipulate the riddle of the day: *Who am I if things social are different?* They understood very well the moral implications of the dilemma, even if their sociologies could not conceive of a coherent solution. Their solution, such as it was, was to conceive of a sociology that served the purposes of the ideal of progress, that of *structuring differences*.

So long as sociology views its work as structuring differences—that is, as participating in modernity's need to structure away real social differences—it will be limited, as it has been for the past century. If differences are real, if they are in the nature of social things, and not just the short-run failure of progressive cultures, then a sociology of structures, whatever its accomplishments, will sooner or later fall short of its goals.

Hence the contradictory situation of academic sociology, and one of the reasons the public might be of two, conflicting minds about it. Since the nineteenth century academic sociology has been a thorn in the flesh of public opinion by forcing it to take seriously the "immense cosmos" of social structures. Yet, having been bred by the culture of that same public, professional sociologies also have been in loyal collusion with modernity's resistance to taking seriously the primacy of social difference. Though a prodigal, still an heir!

▼ ▼ ▼ ▼ ▼

When Immanuel Kant, in *What Is Enlightenment?* provided the Enlightenment its emblematic definition—"Dare to know!"—he expressed in condensed form only part of modernity's foundational culture. What Kant's philosophy expressed, in its most general terms, was the larger moral formula *Dare to know, thus to take the measure of the world such as it is.* To apprehend the world, to know it, means to take moral hold of, to measure, its objective structures. Notwithstanding his extreme skepticism about man's ability to apprehend things-in-themselves, Kant believed that knowing was an activity with moral as well as cognitive implications. Most other modern thinkers, whatever their differences with Kant, have agreed that the human ability to know the world depends mostly on the practical moral attitude of the knower. In most cases that attitude was not all that different from Descartes's moral pilgrimage through his thoughts to consciousness itself, from which he apprehended being itself. But Kant put this demand most succinctly: "Thus the *common reason of man* is compelled to leave its proper sphere and to take a step into the field of a *practical philosophy,* but not for satisfying any desire to speculate, which never occurs to it as long as it is content to be mere sound reason."[10]

More familiarly put, this is the language of the famous subject-object dichotomy of modern theories of knowledge: *Subjects apprehend objects.* For which the corollary in practical moral reasoning is, *The fate of human subjects lies in their moral relations with the object world.* What the individual does in the world is bound up with what one knows; and what one knows of the moral world is what one is. The identity features of the individual cannot escape the world's objective structures. This is the full moral implication of "Dare to know!"

It is perfectly clear that Weber and Durkheim were, in this regard, rigorous moderns for more reasons than their evident debts to Kant and Descartes. In spite of differences in so many other respects, they shared this elementary modern faith. Weber's sociology was an attempt to account for, in his phrase, "the inner justifications" for behavior in the modern world. Why do men obey? was really the question How do modern subjects make inner sense of obedience in a world where free, democratic politics presents itself as little more than "legitimate domination"? Durkheim's sociology was an attempt to account for, in his words, that stratum of "social facts" which "constrains" the moral life of the individual. Why do men kill themselves? was really a question of striking similarity to Weber's How do modern subjects know what to do when the new social order gives them so little normative guidance?

None of the official founding fathers of academic sociology failed to ask such a question in terms more or less similar to those of Weber and Durkheim. Even those at the extreme, like Marx, thought in these terms. For Marx, What is the secret of the capitalist mode of production? ultimately played rhetorically on the prior, if unasked, question: Is it really true that the economic structures of even the most liberal modern political economies exploit and dehumanize human subjects as much as did the feudal lords, the slave masters, and other despots?

Were one to set aside for a moment the apparent differences among Marx, Durkheim, and Weber, it is possible to see the broad similarities in their moral interpretations of the structured world. Each, in his way, denied fundamental differences. As in other ways, the three together compose the triangulated theoretical space of sociology's classic denial of differences. If Marx constitutes the plane of the more serious attempt to get beyond surface appearances, his radical analysis of class divisions was ultimately frustrated by his inability to see class as but one difference among many in the modern world. He believed the workers of the world would throw off their chains and win the world, thus to make it, and man himself, whole again—perfectly classless. Today, we known very well the long subsequent history in which even the most robust experiments at overcoming class differences could not succeed without abusive force aimed at crushing other just-as-real differences—of races and ethnicities above all.

If, therefore, Durkheim constitutes the plane of modernity's most fundamental faith in its ability to work through the temporary evil of the division of social labor, his radical program for a factual sociology in service of progress was frustrated from the start by his inability to see that the constraining forces were many and unreconcilable. Even when Durkheim aimed to prove the validity of his science by demonstrating the differences among the four types of suicide, he was frustrated. In *Suicide*, even he conceded that the differences were negligible. There was, in effect, only one, dominating social force toward self-murder because, for Durkheim, there was only one, remarkably singular double man—against whom the Woman, the Jew, and the Aboriginal were disconcerting, necessary nonentities. And, if Weber was by every measure the most morally vexed of the great originating social theorists, his vexations were caused not by a clear sense of differences in the modern world. Rather, Weber was frustrated by the inexorable unity of the "unalterable order" of the social world—against which the good sciences of the East and the lost humanity of the traditional West were nothing.

Had any of these three been able to think the modern world as differences, things might have been different. What they did, in their time, was nobly done. Marx defined the terms of modernity's radical self-contradiction. Against which, Durkheim defined the terms of its radical self-affirmation. Weber, against both of these positions, defined the moral confusions of modern man trapped between the other two planes. Each made great contributions to the sociology of modern man's dilemma. But each was limited by his prior faith in modern man. Each, in effect, saw the world as progress structuring differences, thus overlooking the more subtle differences that made the world. Instead of structures resolving differences, differences were the structure of things.

It was not until the twentieth century, between the two world wars, that social theory began to reconsider the classic ideas of structures.

▼ ▼ ▼ ▼ ▼

Just after the end of World War I, and shortly after resigning as a member of the British delegation to the Versailles peace conference, John Maynard Keynes wrote:

> I seek to point out that the principle of accumulation based on inequality was a vital part of the pre-war order of Society and of progress as we then understood it, and to emphasize that this principle depended on unstable psychological conditions, which it may be impossible to recreate. It was not natural for a population, of whom so few enjoyed the comforts of life, to accumulate so hugely. The war has disclosed the possibility of consumption to all and the vanity of abstinence to many. Thus the bluff is discovered; the laboring classes may be no longer willing to forego so largely, and the capitalist classes, no longer confident of the future, may seek to enjoy more fully their liberties of consumption so long as they last, and thus precipitate the hour of their confiscation.[11]

These are the words, not of Marx, but of one of the leading liberal economists of his generation. But Keynes, the architect of state-directed structural solutions to economic disorder, was not alone.

In the same period, others as different in their interests and manners of thinking as Reinhold Niebuhr, the American theologian, and Georg Lukács, the Hungarian Marxist philosopher, expressed similarly disenchanted attitudes toward the structures of the postwar world. In the United States, Reinhold Niebuhr's book *Moral Man and Immoral Society* (1932) challenged the traditional pietism of American religious ethics by arguing that society was a structured reality different from and resistant to the moral enthusiasms of the individual. Lukács, whose left-liberal Marxism could not have been more temperamentally different from Niebuhr's radical democratic liberalism, may have put this attitude most succinctly. In *History and Class Consciousness* (1923), he spoke of the "irrational chasm between the subject and object that we find confronting us everywhere in modern life."[12] Lukács, along with others associated with the then newly rediscovered left-Hegelian Marxism, sought to address the more glaring insufficiencies of the classic social theories. In *History and Class Consciousness,* Lukács was among those who rediscovered the younger, more philosophical Marx of the *1844 Manuscripts* in order to revise vulgar Marxism, often in relation to the ideas of Weber and Freud. Lukács had been a visitor to Weber's Heidelberg circle in the years before World War I. Later, the Frankfurt Institute for Social Research (founded 1932) brought together a new school of critical social theorists who were similarly intent upon rethinking the classic theorists—in particular, Marx, Weber, and Freud—in light of the failure of World War I to win the peace that was then threatened by economic failure and the rise of Hitler in Germany. From Max Horkheimer and Theodor Adorno to today's still dominant figure in the Frankfurt tradition, Jürgen Habermas, critical theorists have been chiefly preoccupied with rethinking the classic social theorists of modern culture. From the earliest writings of the Frankfurt School in the 1930s through Horkheimer and Adorno's *Dialectic of Enlightenment* (1947) to Habermas's *Knowledge and Human Interests* (1968) and his more recent writings in defense of modernity, this tradition has established a rigorous practice of critical reevaluation of the most fundamental, liberal principles of the classic, modern era.[13] One of the theoretical purposes of this long tradition has been to deal with the problem Lukács defined as that of the "irrational chasm between subject and object," a problem that had been earlier formulated by Weber. It was, in effect, nothing more than the classic problem of examining the deadly effects of social structures on human freedom. But it was formulated with a new and different seriousness in the interwar era.

With these developments in mind it becomes clear why, in the years just before World War II and then just after, social theorists in Europe and America concerned themselves with renewing their understanding of the structural effects on the moral individual. In France in the first years after World War II, the structuralist method was developed in direct (if not simple) response to the alleged subjectivism of existentialism. Claude Lévi-Strauss and Jean-Paul Sartre are the universally recognized symbols of the issues involved in this controversy.[14] In France the structuralist side won out for a while. But elsewhere in Europe, and eventually in the United States, the same set of concerns enlivened the debates between and among various aspects of the more or less Marxist left. The response to Louis Althusser's structuralism, no less than the controversies over Habermas's revision of critical theory, were not, as it is often said, mere instances of a linguistic turn in social theory. They were, more profoundly, an attempt to come to terms with the question of structured social reality in relation to human subjects. Even controversies associated with poststructuralism (like the feminist attacks on Foucault and the still current confusions over the ideas of Jacques Lacan) are attempts to replace the classic idea of the subject with a richer understanding of the structures of the modern world—its culture, politics, and economic life. Against which have come reactions, particularly among feminists, that insist either on preserving the classic language of the subject and the object or on rethinking the unconscious foundations of subjectivity in the modern world.[15] It would not, therefore, be too far wrong to say that today's debates over postmodernism are the most recent stage of a long history of reflection, beginning in the 1920s, in which social theorists have tried to figure out, and state, the precise consequences of the classic sociologist's inability to understand differences as a structured, primary feature of the modern.

▼ ▼ ▼ ▼ ▼

Modern academic sociology is no exception. Professional sociology began to move beyond its classic period in the interwar years and, in the same fashion as the German and French critical thinkers, by a sustained reconsideration of classic social thought.

The foundational texts of modern sociology were in fact among academic sociology's first attempts to think through in postclassic terms the effects of social structure on individual action. These were, of course, the founding textbook of post–World War II sociology, Talcott Parsons's 1937 book *The Structure of Social Action*, and one of the most widely read essays of modern sociology, Robert K. Merton's 1938 paper "Social Structure and Anomie." From these two, and subsequent, writings came the two dominant schools of sociology in the post–World War II era. Though today opinion has it that these were hopelessly liberal, thus naive projects, the charge is hard to sustain against the facts of their times and what the authors actually wrote.

Merton, most notably, took a position square in the lineage of Durkheim, but with an all-important difference. In *Suicide,* Durkheim's version of anomie was that it was a consequence of society's failure to give normative guidance. The deviant action of the individual, therefore, was a result of the moral quandary created by the failure of social structures. Merton's anomie described a much more complex relation between actors and structures. In the 1938 essay's opening paragraphs, Merton makes a statement Durkheim could not have contemplated: "Social structures generate the circumstances in which infringement of social codes constitutes a 'normal' (that is to say, expectable) response."[16] Even if Merton considered his views on the point similar to Durkheim's, they were not. Forty years before, in 1897, it would have been difficult to imagine Durkheim contemplating the normalcy of suicide. For Durkheim, actions of this sort arose from the state in which his individual was deprived of social instruction. This ultimately is why Durkheim could not distinguish the four types of suicide. They all were caused by some disturbance in the social order that left the individual too isolated from, or too obliged to, the social code. For Merton, infringement of the social code established a very different circumstance because his individual was a more autonomous social character than Durkheim's. In Merton's case the individual was able (creatively, in most cases) to adapt to anomie. Merton's actor, thus, was able to act in the face of anomie because—among other reasons—Merton himself was then more the post-classical thinker. Merton, the student of the classics, was also a sociologist of his times in the 1930s and 1940s—able, thus, to contemplate structures that, however slightly, did more than structure differences. Merton's theory allowed, therefore, for four evidently different, deviant types of individual adaptation—the very sort of differences Durkheim sought to define in *Suicide,* but could not. Though the new theories of structures were still indebted to classic thinkers, one begins to see in Merton's essay the first, gentle signs of a theory of structures that admitted differences upon having first admitted the irrational chasm between subjects and objects.

Though Parsons's early theory of structures may have had, as it is often claimed, a more classical universalizing theme, the basic paradigm of social action there announced is also clearly an advance over the classic model. Like Keynes, Parsons was reconstructing liberal social thought in more structural terms, necessitated by the terrors of the first half of the twentieth century. Parsons, again like Keynes, felt the older, more naive and individualistic liberal values of the nineteenth century had to be reconsidered with a more robust attention to the individual's "conditioned" relations to the socially structured environment in which he lived. Whatever has been said of him, often quite unfairly, Parsons was a man of well-nurtured moral sensibilities. Behind the analytic individual, the unit of his formal theory, stood actual moral individuals whose suffering he could have hardly ignored. To this day, it is far from clear that, beneath Parsons's terrifying abstractions, anyone has put the dilemma of the interwar era more precisely.

In the first pages of *Structure of Social Action*, where Parsons first outlines the conceptual elements of his theory of action, the four essential aspects of the action paradigm are stipulated:

1. an agent, the "actor";
2. a future "end" toward which one acts;
3. a social "situation" (over which the actor has only partial control); and (now to quote him fully),
4. "There is inherent in the conception of this unit, in its analytic uses, a certain mode of relationship between these [four] elements."[17]

One need not pursue Parsons much farther into the increasingly complicated theory that followed to see, already, the centrality of structures in his scheme and, more important, the brilliance of his definition of structure in the last aspect. In effect, in addition to the Durkheimian structural effect in his third aspect (that the individual's situation is partly beyond his control), Parsons composes a definition of structure in the fourth aspect that could speak to the moral needs of the day. The structure of social action was, from this axiomatic set, a structure of structures. Parsons did not view the individual simply as an isolated ends-seeking "unit" but as one situated in circumstances constituted simultaneously by the "situation" but equally by the structured relations between and among these elements. Though Parsons has never been given credit for it, there is an aesthetic as well as intellectual beauty to the idea that would eventually come to be understood as the recursive relation between moral agents and their structural environments.[18]

Were we to imagine that in 1937 Parsons was replying to Lukács's question of the "irrational chasm" hovering then palpably between subjects and their object worlds, only the weight of received opinion would keep us from concluding that Parsons's analytic scheme was a strong and morally good response. It was surely, then, in the late 1930s, among the more courageous and compelling a liberal social theorist could give. Like others, from Keynes and Niebuhr to Lukács and the Frankfurt critical theorists, Parsons too, in his way, recognized that individual actors could no longer be left to their own moral or entrepreneurial devices. They were conditioned and situated.

Thereafter, the questions sociologists put of the relations between subjects and structures were changed. Even if one takes a less generous view of Parsons and Merton, what cannot be denied is that together they did a very great deal to bring professional sociology into sensible contact with structures. Their contributions, when considered against the political and theoretical controversies of their youth, established the centrality of structural thinking to sociological theory.

Still, in some very primal way, both Merton and Parsons then believed modernity's first working principle that subjects apprehend objects. But, now, the relation is somewhat complicated. Both Merton and Parsons, though in different ways, believed in the power of sociology to explain structural effects. This is why both could believe with such confidence in sociology's ability to contribute to the reconstruction of liberal society after World War II. But it was Parsons, in particular, in his first statement of the action paradigm, who confessed his allegiance to the idea that the commanding reality of subjective agents and their structures is, recursively, a structural effect of the thinking subject, the sociologist. For him, the analytic structures created by the sociological subject generated the sufficient reality of worldly structures for extra-analytic agents. Parsons, in *Structure of Social Action*, was moving rapidly away from Descartes, even Kant, and therefore Durkheim. Yet, though he was speeding toward a more complicated structural sense of things social, he remained well within the gravitational pull of modern social thought.

Since Parsons and Merton, few have moved substantially beyond the theoretical position they redefined. Many have tried. In fact, in the generations that followed them, academic sociologists who came into their prominence in the 1970s and the 1980s set about the task of rethinking academic sociology's position on structure. That these later generations might have moved less far from Parsons and Merton than they, in their day, moved from the classic theorists may be illustrated by the following statements gathered from different sectors of the profession's culture and at various points in the period since the first rebellions against the generation of Parsons and Merton in the late 1960s:[19]

[1] The occupational structure is conceived of as consisting of the relations among its constituent subgroups; and these occupational subgroups, not the individuals composing them, are the units of analysis.

[2] In the search for rigor the ingenious practice is followed whereby such expressions [of the definiteness of structures] are first transformed into ideal expressions. Structures are then analyzed as properties of the ideals, and the results are assigned to actual expressions as their properties.

[3] A fundamental weakness of current sociological theory is that it does not relate micro-level interactions to macro-level patterns in any convincing way. . . . We

have had neither the theory nor the measurement and sampling techniques to move sociometry from the usual small-group level to that of larger structures.

[4] A world-system is a social system, one that has boundaries, structures, member groups, rules of legitimation, and coherence. . . . One can define its structures as being at different times strong or weak in terms of the internal logic of its functioning.

[5] An adequate understanding of social revolutions requires that the analyst take a nonvoluntarist, structural perspective on their causes and processes.

[6] Structural aggregates of micro-situations in time and space are on another level of analysis, and play a part in social causation only as they bear upon people's situational motivations. It is within micro-situations that we find both the glue and the transforming energies of these structures.

[7] In this sense, action and order constitute the "structural" properties of social theory.

[8] Structure thus refers, in social analysis, to the structuring properties allowing the "binding" of time-space in social systems, the properties which make it possible for discernibly similar social practices to exist across varying spans of time and space and which lend them their "systemic" form.

[9] Class structure thus remains the structural foundation for class formations, but it is only through the specific historical analysis of given societies that it is possible to explain what kind of actual formation is built upon that foundation.

[10] Social theory continues to be about the functioning of social systems of behavior, but empirical research is often concerned with explaining individual behavior. . . . The focus must be on the [structured] social system whose behavior is to be explained. This may be as small as a dyad or as large as a society or even a world system, but the essential requirement is that the explanatory focus be on the system as a unit, not on the individuals or components which make it up.

[11] Agents are empowered by structures, both by the knowledge of cultural schemes that enables them to mobilize resources and by the access to resources that enables them to enact schemes.

[12] In contrast to the voluntarist view of culture suggested by tool kit theorists, the multicausal explanation I propose takes into consideration how remote and proximate structural factors shape choices from and access to the tool kit—in other words, how these factors affect the cultural resources most likely to be mobilized by different types of individuals.

These extracts, gathered somewhat at random from among the most important writings across a quarter-century (from 1967 to 1992), illustrate the "multiplicity of meanings"[20] associated with the concept structure. Within the community of professional sociologists such variety signals the health of the field itself. Yet, were one to look at the multiplicity from a position outside the culture of professional sociology, it would be possible to conclude (as I do) that the diversity of understandings of social structure is more apparent than real.

Looking closely at the list as a whole, and beyond the differences among its entries, one can see the evident marks of a remarkable continuity, and not just with the particular advances made by Talcott Parsons in 1937. The following general assumptions are still made:

- that structures (whatever they may be) should be thought of as having some relation to individuals or the microworlds most proximate to them (see entries [1], [3], [5], [6], [10], [11], [12], and, implicitly, [2]);
- that however one thinks about this relation, it is one in which the agency of individuals and their most immediate social situations are affected or determined by the bigger structures (see entries [3], [6], [11], [12]; [5] by implication; and [9] by inference); finally,
- that the nature of that relation is sufficiently complicated such that, in order to think it, it is necessary also to think through the structure of social thought itself (see all twelve entries).

The advances beyond the thinking prevalent when Parsons and Merton began to rethink structures are not so great as to suggest anything like a conceptual revolution.

It is not that there are no differences but that they are less than one supposes. There are, indeed, not more than three major positions represented by the twelve examples, and these three largely cover the range of structural theories in sociology today, namely:

1. The best known of the three is the strategy of taking seriously the difference between agents and structures in order to conceive of the difference itself as the problem in need of solution. In spite of a certain inaccuracy in doing so, in the field this is often called the micro-macro problem, of which there are many compelling discussions, most of them organized around the idea that sociologies must adjudicate or otherwise reconcile the relations between big (macro) structures and local (micro) features of social life. It is not, to be sure, all that simple (subjects, for example, cannot be considered either local or little). Just the same, since the views usually gathered around this position aim to keep and remake the classic subject-object distinction, the first way of thinking structures might properly be called the *revisionist*.[21]

2. Others may grant that something like a micro-macro problem is there, but those associated with a second group of related points of view believe there are ways around it. Though this second group may include some who are considered by the first group "micro" theorists, it is the more structural (thus, "macro") members whose solution is of the greater interest here. Though some may consider it a ruthless slur, it is not entirely unfair to label this second position the *reductionist*, a designation that reflects a willingness to focus on but one element in the classic formula.[22]

Not concerned about micro and macro — emphasize on settle·

3. Finally, there is a group of sociologists who, in contrast to the second group, concede there is a problem but, in contrast to the first group, believe it is a solvable one. This way of thinking structures seeks an elegant, even heroic, reformulation of the problem itself. This is the *recursivist* strategy, which aims simply to overcome the classic way of thinking the problem of structures.[23]

The names *revisionist, reductionist,* and *recursivist* refer to the three basic ways sociologists think about structures. Since the days when Merton and Parsons redirected the sociology of social structures, few professional sociologists have failed to exhibit at least a covert allegiance to one of the three ways.

Today, it is difficult, if not impossible, to be a sociologist without thinking structures. This is because, since the end of World War I, the most terrible evils and promising prospects of modern society have been identified with questions of the nature of social structures. In the interwar period, structures of all kinds—economic, political, military, cultural—were, it seemed, arrayed demonically against the better spirit of humanity. In the post–World War II period, in the grand days of the American century, when the schools of Parsons and Merton reigned in sociology, just the opposite seemed true. The structures of society were then thought to be arrayed on the side of human progress. The good society was in view, and structural sociology was high priest of the coming order. Then, suddenly in the late 1960s, after all the consequences of decolonization, urban and racial wars, and political rebellion in Euro-American societies had clashed at once, thus beginning the crisis we are now in, the structures of society were even more the preoccupations of sociologists. Now, in this crisis of some thirty years, the structures of society are evidently neither good nor evil. The crisis is, in effect, a deep moral confusion over whether there can be, any longer, some stable, structured social order. Through these times, Weber's "immense cosmos" of modern society took on more and more definition, as did Durkheim's belief in the moral power of the social. The structures were no longer simply against the individual, as both Weber and Durkheim feared. The individual and social structures were somehow caught in a moral dilemma at the basis of which lay sociology's inability to think structures in classically clear and distinct terms.

These were the historical dilemmas through which sociology passed in its steps from Merton and Parsons to today's multiplicity of understandings of social structures. In its theories of social structures, professional sociology has proven itself capable of attending to the concerns of practical sociologies. Just the same, in this more recent period, practical sociologies have continued to press the question to which there is still no satisfying answer. *Who am I if things social are different?* has become: *Who am I, if social differences are structured against me?*

Therefore, among the three sociological ways of thinking of social structures, each deserves its due, but the third demands particular consideration. The recursivist strategy for thinking about thinking structures is the one that aims self-consciously to break, or at least refigure, the mold of modern culture. It alone among the three sets out to do what Parsons and Merton did in the late 1930s—fundamentally redesign the theory of social structures. That even the radical recursivist theories of structures might not have moved sociology beyond its original modernist culture suggests just how powerful that culture is and how deeply it is caught up in the world within which sociology takes place.

The public may occasionally scoff at academic sociology. But in its three ways of thinking structures, sociology has exhibited a considerable inventiveness, as well as the courage to face a problem few others have dared even consider. That academic sociology may not yet have solved the riddle of modernity does not mean it has not contributed to the thinking through of one of its more confusing implications. This is why sociology's three ways of thinking structures deserve the closer inspection that follows.

Chapter 7

Three Ways to Think Structures and Ignore Differences

T HE PAINTING THAT appears on the cover of this book (see Fig. 1) was executed by the Dutch master Jan Vermeer just as the modern world was taking on its distinctive structure. Vermeer's *Mistress and Maid* dates to the late 1660s when the United Provinces of northern Holland had extended their colonial system across the globe. At the height of its power, the Dutch East India company controlled a fleet of nearly 200 ships, of which 40 were ships of war. The larger number were merchant ships fueling the entrepreneurial ethics of the Dutch spirit of capitalism. The company's own army of 10,000 soldiers secured economic interests principally in India and on the periphery of the Indian Ocean. Its economic successes were astonishing. The thousands of middle-class Dutch who invested in the company gained dividends of up to 40 percent in these years. In Immanuel Wallerstein's phrase, the Dutch were the hegemonic power of the modern world-economy, the very center of the emerging world.[1] The mistress pictured in *Mistress and Maid* was, thus, one of the prosperous Dutch of the seventeenth century, who were among the first generations of fully secular and wildly successful modern capitalists.

In the seventeenth century Holland was also a center of science and learning. Descartes lived in Holland from 1629 to 1648 and published his *Discourse on Method* there. Baruch Spinoza, a second great modern philosopher, was born in Amsterdam in 1632, the same year Vermeer was born in Delft.

Anthony van Leeuwenhoek, the father of microbiology and an inventor of the microscope, not only shared Vermeer's birth year but had his name inscribed on the same page in the baptismal records in Delft. In Vermeer's lifetime, the commerce and culture of the modern world arose as one.

On its surface, Vermeer's *Mistress and Maid* gives little hint of the world structures that made it possible. A maid is passing a note to her mistress. It is likely that the two women share an intimacy that bridges their class differences, for the mistress seems to have been forewarned of the note's message, or at least of its source. Her hand, raised toward her slightly open mouth, closes the blank, unarticulated space between her and the maid. The mistress looks anxiously, not at the letter offered her, but into the dark space that sets her off from her servant. The eyes of the maid are discreetly lowered, again not at the note, but also into the void between her and her troubled mistress.

Whatever is in the note has the power to provoke the crisis that draws the observer into the work of art. Between the maid's extended hand bearing the unsettling message and the mistress's hand raised to her anxious face, the eyes of these two women of such different social position join just off the angle of direct eye contact, in the space of their differences. The observer is awkwardly pulled to this indefinite space above the writing table into the black triangle formed by the letter and the eyes of the women. There are now three lines of vision—those of the two women and that of the observer. Though they meet no place in particular, the uncomfortable coming together of these gazes lends the painting its emotional power. The observer shares the uncertainty of the moment.

But what is in that note? The usual assumption is that it is a love letter, bringing perhaps a word of loss or separation.[2] But, one could wonder, is another vector of difference cutting across the painting? Are the differences between the woman and a man encroaching on the class differences between the mistress and the maid? Are the women coming together in spite of their differences because of a difference between the sexes?

We are drawn to love as the subject matter of life among the women of the prosperous burghers of seventeenth-century Holland. Though Vermeer was not preoccupied with love, it certainly was among the themes of his paintings. The unifying theme of his work was, in effect, the sociology of ordinary life in his day. He took as subjects maids pouring milk, bourgeois women at their music or correspondence, the streets of Delft, various courtship scenes, and the like. *Mistress and Maid,* like Vermeer's work as a whole, portrays the common events of daily life. This invites the possibility that, apart of the subject matter of the note, the crisis in the midst of daily life is one of unrecognizable origins. As is

FIGURE 1 *Mistress and Maid* by Vermeer, Copyright The Frick Collection, New York.

often the case, that which presents itself as the obvious may have explanations which never appear on the surface of things.

Even in those affluent and good times for the new classes of bourgeois people, such crises as there were had some sensible bearing on their positions in the world. Even in the simple confines of *Mistress and Maid,* if the crucial note brings the word of a disappointment in love, the delicate balance of life between the sexes is off. If she is the mistress of the household, what is wrong between her and the master? Who, after all, is the author of the note? And what of her relation to the maid with whom she seems to share some slight degree of intimacy, woman to woman? Who is the woman upon whom the mistress relies for the petty services that provide comfort in her daily life?

Just as in our informed glances about the daily lives in which we today live, we seldom notice the complicated relations that shift just off the canvas. In Vermeer's painting, the play of sexual differences, like the hard reality of class differences, shapes the drama of the event without really being present. The lover is at most a possibility created by a secret note, folded so we cannot ever know its message. The maid, who may well know the secret, is closer to its truth than we can ever be. Yet her proximity is gently proscribed by the plain clothes and her unadorned arms and neck—signs of exclusion from the middle class she serves. *Mistress and Maid* would literally make no sense without these barely visible signs of the structured realities of life between the classes and the sexes in seventeenth-century Holland.

There is still another difference—one so understated that the observer denies its very existence. If one looks closely at the original of *Mistress and Maid* in the Frick Collection in New York City, the notion dawns that the maid might not be European. At the very top of her brow, the hair is tightly curled. Her face, though it is directly illuminated, is evidently darker by several shades than the skin of the mistress. What is Vermeer suggesting in these detectable marks of difference? Is it possible that the maid is African, possibly a Creole offspring from the West Indies? Surely, the middle classes in Holland recruited servants from among the mixed-race classes of the Dutch colonies. This third vector of difference in the painting is just as slightly suggested as is the identity of the note's author. We who are white and middle class are more inclined to insert the lost lover into the painting, while overlooking the signs of racial and class difference. Yet, again, the painting would be of less interest without them. It pulls us in as much for the eerie relation between the women as for the mysterious note. With hard work, we see the class differences because they are sharply accented. But are we meant to see the race differences so slightly hinted?

In those days in Holland race differences were, it must be remembered, the differences imposed by the great capitalist hegemony over the colonized world. Race differences were, in fact, the difference upon which the whole world of Dutch life rested. With the wealth appropriated from the colonies, including the commodity interests represented by the maid, the simple pleasures and crises of daily life in Delft would not have existed. Without the colonial system, there would have been no maids, no jewels to mark the differences between the classes and sexes, and no literary culture to generate telling notes. In the most necessary way, the commonplace life in a small town depended on the whole world structure, which, in that day, the Dutch dominated.

That is the way with social structures. Daily life in the towns depends on such structures for everything, just as the structures of the world economy depend on the rational, capitalist industry of the burgher investors and entrepreneurs who, like the women in their lives, stumble as they try to ignore the unsettling differences of sex and class, of race and the colonial system. As we live the lives we have, we too see these structured differences only in passing. Yet, they are there and we know it—invisible, hulking, shaping, inviting, yet also vulnerable.

The same is true of this painting. Vermeer's *Mistress and Maid* is one of the few he left uncompleted. Many of his works set as this one are filled with fine details, very often maps directly representing some part of the colonized world economy. Why did Vermeer quit this painting, leaving the dark inarticulate space where the eyes meet? In Holland in the seventeenth century, art was no longer subsidized by patrons of the nobility. In this new capitalist society, the vast wealth was distributed among the families of the mercantile capitalists. Art was paid for on the open market. It is likely that Vermeer interrupted work because he lost his commission, or because some other more lucrative venture offered itself. Once again the structures of capital interests intrude, even to cause the artist to think his structure as he did, with this black space where all gazes meet. Had Vermeer finished *Mistress and Maid,* he might have decorated the dark space between the two women, forcing them and the observer to look elsewhere. But that would have been some other, possibly less interesting, work of art. We, the observers, might have been offered a map like the one in Vermeer's *Woman in Blue,* in which a now pregnant woman reads a letter with pensive, almost sad eyes framed by a huge wall map, possibly of the West Indies or of northern Holland poised at the edge of the seas of its conquests. Such a map must have hung in Vermeer's home, reminding him of the world he inhabited even though he never traveled farther from Delft than The Hague, just a few miles to the sea.

In *Mistress and Maid* Vermeer was structuring the differences upon which the drama of his work and life depended. He was in this respect, as in so many others, a modern man. In his way he was thinking the structures of his social and economic world, and thinking them in ways that caused him, and the viewers of his work, to overlook the very differences created by those structures.

Recursivism, reductionism, revisionism—though these three ways of thinking structures are different from each other,[3] each seeks to work around modernity's riddle. Yet, in the end, they all remain on the blind side of modern culture. Though they are inventive in their ways, none can see the reality of differences any better than Durkheim or Weber or the other nineteenth-century sociologists. This is particularly surprising with respect to the recursivists, who take themselves, and are taken, as virtual or near postmoderns.

The recursivist way of thinking structures is, thus, the most compelling instance of the issues at stake in the sociology of structures. This can be illustrated by a text from a moment in the early history of the modern West when ancient structures were about to collapse.

Jean-Jacques Rousseau (1712–1778) completed his *Confessions* in 1770. Rousseau's memoir describes in exquisitely intimate detail the social world of the ancien régime in Europe during its last generation before the Revolution of 1789. The *Confessions* were, principally, Rousseau's defense of his character against attacks upon him. In more than six hundred pages, covering fifty-three years of his life, Rousseau refers to those of his writings that provoked public and official anger—in particular *Émile,* but also *The Social Contract,* the earlier *Discourse on the Origins of Inequality,* as well as countless pamphlets, the novels (especially *The New Héloïse*), and the plays and operas, a dictionary on music, and entries commissioned by Diderot for the *Encyclopedia.* Among Rousseau's many literary achievements were the ideas that contributed to the building up of a new, vigorous culture of opposition to the long traditions of courtly culture.

Though it describes the events and ideas that led to a massive transformation in world culture, Rousseau's *Confessions* is a very human book. It could be said to have been a public revelation of the private, practical thoughts behind this very prominent public life. As a result, the ideas with which Rousseau opposed courtly culture in other writings appear in ambiguous relation to Rousseau's personal circumstances. Throughout his adult life, Rousseau was dependent on the generosity and protection of influential members of the nobility, without whom he very likely would have perished. His relations with the larger cadre of revolutionary thinkers in his day were similarly conditioned by their mutual dependence on the social customs and real politics of the old regime. Rousseau and the Enlightenment philosophes did not form anything like a fabled political vanguard—all for one, one for all—united in opposition to the old order. Rousseau, for good reasons, did not trust Diderot, hated Voltaire, and openly opposed d'Alembert; they in return sought every possible opportunity to aggravate Rousseau's misery. Daily life is complicated in these ways every bit as much among the great leaders of historical change as among less brilliant mortals.

Just the same, Rousseau's personal ideas contributed to building up the new, revolutionary structures that changed the face of Europe and the world. Thus it is evident that the most complicated of the big social structures are fashioned in perverse relation to the mundane details of ordinary lives. One of the sure signs of a vulnerability in the old structures was the extraordinary fickleness of rival members of the noble class who with passing fancy both admired and rebuked Rousseau. Such seeming pettiness could not be unrelated to their inability to make effective accord in the management of France's increasingly desperate economic, military, and diplomatic policies in the two decades before 1789.

There could be no better illustration of the recursive relations between subjects and structured objects than Rousseau's confessional story. Social structures are susceptible to the actions and ideas of individuals just as individuals are susceptible to structural constraints. Who one is in a structured world is the indefinite result of structures that, in turn, are what they are because of what individuals do and think. In the abstract, the concept of recursive structures may seem obscure. In the daily lives of men and women like Rousseau and his rivals, benefactors, and lovers, its meaning is plain, if not quite the full meaning of the concept. Their petty human aggressions, greeds, and desires actually contributed in odd ways to their remaking of the eighteenth-century world, which, in turn, remade them and their successors. The play of individuals on structures and structures on individuals is a very human thing and, thus, indifferent to high-minded discriminations between vices and virtues.

Rousseau wrote his *Confessions* for the expressed, though not exclusive, purpose of demonstrating the moral worth of his personal character against the lies that most of Europe had believed against him. In the brief declaration he made to friendly members of the nobility after completing his *Confessions* in 1770, Rousseau made his purposes plain: "I publicly and fearlessly declare that anyone, even if he has not read my writings, who will examine my nature, my character, and my morals, my likings, my pleasures, and my habits with his own eyes and can still believe me a dishonorable man, is a man who deserves to be stifled." These words conclude the long analytic memoir[4] in which Rousseau goes to extremes above all else to be truthful, as best any individual can. Though the book itself is not viewed as among Rousseau's principal contributions to modern philosophy, its famous opening words are as clear an exposition of Enlightenment thinking as there is:

I have resolved on an enterprise which has no precedent, and which, once complete, will have no imitator. My purpose is to display to my kind a portrait in every way true to nature, and the man I shall portray will be myself.

Simply myself. I know my own heart and understand my fellow man. But I am made unlike any one I have ever met; I will even venture to say that I am like no one in the whole world. I may be no better, but at the least I am different. Whether Nature did well or ill in breaking the mould in which she formed me, is a question which can only be resolved after the reading of my book.

If Kant's "dare to know" is the most memorable slogan of the Enlightenment, then Rousseau's words at the beginning of his *Confessions* might be their most memorable personal expression. Here is every crucial element of the moral culture that modernized the new world: the uniqueness of the individual, the power of what one dares to know in his own "heart," an appeal to the universal understanding of one's fellow man, a republican faith in equality. "I may be no better, at least I am different."

In other words, the ideas that led to revolution in the modern world originated in the agency of individuals—among them, Rousseau. Once established in public opinion, they affected the structured order—disturbing, irritating, ultimately changing its nature. The changes themselves, which began in small ways among a group of difficult men, slowly drawn against their wills toward each other, eventually altered political and economic life, the complete array of social institutions but also the way men and women thought of themselves in the world. Rousseau's *Confessions,* like the personal statements of others of the day—the letters and autobiographies of Thomas Jefferson and the folksy advice of Ben Franklin, among others—prove that the advent of modern culture was announced as clearly in the most personal reflections as in the more famous public declarations. From those first moments in the eighteenth century the specific structural turn taken by the Western world toward republican governments and entrepreneurial economies was set against a welter of free action and thought in civil society that also entailed a sociology of that world.

Rousseau's younger contemporary, Thomas Jefferson (1743–1826), wrote in the most famous public declaration of that age, "We hold these truths to be self-evident, that all men are created equal; that they are endowed by their creator with inherent and inalienable rights."[5] Just as Rousseau, in defense of his character, made appeal to the self-evident truth of his character, so Jefferson expressed a powerful variant of this revolutionary idea. Where exactly did it begin, this idea that subjectively apprehended truths were foundational to the most universal rights? It is difficult to say exactly. Not just with Kant, Jefferson, Rousseau, and the other great thinkers of the eighteenth century; not even, certainly, with Descartes the century before; nor with Martin Luther and Jean

Calvin the century before that. Nor, just as certainly, was it in the nature of things, as Jefferson's proclamation implies.

Sociologically speaking, the origin of the ideal of subjective truth as universal right was in no one place or time. Sociologically, big social things do not begin anywhere in a deep original source somewhere back in history. This was the shared mistake of the giants of classical sociology. Marx, Durkheim, and Weber all referred the fate of the modern world back to some mythic time-place when alienation, anomie, and the iron cage first appeared faintly in the setting sun of a more primitive social order. Whenever origins are located this exactly, it is impossible for sociology to let go of the past. And, a past preserved in order to maintain an idea of the present must be preserved in historical chemicals that burn the eyes that would see the present.

Big structures and big ideas begin more probably in the massive accumulation of mundane details—failed friendships, frustrated loves, improper advances, stupid arguments, and all the other, occasionally more noble, events of daily lives. Recursive theories of social structures attempt to protect the mundaneity of their origins.

▼▼▼▼▼

That today's recursive theories of structures may, in fact, still keep to original principles is illustrated by what was said by another Frenchman in one of the most important public speeches of his life.

Pierre Bourdieu is widely considered, and rightly so, the major sociologist most likely to have edged over the line of modern culture. In his inaugural lecture on April 23, 1982, at the Collège de France, Bourdieu began: "One ought to be able to deliver a lecture, even an inaugural lecture, without wondering what right one has to do so: the institution is there to protect one from that question and the anguish inseparable from the arbitrariness of all new beginnings." Bourdieu continued:

> As a parable or a paradigm, the lecture on the lecture, a discourse which reflects itself in the act of discourse, should at least have the virtue of reminding us of one of the most fundamental properties of sociology as I conceive it: all the propositions that this science enunciates can and must be applied to the subject who practices this science. It is when he cannot introduce this objectifying and thus critical distance that the sociologist proves right those who see in him a sort of terrorist inquisitor, available to carry out all the actions required by symbolic policing. One cannot go into sociology without tearing through the adherencies and adhesions by which one ordinarily belongs to groups, without abjuring the

beliefs that are constitutive of belonging and without disowning every link of affiliation and filiation.

Later, he adds: "Sociology is a science whose peculiar feature is the peculiar
difficulty it has of becoming a science like the others."[6]

Famous as an inventor of reflexive sociology, Bourdieu here makes an art, if
not a science, of the reflexive basis of modern sociology. It cannot be a science
because it must be rigorously reflexive. Those who think of Bourdieu as a
postmodernist could well explain that he exceeds modern thinking by the
very act of drawing so much attention to this foundational act of self-reflection. Though both considered it necessary, neither Descartes nor Rousseau
would have made self-critique the defining feature of modern thought, as
Bourdieu seems to do. Bourdieu thinks in ways Durkheim could not have
conceived. Durkheim, by contrast, hunkered down into the modernist culture
his predecessors invented. Bourdieu claims to be pushing the limits of that
culture, even while he takes with great seriousness the major social thinkers of
his field. His idea of *habitus* is clearly indebted to Weber's idea of an ethical
orientation. His concept *cultural capital,* apart from its Marxian metaphor,
owes a great deal to Durkheim. But, in a surprising way, Bourdieu's theoretical
and literary style is closest to Rousseau's.

Like Rousseau, Bourdieu practices the reflexive art of presenting the truth
of things in relation to the sociologist's character. Unlike Rousseau, he does so
without revealing anything personal. Yet, reading Bourdieu is like reading
texts each of which begins with Rousseau's theme: "I have resolved on an enterprise which has no precedent, and which, once completed, will have no imitator." Though Rousseau's moral tone is different, his moral effect is not
much different from Bourdieu's sense of himself as a "terrorist inquisitor" attacking the terms and the structures of which he speaks, establishing the different, utterly unique, point of view of the subject. Reading Bourdieu (and
unlike reading Rousseau), one seldom gets the sense of being in the presence
of an author seeking common ground with his readers. The moral voice beneath the words themselves whispers to each reader: "Here is how I see these
things; see them for yourself in how I say them; determine their truth by how
well they are said." Why else this title for a book on reflexive sociology: *In
Other Words?*

The brilliance of Bourdieu's sociology lies in the coherence between his
literary style and his theoretical position. Thus, also in "The Lecture on the
Lecture," Bourdieu says with respect to the sociology of social things:

> Through the sociologist, a historically situated historical agent and a socially deter-
> mined social subject, history, or rather the society in which the existing remains of

history are preserved, turns for a moment back on itself, and reflects on itself; and through the sociologist, all social agents are able to know a little more clearly what they are and what they are doing.[7]

Bourdieu leaves no room for doubt. The sociologist is the historical agent who takes history as his theme in order to show others just how social things are.

But what does he mean in that parenthetical phrase " . . . history, or rather the society in which the existing remains of history are preserved . . . "? Does he mean to define society as the structured remains of history? The answer is found elsewhere in his writings, in the programmatic statement Bourdieu makes, over and over, beginning with the theoretical sections of his major transitional book, *Outline of a Theory of Practice.*[8]

This book is locus classicus for Bourdieu's famous concept *habitus.* Just as important, it presents one of his most explicit statements of a formal theory of structures. Since its first appearance, Bourdieu has not modified the definition of *habitus:*

> The structures constitutive of a particular type of environment (e.g., the material conditions of existence characteristic of a class condition) produce *habitus*, transposable *dispositions*, structured structures predisposed to function as structuring structures, that is, as principles of the generation and structuring of practices and representations which can be objectively "regulated" and "regular" without in any way being the product of obedience to rules, objectively adapted to their goals without presupposing a conscious aiming at ends or an express master of the operations necessary to attain them and, being all this, collectively orchestrated without being the product of the orchestrating action of a conductor.[9]

Even if the text seems opaque, it is easy to see that Bourdieu is here somehow putting his own spin on the idea of structures. The chapter in which this passage appears ("Structures and *Habitus*") begins with Bourdieu's declaration of sociological independence from the classic, Cartesian split between subjects and objects: "Methodological objectivism, a necessary moment in all research, by the break with primary experience and the construction of objective relations which it accomplishes demands its own supersession."[10]

In this declaration one sees Bourdieu's sense of sociological terrorism—a science that cannot be a science and also a practice that tells people how the world is. To this end, he moves beyond the modernist formula, subjects apprehending objects, but without moving too far. Thus, the concept *habitus* serves to ground what had before been grounded in consciousness. Just as Durkheim sought to reinvent Kant, Bourdieu tries the same with respect to Descartes. If for Durkheim the collective consciousness was the way out of Kant's mental categories, then for Bourdieu *habitus* is the way out of the

Cartesian critical mediation on objective truths found in the subjective consciousness. *Habitus*, thus, reformulates structures. Instead of seeing structures
as social things over against subjects, Bourdieu explains them with reference
to what can best be called the zero signifier of his social theory of structures—
a null point in relation to which recombinant subjects and objects lose their
separate specific gravities. *Habitus* is, in effect, a theoretically empty meeting
place for the social events in which "structured structures [are] predisposed to
function as structuring structures." These predisposing structured structuring
structures are, like Weber's capitalist ethic, neither a subjective attitude nor a
regular objective rule of the modern world. *Habitus* is that habit of moral action whereby individuals know how to act in a certain manner either without
inventing the action each time they act thusly *or* without being told by any
one or another thing (least of all structured society) just how to act. The
"durable but transposable, structuring but structured, unregulated but regular" habits are ultimately plays on and within the theoretical restructuring of
the thought world between subjects and objects. Neither, yet both, somehow.

Still, one asks: What is it, this *habitus?* Even if one grants it is a theoretical
zero signifier recombining subjects and objects, a question remains. How does
it work? Like Weber's *ethic,* Bourdieu's *habitus* is a disposition to act in ways
that are regular, yet unregulated; structured, yet spontaneous. Dispositions
have verisimilitude but no being—upon which attribute Bourdieu must rest
his insistence that the *habitus* is the way out of the classic dilemma. But this
does not allow Bourdieu better resolution of the problem Weber left unsolved. How do dispositions work? is, in effect, a question of how they come
to be shared, widely and uniformly, across large social groups. The force of the
concept is in its capacity to account for the historically evident correspon-
dences that occur across the actions of large numbers of individuals and the
enduring structures believed to represent those enduring actions. Weber did
not try to answer this question. *Protestant Ethic* began by positing the diffusion of the spirit of capitalism, after which the book explains by describing
the likely prehistory of the ethic back to a plausible origin. Bourdieu, having
begun with the advantage of knowledge of Weber, still must explain what
Weber did not. What *is* his solution?

In one of his most important empirical works, *Homo Academicus,* his study
of the culture of the French system of higher education, Bourdieu seems to
solve the problem with reference to the unconscious: "These are strategies of
the *habitus,* therefore more unconscious than conscious."[11] It turns out, however, that the word "unconscious" is somewhat more figurative than literal.
There is also in Bourdieu's thought a strong inclination to treat shared dispositions as acquired and learned. The true nature of dispositions is not, however,

suggested by the fact that over time they are taught and learned, thus reproduced. Rather, as it was for Weber, it is more a question of how they arise, spread, and endure in times of change.

Bourdieu recognizes this in *Homo Academicus,* his empirical study of French academic culture. In the one chapter in *Homo Academicus* where he discusses the *habitus* explicitly, it is not by accident that the theme of his analysis shifts to the question of dramatic changes in the French university structure in the 1960s. The chapter, "The Defence of the Corps and the Break in Equilibrium," begins:

> The structure of the university field is only, at any moment in time, the state of the power relations between the agents or, more precisely, between the powers they wield in their own right and above all through the institution to which they belong; positions held in this structure are what motivate strategies aiming to transform it, or to preserve it by modifying or maintaining the relative forces of the different powers, that is in other words, the systems of equivalence established between the different kinds of capital.[12]

The changes that disrupted the prior steady state of power relations were, principally, a radical democratization at all levels of the university system. New campuses were created offering university education and certification to students who had previously been excluded—principally those from the lower strata of French society and from its former colonies. Democratization also had powerful effects on the faculties. More students created the need for more faculty who were trained in the new "third-cycle" doctoral programs and took up the new positions—though generally ones in the inferior, less prestigious ranks of the new system. The system thus grew and changed with the important effect that the old structural order, which had been organized narrowly around a few elite schools in Paris, was broken but not destroyed.

Bourdieu's discussion of *habitus* occurs, as the chapter's title suggests, in precise connection with the "crisis of succession":

> The university system in its previous state tended to ensure its own reproduction by producing teachers endowed with fairly stable and homogeneous social and academic characteristics, which were therefore relatively interchangeable over a period of time as well as at any given moment. More precisely, the stability of the system over a period of time supposed that the teachers were endowed, at every hierarchical level, with an academic *habitus,* a veritable *lex insita,* as Leibniz says, an immanent law of the social body which, having become immanent in the biological bodies, causes the individual agents to realize the law of the social body without intentionally or consciously obeying it.[13]

Again, *habitus* appears to entail a slightly self-conscious, certainly oblique theory of the social unconscious. In the pages following, Bourdieu describes the challenges to the old order in the university system with reference to its traditional academic *habitus* as seen from the perspective of heads of academic units during the crisis of 1968. That is, Bourdieu takes the narrative position of those whose power was diluted in the restructuring of the teaching cadres, those who were required, in effect, to give up a familiar *habitus.*

Prior to the democratizations in the mid-1960s and the rebellions of the assistant teachers and students in 1968, the old order functioned (unconsciously it would seem) "on the basis of networks founded on an affinity of *habitus,* common memories, École Normale friendships."[14] When the assistant faculty challenged the traditional elites, the latter's *habitus* changed instantly! "From that moment on, everything that made up the old order, the intangible liberties and connivances which are shared by people of the same milieu, the respectful familiarity which is *de rigueur* between different generations of the same family, were abolished."[15] This, of course, did not mean that the representatives of the old order were left without a *habitus.* They developed a new one.

According to Bourdieu, members of the old order gave up the habit of acting as privileged members of an elite clique to become members of a "non-aligned union"—a syndicate of professional managers. As the well-organized assistant faculty demanded equalities of privilege, pay, and status, the older heads of the system were forced, as Bourdieu's words imply, to enter the modern world by giving up their naive faith in themselves and their privileges:

> And they contributed thereby to reinforcing the very logic which they claimed to combat: by working to reduce the apparent discrepancy between liberties, to minimize the contradictions, conflicts and rivalry between heads which were dissimulated by the non-conspiratorial consensus on common values, by forcing themselves to offer up the united front of a managerial union against the united front of the unions dominated by subordinate teachers, in short, by giving the consistency of a plan to what was only the more or less coherent effect of the spontaneous orchestration of the *habitus,* they reinforced the break between the categories which is the source of the protest against which they intended to struggle, and above all they contributed to destroying one of the main pillars of the old order, ignorance, or, in other words, faith: vagueness has its social function and, as we see with clubs, or with salons in a previous age, the most unimpeachable criteria are those which are the least definable.[16]

The events of 1789 stood behind the political drama of 1968 in France. The old order in the university system was forced to give up a traditional innocence characteristic of "a previous age," for which was substituted the new habit of acting according to a rational plan, precisely in order to salvage what they could of the system's ability to preserve their self-interests. They became, according to

Bourdieu's account, new managerial entrepreneurs, assuming the dispositional qualities of Weber's new capitalists. And, they took on the new *habitus* "from [a certain] moment on." If the *habitus* is unconscious under certain conditions, it would seem to be capable of becoming consciously rational under others.

But how did this miracle happen? It could not have been a long history of cultural diffusion from an original source, as Weber supposed. Nor could it have been, strictly speaking, a result of deeply structured practices nurturing the new *habitus,* for this central implication of reproduction theory seems to be shaken by the suddenness of the 1968 changes. Then, Bourdieu says: "Thus, it is that the synchronic and diachronic homogeneity of the professorial body was based on a harmony among *habitus* which, being produced by identical conditions of selection and training, engendered objectively harmonious practices, and especially selection procedures."[17] The notion of an "identity of conditions" does not, however, explain what exactly unites the identical (or similar) conditions, to say nothing of the actors with similar dispositions acting in otherwise different settings. That explanation would require, as Bourdieu seems to admit, a theory of the unconscious *habitus.*

Bourdieu's *habitus* presses the very limits of the modern sociology of structures to brilliant and instructive effect. Whether it presses them in ways that truly alter that deep cultural theory depends, one might say, on what Bourdieu really means by the unconscious operations of the *habitus.* What is clear is that he has identified a central dilemma in the theory of structures. Yet, neither the classic formula (that changes move from subjects against the object world, or from structured objects against subjects) nor Bourdieu's attempt to get beyond it seems capable of explaining historically specific and all-of-a-sudden changes such as those in France in the 1960s.

Bourdieu's interpretations of the events of May 1968 presuppose that such a dramatic change took place. If it did, it may have taken place not just in France but throughout the Western world. One of the reasons to think the change occurred is reflexive: The traditional ways of thinking about structures and their relations to agential selves seem unable to account for those events without some awkward notion like "the unconsciousness of the *habitus.*" Somehow Bourdieu, the theorist, takes a position at odds with Bourdieu, the sociologist who views society as the "remains of history." For, as reflection on Rousseau's prerevolutionary circumstances teaches, the events of 1789, which Parisians in 1968 had thought they were reenacting, did not occur all-in-a-moment but during a long, obscure preparation. And few today think that the rise of the capitalist entrepreneur or of the new republican actor came in some similarly sudden moment. No one knows for sure whether events in the 1960s in the West were changes of a different, more dramatic sort than these classic examples. What we know, however, is that Bourdieu interpreted those events as though they were quite sudden because, it would seem, his leading concept can account for change in no other way. The *habitus* explains the enduring reproduction of social structures quite nicely. But it seems able to explain the disruption of structures only through recourse to the unconscious, on the one hand, and to an arbitrary historical interpretation, on the other. In effect, *habitus* cannot account for change in *habitus.*

The most intentionally inventive sociologist of structures—the one individual who, more than any other academic sociologist, sought to change the way these things are thought—could not succeed without reliance on a concept his theory could not explain. It is possible that no sociology of unconscious habits can explain either itself or the differences that arise in it when history changes. Though the *habitus* was invented to account for spontaneous differences in structured actions, it turns out to be a global attribute utterly devoid of gender, race, or sex. Even its recognition of class differences recedes into the dark mass of universal human nature.

It is possible, furthermore, that sociologists, like astrophysicists, must rest their case on black holes like the *habitus,* into which all social matter enters, creating a weird lurking density—social mass without volume.

If Bourdieu's terrorist sociology invents, in the manner of Rousseau, the utterly unique, nonreplicable theory of the *habitus,* then Anthony Giddens's approach to the same set of concerns takes a different form. It is hard to judge to what extent their differences may represent those between elite French and elite English academic cultures—between the prowess of near hermetic finesse and the demanding exposition that opens an inner logic.[18] What is not hard to see is that Giddens takes a literary and theoretical strategy nearly opposite to Bourdieu's. Few sociologists of his generation have attempted as massive and multifaceted a literary project as Giddens's, one that reinvents sociology *tout court.* It is necessary to go back to Parsons and Merton to find anything comparable. Such a comparison, fancifully made, might also cast Bourdieu, the empirical sociologist of the habitual middle range, as a Merton to Giddens's Parsons, the grand theorist of the social whole. Yet, unlike their predecessors in the post–World War II period, Bourdieu and Giddens in the post-1968 period have no strong personal connections, and fewer similarities of style. Both, however, seek to reinvent sociology by means of a recursive theory of social structures that aims to get around or beyond the dualism of subjects and objects.

Giddens's first rigorously synthetic statement appeared in 1976. Its title made its purposes clear: *New Rules of Sociological Method*. Here Giddens made his most open, yet simple, definition of the new sociology: "*In sum, the primary tasks of sociological analysis are the following: (1) The hermeneutic explication and mediation of divergent forms of life within descriptive metalanguages of social science; (2) Explication of the production and reproduction of society as the accomplished outcome of human agency*."[19] In the short book thus summarized, Giddens began systematically to develop a new sociology of modern society in which the single most decisive questions are, What are structures? How do they work in relation to subjects? The culmination of this effort was *The Constitution of Society* in 1984, Giddens's most complete working through of his social theory of *structuration*.[20]

The concept *structuration*, like Bourdieu's *habitus*, seeks to reformulate the sociological understanding of structures by getting beyond the classic dilemma: "I wish to escape the dualism associated with objectivism and subjectivism."[21] Why, again, get around this dualism? Bourdieu's answer is relatively clean. He thinks the subjectivism/objectivism duality freezes sociological thought, preventing the theorist from getting through to the null point of reflexive uniqueness, from which, Bourdieu believes, one gains the more perspicacious view of society. But Giddens's purposes are different to a slight, but important, degree. In the comparison it becomes evident that, to a far greater extent than Bourdieu, Giddens sees sociology as *the* sociology of "advanced or modern societies."[22] Uncannily, in the comparison, it appears that Bourdieu wants more to invent the new *general* sociology of *all* things social; while Giddens seems more preoccupied with the sociology of *modern* societies. If we take Durkheim (to whom both are obligated) as the measure of this comparison, it is clear that Bourdieu's writing is much more that of the culture of Enlightenment—trying to say everything necessary, to say it beautifully and well, and to say it as never before. Bourdieu's reflexes are, like Rousseau's, to the privileged subject in order that he might, like Durkheim, describe the universal of social things. By contrast, Giddens engages the reader more directly. This is not to suggest that Giddens's language is plain, only that he aims somehow to make himself understood in terms that are, in principle, shared. Bourdieu's writings are a continuous series of special insights loosely organized by the *habitus*. Giddens's are much more the continuous pursuit, through a series of literary and conceptual obstacles, of the completely articulated theory of modern society. In this one regard, Bourdieu is more classically eighteenth century and Giddens more instrumentally twentieth. But the clue that both might be well within the culture of modernity is that both seek the universal truth of some social reality: Bourdieu from the utterly distinct discursive insight, Giddens from the heroic search for a new common language.

This quality of Giddens's writing and thinking is evident in what may be his most unsettling and thus memorable interpretation of the concept *structure:*

> Structure thus refers, in social analysis, to the structuring properties allowing the "binding" of time-space in social systems, the properties which make it possible for discernibly similar social practices to exist across varying spans of time and space and which lend them "systemic" form. To say that structure is a "virtual order" of trans-formative relations means that social systems, as reproduced social practices, do not have "structures" but rather exhibit "structural properties" and that structure exists, as time-space presence, only in its instantiations in such practices and as *memory traces orienting the conduct of knowledgeable human agents.*[23]

Opaque from one point of view; clear enough from another. Where Bourdieu is slightly more intent on putting his own gloss on sociology's vocabulary, Giddens is somewhat more concerned to *redefine* it altogether. Thus the series of qualified, neologistic terms in Giddens's discussion of *structuration:* "'binding' of time-space," "'virtual order' of transformative relations," "[not] 'structures' [but] 'structural properties.'" But even in these few lines, there is something a little off. The flurry of quotation marks qualifies an otherwise supremely confident prose, as if to signal the approach of something that could be its undoing.

What Giddens is signaling in these literary apologies may be the most distinctive feature of his theory of structures. He writes about structures as though he were writing of them in more or less the same terms in which they are normally thought. But, in fact, he does not think structures as others do. Structures, for Giddens, are not so much things in themselves as, to use his words, "virtual order" properties that exhibit themselves only in concrete instances of social practice, as "memory traces orienting the conduct of knowledgeable actors"! This turns out to be a big and courageous theoretical step.

In his theory of structures, Giddens proposes to overcome the duality of subjects and objects because he believes that his predecessors in the sociological tradition gave overly objectivist definitions of structures, which, in turn, had the effect of distorting their views of subjective agency. In this regard, Giddens has Durkheim's definition in mind when he describes structures as rules and resources, simultaneously. Yet, he expressly separates himself from Durkheim's more restricted idea of structures as constraining rules, just as he puts the same critique to Marx and Parsons and the French structuralists.[24] Like Bourdieu, Giddens does not believe the tendency toward objectifying structures or its corollary of subjectifying agents solves the problem of ethical behavior in modern societies. *Structuration* theory is Giddens's way of doing what Bourdieu tries to do with *habitus,* but with a crucial difference.

Where Bourdieu balks before the unconscious as a solution, Giddens ventures forth, as is already hinted at in the premise behind his view of structures as virtual order properties. Structures are not real social things. Giddens is one of the first to admit this disconcerting fact that prior generations of sociologists had repressed. Durkheim, who was consumed with interest in the reality of social things, avoided a positive description of the structure of modern society perhaps because, in some reflexive way, he knew they were not as real as they are felt to be. Likewise Bourdieu, who clearly agrees with Giddens on the virtuality of structures, avoids saying so in so many words. Bourdieu, who wants most of all to be known as an empirical sociologist, sets up the inscrutable black hole of *habitus* in order that he might explain the agential aspect of structures without having to consider it in so many words. Giddens, by contrast to both, wants nothing so much as to say the complete theory of modern societies. Giddens takes the more heroic, if riskier, approach. Structuration theory is a sociology of structures that grants the irreality of social structures in order to define "structural properties" in the only place they can be observed: practical actions and memory traces.

Giddens's attempt to solve the problem is not without its problems. A cynic might argue that the reason he remains entirely within the discourse of social theory, never writing what others consider empirical studies, is that it is impossible actually to describe a virtual structure, thus to prove his theory. This, I think, would be a cheap shot. Giddens is among those who believe that the discursive activity of writing, and saying, the social theory of things in modern societies is a nearly sufficient, certainly necessary, hence good enough, way to do sociology. Giddens gets to this point for the same reason as does Bourdieu, but Giddens's theoretical style of saying everything that can be said allows, even requires, him to account for the virtual unconscious as corollary to his virtual structures.

When Giddens actually writes about sociology, as in his inaugural address at Cambridge University ("What Do Sociologists Do?"), he writes of it as though it were a social science among other social sciences, differing only in its greater capacity for reflexivity. He, thus, assumes a strategic narrative position within professional sociology—one from which he looks out on the social world sociologists presume to see better for reason of their trained reflexive eyes. As a consequence Giddens frequently makes "empirical references" (especially in books like *The Nation-State and Violence*). But he makes them, strictly speaking, ex officio, that is, by virtue of his office as a reflexive sociologist. One must go back to Talcott Parsons, against whom Giddens situates himself, to find a sociologist who assumed a similar literary and theoretical position.

It is not, therefore, by accident that Parsons was also the early modern sociologist who came closest to treating structures as though they were virtual properties. The difference is that Parsons tried to reproduce those structures within the body of his writing, an ultimately foolish enterprise that drew him inevitably deeper and deeper into the unending layers of the AGIL paradigm.[25] By contrast, though Giddens seems to be providing the exhaustive representation of structures in the text, he is always aware of his public, of the reader he addresses, the one who bears the prior responsibility for the reflexive attitude in daily life. This, then, is the precise objection Giddens makes to Parsons. Indeed, Parsons did not address the reader's practical authority because, within his theory, the virtual reality of structures was sufficient. For Giddens the virtual reality of structures is always outside, even over against, the natural reflexive capacity of the most ordinary human subject. Though a society's structures are virtual, they are necessarily a redoublement of a primary, if inaccessible, reality of social life. Thus, the world of difference from Parsons—a difference that entails, on the one hand, a recursive theory of structures and, on the other, a theory of their necessary duality. Though Parsons allowed, at least by implication, for the former, he could not acknowledge the latter. Giddens can; in fact, he must if he is to speak about the social world to those who, in his view, build it.

Thus the dualism of subjects and objects is overcome by recourse to the double nature of structures themselves. "According to the notion of the duality of structure, the structural properties of social systems are both *medium and outcome* of the practices they recursively organize."[26] The statement is amazing and beautifully so. Having defined structures as properties of practical actions (and the memory traces that may orient those actions), Giddens still speaks of them as though they have real effects. Structures, being resources as well as rules, do "recursively *organize*" social realities. They are, thus, real players, perhaps actors. This is a coherent view, perfectly defensible given its own logic. But it comes onto shaky ground soon enough.

It is very difficult to describe the recursive properties of structures, as is evident in the figure of speech to which Giddens resorts when attempting to simplify: "We should understand human societies to be *like buildings that are at every moment being reconstructed by the very bricks that compose them.*"[27] When compared to the inscrutability of *habitus*, Bourdieu's key metaphor, Giddens's is clumsy. He is trying to describe the most subtle of human processes with reference to the long, laborious construction of a building. This is already a slight clue to the difficulty of the task he has set (or, perhaps, to Bourdieu's wisdom in avoiding it).

Within the language of sociology it may not be possible to say what Giddens wants to say. The duality of virtual structures means that knowledgeable agents, being the only real actors in society, act partly under the direction of structured rules and partly in reliance on structured resources. But structures are never observed in themselves, only as reflected in the practical actions of individuals. The structured inequalities of the class system of modern urban societies are not in themselves observable, except *through* the obvious instances of actions in which real people defer or condescend, starve or stuff themselves. Virtual realities are nonetheless real, though without their own specificity.

This is why Giddens takes so seriously the idea of sociology as an extended conceptual discourse on the nature of modern societies. More specifically, this is why discourse (the ability to say things in so many words) is the key to consciousness, which in turn is the theoretical key to virtual reality. It is plain to see that, if there is no literal, positive reality to structures, the only place one can observe them is in what people say about their actions. Observing actions themselves is insufficient. A poorly clad young person with unkempt hair, wandering about and begging for food, might appear to be hungry and thus an instance of the structural properties of the system's virtual inequality. Yet, he could also be a middle-class person of means who, for his own political or personal purposes, assumes the appearance of poverty—an act he would be able to execute over time not *in spite of* his relative wealth but *because* of it. (Alex Supertramp comes to mind.) One could only determine such a character's place in the scheme of virtual structures by talking to and with him, or about him and his kind. Even then, the results would be uncertain because the reliability of the conversations would depend utterly on the state of his, and his interpreter's, consciousness. Discourse always bears some relation to consciousness, even if the relation is perverse.

This is the insight that brings Giddens to the unconscious aspect of social life. He distinguishes practical from discursive consciousness, without which distinction there could be no reflexivity and thus no recursivity in society. Practical consciousness is that awareness of structured reality one holds in the head without necessarily being aware of it at any given moment even though it is the resource by which one goes on and gets by.[28] We speak a language grammatically without being able to list the grammatical rules we use. We may, depending on our social background, defer to others of presumably greater status without knowing exactly why. That people hold in their heads a practical consciousness is illustrated by the degree to which Larry Hogue infuriates and befuddles so many people. The practical code says, tacitly: "A homeless, mentally ill, Black man ought not even know, much less act, on his rights to go where he pleases and do what he wants." Hogue breaks the practical rules. When such rules are broken, people figure out the rule if they can, or call in the experts. Thus, discursive consciousness is the capacity to talk coherently about social actions. It encompasses the ability to understand and, if called upon, to recite the grammar of those actions. When, and if, they do, they exhibit discursive consciousness.[29]

Here is where the sociologist enters as the crucial actor in society. "Human actors are not only able to monitor their activities and those of others in the regularity of day-to-day conduct; they are also able to 'monitor that monitoring' in discursive consciousness."[30] All human actors (in principle) and professional sociologists (by definition) are capable of talking about their social actions and the actions of others (and talking about that talk). Otherwise, there is no way to know structures; thus, for all intents and purposes, there are no structures. The ability of persons to put into words what they, and others, are doing is the only reliable way one has to know the virtual reality of structures. But (and Giddens refrains from putting it this radically), it would seem that the capacity of ordinary, untutored individuals to put into words what they think about social actions is the principal means unto knowledge of virtual reality. If so, then discursive consciousness *is* the sole basis for that virtuality. Virtuality of structures in social life must mean "mediated for all sufficient purposes by talk"—by discourse about structures.

Only those who hold fast to the original formula whereby subjects are considered capable of apprehending *real, available* (as distinct from *virtual*) objects need be put off by this interpretation of Giddens. Even if Giddens might not go quite as far as I have in interpreting him, his theory would seem to entail some central elements of this characterization. Certainly, for a salient example, the virtual reality of his structures has not in the least prevented him from engaging in exceptional, and convincing, discursive practices with respect to modern social structures—nation-states, capitalism, the modern state and the class system, modernity itself[31]—and to do so with utter seriousness. Theoretical seriousness has little necessarily to do with the hardness of one's theory of reality. Giddens's refusal to allow his theory of virtual structures to inhibit his theories of real structures is one of his most generous contributions to sociology—one that, just the same, falls short of solving sociology's problems with structured differences.

Discursive consciousness clearly requires some sort of theory of the unconscious life. Giddens, in the few places he discusses the Freudian theory directly, makes a simple, popular interpretation of the psychoanalytic view. In effect, if discursive consciousness is that which is available to be put into words, then practical consciousness is that aspect of the not necessarily conscious life available for use in practical life. Though Giddens grants that there is a deep unconsciousness that resists practical life, he is, quite understandably, very much more interested in the unconscious play between practical and discursive consciousness. When he sets about to discuss the unconscious,[32] Giddens's interest turns much more directly to memory than to Freud's notion of the perverse, resisting unconscious. The unconscious aspects of social (or does he mean mental?) life come to the fore of his argument only because some version of the unconscious life is required to account for what he considers the fundamental dilemma of modern life. If for Weber that dilemma was "Why do men obey?" for Giddens it is "Why and how do they trust?"

For Giddens, the most fundamental fact of modern (especially late-modern) societies is that individuals are disembedded from primary relationships. The corresponding existential problem of the modern is "trust versus risk": "Modernity, as everyone living in the closing years of the twentieth century can see, is a double edged phenomenon."[33] For Giddens this becomes the ethical question of late-modern societies because these are social worlds in which individuals are, as he puts it, disembedded. Trust is not the same ethical issue when persons live face-to-face where actions can be monitored directly. It makes less difference what the actions of others mean if in village or neighborhood life of early modernity one can observe, hence control, directly. In late-modern societies everyone is a virtual stranger to everyone else because even those who have not left the village are connected to others as much by virtual media of communication as by personal knowledge. This fact even undercuts the power of personal knowledge of another. If in a matter of seconds I can call or fax another in some distant place to verify what you *seem* to be and what you say you are, then your ability to pass with strangers on the strength of your word, or the visible qualities of your actions, is always open for inspection. Thus trust becomes the major, critical issue in late-modern life. One never knows.[34]

This is the sense in which the practical ethic of daily life is just as central to Giddens's idea of sociology as it was to Weber's (and, by implication, to Bourdieu's). But, for Giddens, much more explicitly than for Weber (and even for Bourdieu), the practical sociology of daily life is, at once, the resource and the rule of *professional* sociological knowledge. The sociologist—whether practical or discursive (that is, whether lay or professional)—is the universal person of modern society. Sociology, in other words, is the competence whereby persons monitor their actions and the actions of others.

Sociology, therefore, is the sine qua non action in the recursive building up of structures and the maintenance of their virtual reality. Sociology, necessarily, is the means whereby those structures in all their virtuality recourse through the life of society. Yet, as Giddens recognizes, sociological discourse cannot do its powerful work of carrying forth the structure of modern societies without the unconscious, however minimally defined. Even though conscious talk about their structures is the constitutive practice of modern societies, conscious talk (and the virtual structures it composes) cannot escape its symbiotic dependence on practical consciousness, which is, as we have seen, effectively a practical *un*consciousness.

In Giddens's scheme of structured social things, the unconscious serves two necessary purposes: (1) It accounts for the fact of practical action, which would not take place at all if actors were obliged at *each and every moment* consciously to monitor, hence talk through, what they thought they were doing. (2) The unconscious, thereby, accounts for the virtual, recursive nature of social structures, which—because they are acknowledged to be virtual— would have no practical reality as rules and resources if, similarly, they were *nothing but* discursive facts. In the former respect, the unconscious allows actions their practical freedom; in the latter, it allows them their real weight— rules and resources available to structured action over time, across space.

But the key to Giddens's idea of the unconscious is the *potential* availability of that which is kept ready for discursive presentation. Giddens's unconscious, therefore, is always in ready service. That this is so is evident in his failed attempt to come to terms with Freud.[35] Giddens's unconscious is a reservoir of memory, a resource. Freud's is the internal Other, a force aggressively resistant to the conscious mind (and, thus, the internal Other of civilization itself). Giddens cannot go so far as Freud because that far would wreck the theory of modern structures. If virtual structures exhibit their properties only in instances of practices and "memory traces" guiding an agent's conduct, then social memory must be "for," not "against," modern consciousness. In this delicate theoretical distinction, the fundamental fact of differences must be denied.

It is now not difficult to see why modern theories of structures and agents, objects and subjects, resist ideas like Freud's of a perverse, resistant, distorting unconscious force, the effective limit of social and mental life. Bourdieu and Giddens among professional sociologists have come as close as any to pushing the idea of structures to this limit, which is, after all, the same limit with which Durkheim contended but could not manage: differences.

The unconscious is the ever-present, covert Other upon which both the recursivist sociologies faltered. Bourdieu's *habitus* and Giddens's *structuration* are attempts to account for that which the subject-object formula excludes: the not entirely explicable and not quite conscious null point where structures arise from and intrude upon human subjects. Both concepts attempt to describe the undescribable in modernity's riddle. *Who am I if things social are different?* entails an impossible moral anxiety. What becomes of individuals if they are thrust alone into a social world so poorly structured as to frustrate their need to know who they are by identification with some larger social whole? This old question, and all its permutations, is the one contemporary sociologies of structures (including Bourdieu's and Giddens's) can answer no better than could Durkheim.

The recursivists are on the right track in seeing that the riddle cannot be worked through so long as one thinks of the subject "I" as though it were of a different order of things from the structured "social." Where the recursivists lost their way was in trying, by the most brilliant and creative means, to define the null point of reconciliation between the opposing terms of the classic dichotomy. While throwing out the subject-object formula, they sneaked it back in by describing the mysteries of the unspeakable, recursive disposition—that place of habits one cannot know but without which one is either squashed by or cut loose from constraining structures. For this, Bourdieu and Giddens are thrown back onto a concept that seems like the unconscious but is not. The recursivists want to tame or simulate the unconscious or to habituate it to the familiar terms of modern thinking.

But the unconscious is not so readily domesticated. It intrudes deceptively, but regularly, on the hope of Enlightenment reason, reminding even those who resist it that social differences are as much within as without. If we cannot count on our own *selves* to remember accurately, to refrain from slips and distortions, to keep in check the native aggressions and desires, then how can it be supposed that we are one within ourselves? The human subject is, thus, differences—those of the unbreachable divide between that which we know we know and that which, pretending aside, we know we do not and cannot know. If social individuals are different within, that difference must then be a source of their eagerness to avoid, exclude, punish, or at least iron out the differences occurring in their social worlds. When a culture like the modern comes along, devoted as it has been to unifying the world as though it were one, the denial of the difference within is enforced by social pressures. Under these conditions the riddle has no answer. It is instead the symptom of the denial.

What Giddens and Bourdieu have accomplished is a considerable advance, nonetheless. Durkheim, by comparison, took the pitifully awkward way out. Durkheim knew that the crucial fact of the modern division of social labor was the structured salience of differences—what Giddens might call the disembedded nature of practical social life in modern societies. But, even Giddens and Bourdieu, having resisted a strong theory of the unconscious as the resisting Other, do not advance far enough beyond Durkheim. Neither, therefore, is able to concede the disturbing structural effect of social differences on the categories of social thought. Differences are structured away, which is why each views the modern world from his own special variant of the view from nowhere.[36]

Yet, Giddens and Bourdieu, by pushing their sociologies to the cherished limits of modernist sociology, demonstrate that other sociologies of structures are embedded ever more deeply than theirs in the primitive assumptions of modernity.

What the recursivists do and do not accomplish becomes clear upon returning to the other two approaches to a sociology of structures: the reductionist and the revisionist. Where Bourdieu and Giddens demonstrate the promises and frustrations of exploring the limits of modern social theory's dichotomies, the other two illustrate what is gained and lost by remaining well within them. Though the reductionists and the revisionists take common comfort in sociology's traditional language, they take it in different ways. Reductionists, in effect, grant the problem but believe it is sufficiently well solved by simple recourse to one of its aspects, the subjectivist or objectivist. Revisionists disagree. They believe that the classic terms of the theory of social structures can be renewed by careful revision—by a reworking of the relations between subjects and objects, agential selves and constraining structures. Revisionists seek, therefore, to link the microreality of subjects to the macroworld of objects, while reductionists are prepared to restrict their attentions to one or the other.

Reductionists, thus, take the attitude that since not all things can be done at once, it is best to do what most needs doing if the doing is sufficient to the task. Where recursivists are serious but playful, reductionists tend to be sober and hardworking. But what the reductionist gains by a more focused attention may be lost to the costs of the strategic exclusion. Within sociology, however, there are very few reductionists on either side of the dichotomy who are unaware of the risk most take to meet the objection. As an example, one might consider the most belligerent of the subject reductionists, George Homans. Homans insisted that it was entirely possible to explain everything any social scientist might need to explain by reference to the elementary principles of behavioral *psychology*! (Imagine Durkheim turning in his grave.) In one deadly serious rhetorical moment, Homans claimed it was possible to account for William the Conqueror's decision not to invade Scotland by exclusive reference to the principle of behavioral psychology, which stipulates that all behaviors are responses to a rewarding stimulus. Since Scotland did not stimulate the interests of William, the course of its history was different.[37] It would be hard to imagine a more extreme instance of methodological individualism. But even Homans, who was capable of play,[38] was mostly sober in his conviction that Durkheim was wrong. Everything social, including the structures of society, was, he thought, *better* explained by reducing one's attention to the more parsimonious principles of behavioral psychology. Such an attitude may be wrongheaded in certain ways, but it cannot be accused of a failure of nerve. The same can be said, with even deeper conviction, with respect to methodological individualism's reductive corollary, structuralism.

When the sociological task at hand is to explain the structures of the modern world, then it seems reasonable to conclude that what is needed most is a thoroughly structural account of things. In the years following the 1960s, many sociologists shared the widespread enthusiasm for one or another variety of structuralism, and for good reason. If doubt about world structures in the years following the failures of the world powers to impose themselves in Vietnam and Afghanistan is among the most important social dilemmas of the era of crisis, then it would seem entirely reasonable to organize sociological work with focused attention on structures—how they arise, change, and exert their constraining force. To cite but one example among many that could be given, Immanuel Wallerstein's three-volume study, *The Modern World System,* has taught an entire generation to think differently about the structure of the world—to think of it as a dominant political center extracting resources and economic gain from the peripheral areas. Though Wallerstein has not been alone among those who sought to write modernization theory out of and a more honest theory into our way of imagining the path of economic progress, he has been a salient figure in that project, surely among sociologists. Because of Wallerstein and others associated with the various traditions in development studies, it has been more and more difficult to imagine the world as progressively modernizing along a linear historical path from weak to strong, from poverty to wealth.[39] Just the same, from the point of view of a theory of structures, Wallerstein's accomplishment was built on a reductionism: "I was looking to describe the world-system at a certain level of abstraction, that of the evolution of structures of the world system."[40] This he did without explicit preoccupation with questions of the modern subject.[41] Just as the methodological individualist sets aside structures because he believes subjectivist solutions are sufficient, so the structuralist reduces away the subject to focus on the sufficiency of structures. Where the methodological individualist aims for the parsimony of reference to concrete observable subjects, the structuralist strives for a comprehensive account of social wholes.

They each give up something to gain something else. The question is whether the gain is sufficient to the loss.

An instructive example of the accomplishments of structural reduction is Theda Skocpol's 1979 book *States and Social Revolutions,* which she prefaces with a personal confession:

> Books grow in unique ways out of the experiences of their authors, and this one is no exception. The ideas for it germinated during my time as a graduate student at Harvard University in the early 1970s. This was—however faint the echoes now—a vivid period of political engagement for many students, myself included. The United States was brutally at war against the Vietnamese Revolution, while at home movements calling for racial justice and for an immediate end to the foreign military involvement challenged the capacities for good and evil of our national political system. The times certainly stimulated my interest in understanding revolutionary change. And it was during these years that my commitment to democratic-socialist ideals matured. Yet it would be a mistake to imply that *States and Social Revolutions* sprang immediately from day-to-day political preoccupations. It didn't. Instead it developed in the relative "ivory tower" quiet of the library and the study.[42]

It would be hard to find a more perfect statement of the reasons that led so many of Skocpol's generation to the sociology of world structures.

Like many of her generation who entered professional sociology when she did, Skocpol responded to the political struggles of her youth by committing her adult career to studying the structures of a world they helped disrupt. What she calls "The Uppity Generation" devoted itself to practicing C. Wright Mills's dictum—let sociology be the work of imagining the structures that affect personal lives. Some, Skocpol notably, emphasized one side of Mills's formula.[43]

The purposes of *States and Social Revolutions* were all structuralist: The first was to explain social revolutions as structural phenomena. The second, corollary to the first, was to demonstrate the strength of structural explanations. The third was to account for the three social revolutions that had shaped the modern world as it was in the post–World War II period—the French, the Russian, and the Chinese. And fourth, she sought to develop a theory of social change that was more adequately structuralist by demonstrating the interplay of class *and* political forces.[44] These purposes are suggested in the definition with which she begins: "Social revolutions are rapid, basic transformations of a society's state and class structures; and they are accompanied and in part carried through by class-based revolts from below." To which she adds:

> I shall argue that, in contrast to the modes of explanation used by the currently prevalent theories, social revolutions should be analyzed from a structural perspective, with special attention devoted to international contexts and to developments at

home and abroad that affect the breakdown of the state organizations of old regimes and the buildup of new, revolutionary state organizations.

A great deal is revealed about this theory of structures in these two statements and the personal comments preceding them.[45]

Skocpol, like Giddens and most other theoretical sociologists, works toward a new theory by working through those of her predecessors. Unlike Giddens, she insists on either primary empirical data or at least the fresh interpretation of the evidence of others—thus, the contrast of her writing with Giddens's. His is a discursive working through of the theories of others in order to compose the virtual reality of structures. Hers is more classically scientific. She writes much more in the format, if not the style, of Homans than of Giddens. Though she grants that sociology is a "critical enterprise," she also believes it is an "objective and cumulative science."[46] She, thus, patiently leads the reader through the scientific literature, to the scientific question, to the evidence. In the end, however, the reader is not so much brought into a virtual world as given the information upon which she may decide of her own enlightened accord. This is a difference between writers who believe in plausible reality and those who believe reality is virtual. Skocpol's social structures are defined and drawn up for all to see. Those of Giddens and Bourdieu are created as virtual spaces to be entered.

But in Skocpol's modest confessional preface, there is another, easy-to-overlook clue to the structuralist position. Her book, as she says, grew out of her experience as a politically engaged student. But it was not written out of that experience. Rather, her theory of state structures was a product of the solitary graduate student thinking between different teachers and, more importantly, differing rival traditions of social theory. Skocpol makes it plain (in the first chapter of *States and Social Revolutions*) that the theory itself is an attempt to find a new way out of the failures of the old. In general terms, it is an attempt to link Marx and Weber, classes and states, world systems and politics, economic and political histories, Immanuel Wallerstein and Charles Tilly, among others. Skocpol's confession is modest compared to Rousseau's. Yet, she believes, as did Rousseau, that the truth of her theory, including the validity of her interpretations of the evidence, depends on the virtuous discipline of the self. She was stimulated by experience in politics, but she retired as an individual to think through the world and its literature. The result of her effort is so pervasive in its own right that it is difficult to see the contradiction between the book's manner of authorship and its argument. If, as Skocpol says, "books grow in unique ways out of the experience of their authors," then why should the social production of books be different from the social production of revolutions?

Though any particular book is surely not as complex a structure as a social revolution, books and other writings are important to structural changes. The text from which Skocpol derives her title, Lenin's *State and Revolution,* is one example. While Skocpol's *States and Social Revolutions* did not lead to a revolution in state structure, it did contribute mightily to the restructuring of social and political theory in the last generation. How can it be said that Skocpol's writings, and those of others (for example, C. Wright Mills's), are not effective forces in the structural transformation of some part of her world as, the differences being noted, Rousseau's writings were in his?

Recursivists like Giddens may or may not succeed in bringing the real world into his virtual reality of recursing structures, but it is certain that they would not neglect what structure-reductionists do. If Skocpol's book grew out of her experience in the 1960s and was written in the quiet of (as she puts it) Harvard's ivory tower, then is not her subjective experience a fact without which the book's structural effect could not be explained? By inference, the question to be asked of the structuralist approach is, How is it possible to account for structural change, whether modest or great, without recourse of some kind to those whose individual actions helped make them, as they in turn were made by them? The recursivists insist on this question.

For methodological reasons, reductionists take the risk of denying facts that may ultimately be necessary to the explanatory account for which the strategic reduction is made. The modest excusing of the author's personal experience may be required by scientific protocols, but such manners may still wreck the party if, in the actual scientific work, they reappear to limit the sufficiency of the explanation. Skocpol aims precisely to exclude voluntaristic explanations of revolutions. She, therefore, quotes in her favor the words of two fellow nonvoluntarists: "Revolutionary movements rarely begin with a revolutionary intention"; and "Revolutions are not made; they come."[47]

Is this so? Are revolutions unintended, passive effects of structural shifts? If this is so, then its proof can be decided by direct reference to the results of the method the position requires; that is, with reference to the effects not of an author's intentions but of the exclusion of voluntarist factors. What, then, are the effects of the reduction Skocpol makes?

Consider, for example, her account of the French Revolution of 1789.[48] The old regime collapsed in the face of rising protest from below because the dominant classes fell into a structurally weak position. France's state power was unable in 1789 to resist the rebellions rooted in the inferior classes—most especially of the rising class of bourgeois merchants and their cultural elite influenced by Rousseau and that crowd. The old regime's power had been slowly depleted by a series of events over time. Internationally, France's geopolitical position had been weakened by its support of the American

Revolution in 1776. Among other effects, the alliance with the American colonies against her world rival, England, drained the French treasury. This forced the throne to increase taxes beyond a point that already restless merchants and peasants, even migrating intellectuals, were likely to tolerate. The emergent bourgeois class had already gained a strong hand in the National Assembly, further limiting the power of royal and noble political forces. Then, the famines of 1788 aggravated an already critical situation. By 1789, therefore, the sovereign and those who shared his political and class fate were unable to suppress the revolution because the structural basis of dominant class power was broken. Much as the heads of academic departments in the rebellions of 1968 described by Bourdieu, the members of the dominant class, even those close to the throne, began to struggle with each other as they saw their powers at risk, thus weakening their capacity to obey normal habits of administrative control of the social mechanisms. Skocpol summarizes one crucial aspect of the structural break:

> Thus by the early summer of 1789, the quarrels within the dominant class over forms of representations culminated in a victory for the Parisian National Assembly and its various liberal, urban supporters through France. And a concomitant of this victory was the sudden devolution of control over the means of administration and coercion from the normally centralized royal administration into the decentralized possession of the various cities and towns, mostly controlled by the National Assembly.[49]

At this moment in 1789 Rousseau was long dead. Had he been alive it would be hard to imagine that he would not have taken satisfaction from the crumbling fortunes of those who had treated him so badly. While he lived, he was anything but a revolutionary in the practice of his daily life. In his *Confessions* he revealed that the troubles he made of his own well-publicized intentions were mostly due to his wild, passionate loves for women with prior commitments. Yet, there remains the fact of Rousseau's writings, nearly all of which were composed in the calm of a provincial life.

It is accurate to say that Rousseau and the other philosophes did not "intend" the Revolution of 1789, certainly not the way Jefferson intended the one he declared in 1776. But it is difficult to suppose that the events of 1789 just "came and were not made." Rousseau and those other liberals of his generation, notwithstanding their inability to get along with one another, surely had some decisive effect on the French Revolution. At the least, the passages in Rousseau's *Social Contract* on the limits of the monarchy, passages that had infuriated Rousseau's opponents when he lived, were well known throughout the land. Did he write them precisely because he intended to produce the structural effect of 1789? Certainly not. Most of what he wrote was for money, secondarily fame, tertiarily culture and morality. But that Rousseau and others who prepared the liberal classes for what they did in 1789 did not form in their conscious minds the precise intent to revolt does not mean that, whatever they had in mind, their actions were not as effective a force in the Revolution of 1789 as, say, the structural effects of the 1788 famines.

What the structuralist perspective can do is important in itself. The reason it is questioned here is more to examine in fresh light the fortunes of modern culture's structural theories of itself. Since Descartes, modern sociology has not been able to think its world without thinking a theory of its way of thinking. The structuralists, as illustrated by Skocpol, develop their theory of thought in a definite manner, as do the recursivists. Hers is a sociology that issues from the informed subject who, though she gains perspective from experience, must isolate herself in order to contend with the strengths and weakness of what others have thought about revolutions and structures. In this attitude, the subjecthood of the author is the source of the structures described. Though the authorial subject is suppressed in writing of the sociological subject matter, the latter is dependent on the former. The direct or secondary historical observations out of which the structural theory is composed are, as they always are in intensely empirical sociologies, made by the observing author. Techniques for certifying their reliability and validity are nothing more than measures of the degrees to which other subjects are likely or not to observe the evidence and compose the structures in a fashion tolerably close to that of the originating author. Comparing one's observations with others' is a well-regarded method of theory construction. But, when it is used for the announced purpose of composing a structuralist theory of structures, the theory bears an unusually heavy burden of proof. Can it provide assurance that its prior commitment to a theory of structured structures (to use half of Bourdieu's formula) is not a consequence of the authorial subject's prior decision to exclude the effects of structuring subjects, beginning with the decision to exclude herself as the necessary source of all sociologies of structures?

In other words, can the structuralist theory of structures, its sober ambitions notwithstanding, account for the null hypothesis of any structural theory of modern societies?—*What if the world, rather than being one that structures differences, is instead structured differences themselves?* The recursivist does not allow the null hypothesis because it works within its own null point of virtual reality. The structure-reductionist does not because, having decided as a condition of sociology's objectivity to exclude herself, her claims for the structuralist approach ignore the very originating difference she herself makes in the making of structures.

▼▼▼▼▼

The revisionist sociology of structures, the third of the three, frankly seeks to salvage the classic concepts. Though not all revisionists could be considered Durkheimian, each in some way explicitly attempts to build a way out of the puzzle Durkheim could not solve. *Who am I if the world is different?* was not well solved by Durkheim's reconstruction of moral consciousness as though it were, always, one and the same, changing only according to the dividing pressures of history. Though other classic writers considered the same problem, Durkheim's failure remains a compelling challenge to professional sociologists.

Durkheim, writing in the 1890s, might be forgiven for believing that modern society's divisions were a temporary, early stage of modern life that would be progressively overcome through the good efforts of sociologies. In the 1990s, revisionists responding to Durkheim's unsolved riddle seldom think so naively. They are much more likely to face the task of building a link between micro- and macrorealities with due respect for its difficulties. As one revisionist, Randall Collins, puts it, "Macro and micro levels are implied in each other, and it is a tricky task even to set forth the issues of how this is so."[50] Few revisionist sociologists, even in their disagreement with each other, would disagree with Collins on this.

One of the trickiest aspects of the task is that involving the use of words like "level" to describe differing realities to be "linked." Jeffrey Alexander, for example, recommends theoretical caution and care when speaking of levels in order not to create the impression that the things linked are free-standing small and large sectors of a mechanically structured world:[51]

> [The] equation of micro with individual is extremely misleading, as, indeed, is the attempt to find any specific size correlation with the micro/macro difference. There can be no empirical references for micro or macro as such. They are analytic contrasts, suggesting emergent levels within empirical units, not antagonistic empirical units themselves.

In order to speak of a micro-macro link, one must speak of an analytic relation in which the relation of the "realities," if not virtual, is also not "real" in the usual sense.

Such a view as Alexander's, however, unnerves those in still a third region of the revisionist enterprise.[52] James S. Coleman, in decided contrast to Alexander, is among those who are willing to let micro and macro stand within an equation expressing different sizes and levels. From one point of view, his sociology appears to be reductionist. Still, Coleman (like Alexander) wants to work with the distinction as though it were analytic but (somewhat like Collins) to maintain the separateness of real levels. In effect, Coleman seeks to build a sociology that attributes the analytic resources of the individual to the socially structured levels. His purpose is, thus, to overcome the restrictions of the methodological individualist position without sacrificing methodological individualism's commitments to the clear observation of individuals. Thus, Coleman proposes a rational choice theory of socially structured actors:

> The principal task of the social sciences lies in the explanation of the social phenomena, not the behavior of single individuals. In isolated cases the social phenomena may derive directly, through summation, from the behavior of individuals, but more often this is not so. Consequently, the focus must be on the social system whose behavior is to be explained. This may be as small as a dyad or as large as a society or even a world system, but the essential requirement is that the explanatory focus be on the system as a unit, not on the individuals or other components which make it up.[53]

It is not a mere quibble to ask, What, after all, is demarcating about a dyad? Is it not the most artificial of analytic lines, as though there might be somewhere a human monad free of any dyadic or other entanglements?

Such a question arises, sooner or later, from confusions faced by any attempt to revise from a position that is *both* analytic and realist. With rare exception the revisionist theory of structures is one that believes it possible to distinguish levels in the analyst's mind in order to borrow social things from one level (agency, rational choices, motivation—for examples) in order to describe and explain things in another level (structural force, constraint, the corporate actor—for examples). Coleman would be among the first to point out that the temptation is strong to take empirical observations "below the level of the system to be explained."[54] Yet, his idea is to build the theory that will allow and encourage observations at the more systemic, hence structured, levels. "A minimal basis for a social system is two actors, each having control over resources of interest to the other."[55] This, then, is Coleman's minimal dyadic system; below it no sociological observations should be made. But, immediately, the contradictions of his ambitions are apparent. Having said that empirical observations are "often" made at the level of individuals, he believes they *can* be made at that level. Yet, *social* scientific explanations can only be made at the "1 + 1 level," where individuals are already linked by competing interests in scarce resources. One wonders, given this, what would constitute a real individual observable apart from at least a dyad? Even Tarzan of the Apes is said to have borne the traces of his noble birth while being raised in the social systems of the apes.[56] Not even one of Freud's analytic patients could be said to be a pure individual observed by the analyst, since this sort of analytic observation is made within a transferential relation between patient and analyst. Having it both ways between the analytic and realist attitudes is extraordinarily difficult. This is the tricky part of the revisionist challenge.

Surprisingly, given the strength of the revisionists' purposes, their categories are more than just tricky. They are analytically unstable.[57] A full century after Durkheim's effort to construct a scientific sociology well within the rules of modern social thought, attempts to make some version of his project work come unsettled at their foundations. Today Durkheim's avoidance of social difference works less well, especially when it is pursued within the Durkheimian vision of the moral necessity of a strong professional sociology. The professional sociology Durkheim and Weber founded, in their related but different ways, was itself built, to recall Bourdieu's words, on an "innocent faith."

Durkheim naively believed in progress, sociology, and thus in the final overcoming of social divisions. Few of today's revisionists believe in so innocent a world. Faced with the necessity of acknowledging current reality, which contradicts the dreams of Durkheim's generation, revisionists must qualify their terms. This, as we have seen, has been a necessity since, at least, the interwar period of this century. Parsons was the first major sociologist to make the concession. He attempted to reconstruct the sociologies of the classic age using the old language of structurally conditioned actors by introducing the use of "analytic units," with which he founded the tradition of analytic realism in sociology. Parsons's admission that the units used for thinking do not *necessarily* (in the logical sense) correspond to social realities was a deceptively strong move beyond the classic age. Durkheim, by contrast (speaking ex cathedra as the father of fathers of official sociology) simply stipulated that suicide rates were what he studied, and because he studied them they should be taken as though they were suicide itself. No analytic concepts were required either by Durkheim or Weber, not even by Marx, possibly not by Freud. Though one could well trace the idea of a virtual reality back to Freud's study of dream language, Marx's of hidden modes of production, or Weber's of the virtuosity of ideal types, the fact is that the self-conscious idea of a distinction between real social things and virtual analytic ones came into sociological thought with Parsons. Thereafter, like it or not, one had either to admit the analytic status of sociological concepts or to pretend one's way around them. But in the long run the analytic nature of concepts and observations cannot be gotten around.

Where the recursivist way has been to reinvent the conceptual world, the structure-reductionists have attempted to ease the tension by assuming the reality of the structures they invent. By contrast to the other two, the revisionist way is the least stable because, in relying on the analytic distinction between levels, it relinquishes the confidence of the positive reality of the reductionist without purchasing the freedom of the virtual reality of the recursivist.

It now becomes apparent just how far the recursivists have moved from, without actually escaping, the controversial space that binds the other two ways of thinking structures. In the comparison, the most radical of the sociologies of structure suddenly becomes visible in another light. Though it thinks of itself as an attempt to get beyond the troubles of the others, which remain within the classic formulation, the recursivist way does so only by assuming what might well be called a false-transcendental perspective. The irony of recursivism in sociology is that it is well aware that recursivity itself moves back and forth, from and upon the theorist. Yet, in creating virtual realities of the well-disposed world of *habitus* or the conceptually articulate one of structuration theory, the new recursivists are forced to assume an idiosyncratic position within a classic space. The recursivist theorist is one who sees everything uniquely. This is a position much like Rousseau's. But it is not the classic transcendental attitude that Jürgen Habermas wants to define. Recursivists, far from claiming to be in the universal pragmatic position, are in fact in the utterly unique, not-to-be-imitated one.

But, none of the three ways of thinking structures faces up to the differences that tug from within the individual while unmaking, for better or worse, the world without. Recursivists, in spite of their quest for the purely unique, dull the effect of differences by inventing a virtual reality that mystifies the universal human. Structure-reductionists revert to a strong conviction that structures are the most real, if not universal, fact of human life, thus denying the most fundamental of all moral differences—that in their hearts, anxious subjects want to be, at one and the same time, somehow both unique and the same as their world. Revisionists seek heroically to work and live between different levels—an analytic distinction that in the end only serves to deny the felt moral conflicts recursivists reinvent and reductionists avoid.

Sociologists have two choices in building a sociology of modern "man" from within the language of that man—to assume either the perspective of universal humanity (as reductionists do) or the null perspective of the uniquely astute maker and observer of his virtual reality (as the recursivists do overtly, and the revisionists do covertly). Though the intentions and results are different, the theoretical effect is the same. Social differences are effectively ignored and the riddle is unsolved. *Who am I if structured things are different?* is the effect of modernity's denial of those differences.

Rodman's complaining father in Stegner's novel would be satisfied by none. He might, surely, be variously impressed, as many are by professional sociology. And he was certainly wrong in his characterization of sociology as nothing more than the abstract manipulation of Xs and Ys. On the contrary, sociology's difficulties with its public critics have much more to do with the frustrations it understands very well. So long as it construes a theory of itself within the terms of the culture it seeks to change, sociology is not likely to deal with the fundamental dilemma of the modern world.

So long as it seeks to structure differences, sociology will not be able to consider the now more likely proposition that the world it studies is no longer, if it ever was, amenable to reconciliation of its inherently divided natures.

Chapter 8

Measuring the Subject's Secrets

In order to do their work properly, sociologists frequently find they must be so lucky as to discover, or so creative as to invent, human subjects who become the characters in their stories.

Max Weber, we have seen, was lucky enough to find Ben Franklin, who in *Protestant Ethic* became the historical individual of the spirit of capitalism before capitalism. Though it is seldom thought of this way, Marx did something similar in his whimsically nasty character Mr. Moneybags.[1] Likewise, what would Freud have done without Dora or the Rat Man?[2] Subjects like these are sometimes evident even when they are nameless: Durkheim's agnostic generic man soullessly facing a divided world at the end of last century; Parsons's postwar modern man, chastened by structured conditions, yet bold in action; Giddens's end-of-the-American-century recursive man, caught between busily building structures and resisting the lapse into pure simulacra; and so on. From the earliest moments of modern life, theories of the social have been discovered or invented by a disciplined pilgrimage back to a subject. When the subject of their quests was not one's own self, it was often another's—a subject meant to stand for the social circumstances of modern man.

The secret of the modern world lies within. There is no more fundamental assumption among moderns than that the best way *out* to the world of objects is *in*—to the true consciousness of subjects. Descartes traveled into the silent, reduced axial point of his clearest, most distinct idea. The idea was, in effect, that his moral journey was *the* most universal truth. Kant's regular walks in Königsberg, interrupted only twice (once by the events of 1789, once by reading Rousseau), ordered his outer life so that he could descend to the deep structures of his consciousness. He, like others of his day, dared to know not so much the outer world as such, but the outer world as revealed in the light of subjective consciousness. Rousseau and Ben Franklin, with greater autobiographical courage, did much the same.

In the summers of 1886 and 1887, W.E.B. Du Bois, while he was a young student at Fisk University, taught school "in the hills of Tennessee where the broad dark vale of the Mississippi begins to roll and crumble to greet the Alleghenies."[3] In this hilly backwoods, he met people who knew nothing of the outer world, one of whom was the subject of Du Bois's early theory of progress:

> Best of all I loved to go to Josie's, and sit on the porch, eating peaches, while the mother bustled and talked: how Josie had bought the sewing-machine; how Josie worked at service in the winter, but that four dollars a month was "mighty little" wages; how Josie longed to go away to school, but that it "looked like" they never could get far enough ahead to let her; how the crops failed and the well was yet unfinished; and, finally, how "mean" some of the white folks were.[4]

Ten years later, Du Bois returned to those Tennessee hills. Josie had died. "We've had a heap of trouble," her mother said, "since you've been away."[5] In those ten years, Du Bois had enjoyed the best fruits of Western civilization—study and travel in Europe, a Harvard Ph.D., a brilliant beginning to his career as a college professor and sociologist. He, in this time, had seen the world, which still had not seen the people of his youthful summers. Upon leaving, he said:

> My journey was done, and behind me lay hill and dale, and Life and Death. *How shall man measure Progress there where the dark-faced Josie lies? How many heartfuls of sorrow shall balance a bushel of wheat? How hard a thing is life to the lowly, and yet how human and real!* And all this life and love and strife and failure,—is it the twilight of nightfall or the flush of some faint-dawning day? . . . Thus sadly musing, I rode to Nashville in the Jim Crow car.[6]

There could be no better statement of the centrality of measurement to modern civilization. "How shall man measure Progress there where the dark-faced Josie lies?" Though measurement is considered the domain of serious empirical science, it was first the moral property of men and women attempting to understand the inner secrets of their being against the terrible demands of the modern world. "How many heartfuls shall balance a bushel of wheat?" The foundational fact of sociological measurement is that of the immeasurable reality of human differences, for it is only in relation to them that the true, exact nature of human life and progress can be measured. "How hard a thing is life to the lowly, and yet how human and real!"

Du Bois was, in his early days as a sociologist, one of modern sociology's most meticulous measurers. To this day, *The Philadelphia Negro* is a model for the sociological study of urban groups. In but three months in 1896, Du Bois walked the streets and climbed the stairs of Philadelphia's Seventh Ward to take interviews in 2,500 households, which he then measured, analyzed, and wrote up. The book of over 400 pages was researched and completed, from beginning nearly to the end, in just over a year, with little help beyond that of his devoted wife, Nina. No one quite matched Du Bois's work ethic, and no one worked quite so alone. Research, however, was like that in those days. Marx worked alone in the British Museum, though with the support of Jenny, his wife, and Engels, his friend and sponsor. Weber, with the encouragement of his wife, Marianne, and the brilliant intellectuals in their social circle, nonetheless did all those endless calculations, translations, and historical researches mostly on his own. Even Durkheim, who in the Paris years had the best organized circle of fellow workers, in his earlier years in Bordeaux did many of the calculations in *Suicide* by hand. Today, sociological measurement is, if not easier, at least less labor intensive.

It is possible that the technologies that support sociological measurement today contribute to the profession's occasional loss of connection with the first and fundamental problems of social measurement. The advantages of computer-driven data processing and statistical double-checking of data are real. What might have been, for example, if Durkheim had had a machine capable of reducing his work so that he could have gone back to recalculate his numbers in support of egoism to determine if, perhaps, the Protestant entrepreneur vulnerable to egoistic suicide was the same, or a different, subject from those anomic businessmen who killed themselves in times of economic crisis? Yet, whatever Durkheim and his contemporaries lost to the inefficiencies of having to measure and calculate by hand, they were somehow closer to the deeper, moral aspects of social measurement.

There could be no better testimony to this advantage than Weber's words in his first Munich lecture (1918), "Science as a Vocation":

> Nowadays in circles of youth there is a widespread notion that science has become a problem in calculation, fabricated in laboratories or statistical filing systems just as "in a factory," a calculation involving only the cool intellectual and not one's "heart and soul." . . . Certainly calculations [are] . . . an indispensable prerequisite. No sociologist, for instance, should think himself too good, even in his old age, to make tens of thousands of quite trivial computations in his head and perhaps for months at a time. . . . But if no "idea" occurs to his mind about the direction of his computations

and, during his computations, about the bearing of the emergent single results, then even this small result will not be yielded. . . . Ideas occur to us when they please, not when it pleases us. . . . However this may be, the scientific worker has to take into his bargain the risk that enters into all scientific work: Does an "idea" occur or does it not? . . . Ladies and gentlemen. In the field of science only he who is devoted *solely* to the work at hand has "Personality."[7]

One of sociology's greatest measurers understood measurement to be a matter of the heart and soul, above all else.

The first and fundamental fact of measurement in modern societies is differences, beginning with sociology's classic, necessary fascination with the social differences arising in the transition from traditional to modern societies. Where human societies are relatively well covered by a sacred canopy of some kind, social differences, such as they are, do not constitute a moral dilemma. This was Durkheim's idea in *Elementary Forms of the Religious Life* as well as in *Division of Labor.* Where there is a definite collective conscience, men know exactly who they are and where they stand. When the traditional moral bond breaks down under the pressure of the modern division of labor, the moral basis of this knowledge must be constituted anew. Marx held the corollary idea: Powerful religious ideas are opiates. They drug the mind's moral insight into the true, aggressive divisions of class conflict. But it may have been Simmel who best described the difference differences make in modern life:

Man is a creature whose existence is dependent on differences, i.e., his mind is stimulated by the difference between present impressions and those which have preceded. Lasting impressions, the slightness in their differences, the habituated regularity of their course and contrasts between them, consume, so to speak, less mental energy than the rapid telescoping of changing images, pronounced differences within what is grasped at a single glance, and the unexpectedness of violent stimuli. To the extent that the metropolis creates these psychological conditions—with every crossing of the street, with the tempo and multiplicity of economic, occupational and social life—it creates in the sensory foundations of mental life, and in the degree of awareness necessitated *by our organization as creatures dependent on differences,* a deep contrast with the slower, more habitual, more smoothly flowing rhythm of the sensory-mental phase of small town and rural existence.[8]

Against the simpler circumstances of traditional life, the modern is defined as that society in which differences themselves redefine the mental life, the subjecthood of man. In his way, Simmel put acutely what most other thinkers then thought—Marx, Weber, and Durkheim included.

It would be accurate to say that sociology came into its professional being in response to the demand for well-measured accounts of the disruptive differences that were the salient feature of modern social life. But, of course, we know very well that the actual professional practice of measurement took a largely tendentious attitude toward this serious responsibility. Empirical measurement, as it came to be practiced, especially in the tradition of Durkheim, served largely to efface the real differences. The increasing power of statistical measures served this tendency all too well. The arithmetic culture of statistical analysis, to put it simply, determines central tendencies.[9] Or, somewhat more exactly, it certifies the extent to which a measure of empirical events is more or less likely to be accurate. But what, in effect, is the social basis of this accuracy? Nothing more than the expression of degrees of confidence that measures are reliable and valid, where "reliability" and "validity" are, in further effect, expressions of the degree to which any subsequent measurer is likely to see and record the events in just the same way as did the first measurer who presented his observations, well measured, as the truth of a matter. In social measurement, in other words, statistical operations, no matter how subtle their workings, come down to a verified answer to one question: Did I in fact see what I think I saw? This question is good to ask. Much important descriptive work has been done in its name. But, statistical cultures are strongly predisposed to discover the central tendency among social things. As a result they suffer the extreme costs of an inherent aversion to exploring differences.

Social measures that seek recourse in the statistical certification of central tendencies are necessary but insufficient to sociological work. If sociologists are to take account of the possibility, let alone the probability, of real, unresolvable differences, they must formulate a social theory of measurement in a sympathetic, but perverse, attitude toward the inherent desire to find the single moral truth of social things. Among professional sociologists the need for a more satisfactory theory of measures has been recognized, if not widely heeded. In what is still the most important, explicit attempt by a sociologist to restore measurement to its central place in moral life, Aaron Cicourel has said that measurement in sociology "cannot be rigorous without solutions to the problems of cultural meanings."[10] By this he meant that measurement is the process whereby social actors attempt to explain, correct, and otherwise account for the first fact of communication in daily life: We don't often get it at first! That is, social communication is not a process of simple, direct conveyance of meanings from A to B. Instead, it is the more complicated process whereby A's communications to B are typically indexical rather than direct. They point to, or suggest, the implied meaning, but seldom, if ever, contain it fully present. A simple utterance such as "The whole world is garbage, lady!" is not full of meaning without social work. Whoever hears the utterance can determine Larry Hogue's meaning only by inquiry into the meanings it points to without containing.

It is, in this way, no different from the meanings hidden in most daily conversation.

Not long ago I had a conversation about a reasonably mundane affair in the lives of college teachers, a failed meeting. It proceeded more or less in this way (names except for mine being fictionalized):

L: Charles, Sam has scheduled something else at the time of our meeting. . . . What do we do?

C: Got me, what do you think?

L: Well . . .

C: I guess we'll have to postpone. But it has to be in the next two weeks. . . .

L: Yeah . . . will you let me know?

C: Well, sure. . . . I don't know. Maybe it would be easier if you asked Karen to call Mary . . . well, I mean Joan because Mary is away this week. She has the agenda and can also tell David. Is that okay with you?

L: . . . Sure.

C: I mean . . . I'm not on campus today and it might get done better that way.

L: Yeah.

Communication begins and continues in this way. It is obvious that the full meanings are only partly disclosed in talk. But enough is said to get the job done without going into what both L and I actually thought about the cancellation of the meeting. To be honest, I am not sure what L knows about what I thought (much less what I felt). I am not even sure I know what I felt, though I know the fact of the failed meeting meant much more than words can say. Then there are the social facts that occur only upon reflection from outside the conversation. What, for example, is the cultural meaning, if any, of the social fact of a short conversation in which it was L and Charles, both men, proposing to ask women to arrange their affairs while, possibly, excluding for the moment still other women from their decision? It may mean nothing. Or, it might. Who knows? And so on.

Cicourel, and others, believe that this structured failure to say what is meant in so many words is exactly the way social communication works. If this is so, then whenever social beings seek to judge the meanings presented obliquely to them, they are engaged in social measurement. The daily work of linguists, judges, social workers, and sociologists is, in effect, no different from the work of daily life performed more or less competently by most folk in social settings.

Social measurement is, therefore, a ubiquitous, unavoidable, though artful, fact of social life.[11] It is also a potentially disturbing and always disruptive activity. Thus, it would not be unreasonable to suppose that all cultures with the means to do so will build into their general moral code permissions to ignore some meanings. That may be as good a general definition of culture as there is. Culture is the well-organized, if not well-advertized, code of practical instructions whereby members are given permission to talk meaningfully about some things while ignoring others. It may even be, under certain conditions, that cultures actively prohibit talk of certain meanings. How else could it have happened that modern culture would have placed such wildly unjustified faith in the meaning of progress, refusing all the while to speak seriously of, to, or for those, like Josie, to whom that hope was not truly offered? It could not have been simply that modernists were evil people (though some were). It was, to a large extent, that the culture itself gave what it thought was benign permission for the silence. "How shall man measure Progress there where the dark-faced Josie lies?"

It is not, therefore, entirely surprising that more attention has not been paid to theories of social measurement. Were such theories to become explicit, they would necessarily disabuse the techniques of professional measurement of their privileges. If all social persons make their daily lives by measuring social differences, then the formal search for fine propositions expressing the truth of central tendencies will cease to be the standard by which measurement is measured. It will become, then, but one important, though necessarily local, activity amidst a wider array of measures.

It is possible, and certainly necessary, to describe at least the outline of a social theory of measurement:

1. Social measurement is a serious and ubiquitous activity whereby events in a purportedly real world are provided a sense of order consistent with the social accords of the culture in which the measures are conducted. In other words, measurement is a theory of social order whether expressed numerically or discursively.
2. Measurement as the organized social practice whereby a certifiably disciplined group of workers applies agreed-upon standards to an available field of objects is but one form of social measurement—an important one, but only one.
3. The reality of the worlds measured (by whomever for whatever purposes by whichever means) is, by tacit agreement (since Kant at least), probable but unprovable, therefore, uncertain.

4. Fortunately, assurance of the reality of the worlds is unnecessary to the conduct of successful measurement, which is proven by the fact that measures (whether practical or certified) hardly ever inquire into the reality of worlds.

5. Cultures bequeath to all measurers permission to believe in the reality of their worlds (that is, to believe there is a definite nature to the order of social things), so long as they do not press the point too far.

6. As a consequence, even when it is conceived of as the earnest hard work of science, measurement as practiced is an attempt to apply culturally acceptable protocols for the purposes of observing, recording, and evaluating culturally meaningful "events."

7. Therefore, put simply but adequately, measurement begins always and everywhere as the application of practical, cultural standards for the sensible purposes of discovering, inventing, and otherwise describing the ineffable secrets of social practices.

8. Therefore, social practices are always, necessarily, ineffably secret because in the practice of daily life people take the measure of their worlds by means of culturally acceptable protocols. These cultural protocols are the elegant means whereby cultural members hold out hope that there are "real," "true," and "worthy" meanings even though experience in daily life, especially conversation, does little to encourage that hope.

9. Further, between the measurer and the measured there is nothing certain but the shared accord to ignore the fact that there is nothing real but secreted meanings.

10. Consequently, a sensible theory of measurement must begin with a fictional character, namely, the research subject whose role in the measurement of things is that of characterizing, as though they were knowable and observable, the ineffable (and sometimes perverse) secrets of human motivation and action.

In a word, measurement, like cooking, is a universally necessary endeavor that produces dishes of wildly uneven quality. Even the worst meals, like the poorest measures, tend to support one's daily life.

▼ ▼ ▼ ▼ ▼

That such a theory of measurement as the one just enunciated might be plausible can be seen from a close examination of an important attempt to explore the mysteries of social measurement. If it can be shown that even the most scrupulous examinations of professional social measures are tolerably within the previous outline, then there is good reason to suppose that its foundations in practical life are, to use the word, real.

In professional sociology the research subject might be defined as the presumably "real" individual subjected to controlled analysis in order that science can measure her difference from the considered truth of social things of her kind. Once thus controlled she ceases to be "real," but in ways that allow her analytic irreality to make culturally meaningful sense. Thus, all forms of scientific measurement are concerned with one question: *What are the secret degrees to which this subject is (or these subjects are) different from central tendencies—that is, from whatever is taken to be the universal norm of social things?*

The research subject, whether single or collective, is the one who bears the hidden secret of social differences, which, after all, are the matters of scientific interest to sociologists. For example, take a striking case of a sociologist's subject, Dorothy Smith's "K" in "K Is Mentally Ill."[12] In the following selection from Smith's article, a written report on an interview is characterized by Smith as "raw" data. That is, the data are acknowledged to be naturally dirty, unfit as such for scientific consumption. Smith's raw data are, therefore, like all other data that eventually form the object fields of measurements. Nothing we measure ever comes to us in a well-cooked, pure, and sterile state. Thus, it might be said: *Professional measurement is the disciplined, artful process of cooking raw data.*[13]

Here then are Smith's "raw data":

17 ANGELA: My recognition that there might be something
18 wrong [with K] was very gradual, and I was actually the last of
19 her close friends who was openly willing to admit that
20 she was becoming mentally ill. Angela found it easier to
21 explain things chronologically, and, in retrospect, it
22 appears that this would make the observations fall
23 more easily into place.
24 We would go to the beach or the pool on a hot day, and I
25 would sort of dip in and just lie in the sun, while K
26 insisted that she had to swim 30 lengths. It was very
27 difficult to carry on an intelligent conversation with
28 her, this became apparent when I wanted to discuss a
29 particularly good movie, and she would make childish
30 inane remarks, completely off the point.
31 Slowly my admiration changed to a feeling of bafflement.
32 I began to treat her more like a child who was perhaps
33 not too bright, and I became protective of her. I
34 realized that this change had taken place, when a mutual
35 friend, Trudi who was majoring in English, had looked
36 over one of her essays, and told me afterwards: She
37 writes like a 12 year old—I think there is something
38 wrong with her.[14]

In this extract from a 163-line data chunk in a scientific paper, a sociologist presents data in the form of a verbatim account by a student researcher reporting on her interview with Angela, who in turn reports on the behaviors of K—which reports are confirmed by Angela (and the interviewer) and by parallel reports, such as Trudi's, on K's behavior.

The author of the paper, Dorothy Smith, intends to demonstrate the complicated dynamics associated with the establishment of what she calls "factual accounts." Smith holds, in her words, that "the actual events are not facts. It is the use of proper procedure for categorizing events that transforms them into facts."[15] In other words, though the eventful behavior of K—as reported by Angela to an interviewer, to Dorothy Smith and by Smith to *her* readers (and by me to you)—is the "subject" of all these communications; the events themselves are not factual outside these complicated communications. For the intents and purposes of the sociology Smith is writing, this means that whatever events K performed are not the "real" social things of interest to sociologists. They may or may not have been real in themselves. As a matter of fact, the first fact that struck Smith, and led to the writing of her paper, was that the account of K's mental illness seemed much more convincing when the student reporter represented it orally (without the interviewer notes) than it did when Smith first read the written report itself. This curious incongruity between two different accounts by the same interviewer of the same events is what led Smith to write the paper subtitled "The Anatomy of a Factual Account." The study's premise is that facts are constructed by mechanisms of social interaction such as instructions to the reader (or auditor) of the account and subtle devices for authorizing the validity of observations and normative judgments contained in the report. Smith's paper is an analysis of just how, within the written report, the assumption that "K Is Mentally Ill" came to be taken as factual. Yet, one might say, the facts in the report on Angela's interview are not measured by Angela, but by Smith. Technically speaking, they are not even measured by Smith but, ultimately, by her readers—those within the sociological community who find them of sufficient plausibility to outweigh the doubts of others who may find them implausible.

Still, as in all reports of measured social things, the quality of the measurement determines whether observations achieve the elevated status of *facts*. Thus, it is the sociologist's account that counts most. In the example, it is evident that few nuances in Angela's full report escape Smith's observing eye. For example, Smith notes, in the previous extract, that the interviewer, in writing the report, describes Angela's normative sense of what one *ought* to do while at the beach or swimming pool. Angela "would sort of dip in and just lie in the sun, while K insisted that she had to swim 30 lengths" (lines 25 through

26). These "events" took place in the early 1970s. Had they occurred today, swimming thirty laps might not be strange behavior for a young woman. On the contrary. But, even in the 1970s, when the article was first published, Smith observed that what was going on was that the writer of the report was establishing her sense of the normal, against which K's behavior was pictured as deviant. What was going on here was that the report used Angela's "sense" of normal pool or beach behavior as the measure of K's deviance. But, as can be seen, the first and crucial moment of measurement in this factual account was highly susceptible to a surprisingly variable cultural influence lying completely outside the protocols governing valid data taking.

Smith is well aware, as all good measurers must be, that good measures must attempt to control for such natural dirt in the raw ingredients to be cooked. In fact, it would seem that not only was Smith aware of this responsibility, so were Angela and the largely untutored student interviewer. The validity of Angela's measured sense of K's differences is promptly subjected to a reliability test by the introduction of the English major, Trudi (line 35), who, after judging that K's writing is like that of a twelve-year-old, concludes: "I think there is something wrong with her" (lines 37 and 38). Trudi's conclusion, certified by her status as an English major, thus completes a first cycle in the account of K's behavior, which is introduced at lines 17 through 20: "ANGELA: My recognition that there might be something wrong was very gradual, and I was actually the last of her close friends who was openly willing to admit that she was becoming mentally ill." These lines, of course, are composed by the interviewer (who wrote them from memory). They are attributed to Angela and purport to represent the "facts of the matter," but they are composed into a story told by the student researcher/interviewer, who was instructed to produce her account for Smith, who then presented her account of the factual account of K's state of mind to her colleagues in the professional sociological community.

It could be said that Smith's astute account of the construction of a factual account is also an excellent account of the sociology of measurement among professional sociologists. Measurement, as Smith's paper suggests, is the procedure by which facts are established to be authoritative. This involves a clear and precise use of a normative standard in order to measure the difference (or proximity) of the observed subject from that standard. Facts thus constructed may then be compared, by a variety of techniques, to an aggregate norm in order to determine the degree of their scientific value. In Smith's case study, the aggregate norm is, among other things, the ready assumption that Angela's and Trudi's sense of normal swimming pool and writing behaviors are reliably shared by others. Smith—as the off-stage commentator on the measuring work of the reporter, the interviewer,

Trudi, and others—keeps herself in the skeptic's position. Just the same, anyone in the line of auditors privy to this report may be justified in wondering if Smith's readers do or do not share an aggregate sense of the correctness of the norms Angela and Trudi assumed sufficient to the fact of K's mental illness.

But, here, a remarkable fact about the factual account becomes more important than at first one might have suspected. K is the "subject" of the article (in several senses of the word "subject"). But K is not there—at least, she is not there outside layer upon layer of accounts of her behaviors, each interpreted. In one sense, K's mental illness is the subject of the investigation. But, as Dorothy Smith makes clear from the beginning, even this "fact," so boldly insisted upon by the interviewer, is of dubious value. What is dubious? At the least, once one reads Smith's account of the construction of a factual account, it becomes clear that the subject herself (that is, the research subject) is very, very far away. The layer upon layer of secondary accounts of K's behavior are designed to tell her secret. In reality they hide it all the more. Whatever her own behaviors may have meant to K is totally, and without remorse, excluded from the account. Were K not a human subject, this might not matter. Were she not a human subject in a paper that is now part of a social theory of the importance of women's experience in sociology, this might not matter. And, as far as K herself is concerned, had the factual account of K as mentally ill not resulted, in the least, in her exclusion from a circle of friends and eventually in treatment for mental illness, it might have mattered less. But, in all these respects, the remarkable indifference to the actual research subject does matter. The last lines (162 and 163) of the report are, "It was arranged that K should go back to the psychiatrist." One wonders who exactly was the unidentified subject whose actions are hidden in the passive construction, "*It* was arranged."

We are never told how K felt about all this. In fact, throughout the paper, there is a studied delicacy toward K. Clearly Dorothy Smith, her reporter, and the informants (Angela and Trudi) all shared a concern for K. At the same time, they are put off by her behavior *and* each was willing to treat K as a research subject, that is, as an object of work that has nothing to do with K's plight. Just before introducing the report, Smith makes the statements:

> Thus the interview as we have it must be regarded as a cooperative working up of a now rather distant and wholly indeterminate set of events. *In addition, I have myself done some very minor editing to ensure further that the subject should be identifiable.*[16]

In the first of these sentences Smith is acknowledging, at least obliquely, just how far K is from the factual account of her supposed illness. But then she makes a statement that would cause most sociologists to take a second look. Does Smith mean to say that she edited the data to "ensure further that the

subject should be *identifiable*"? Does she not mean "should *not* be identified"—that is, that her identity be kept a secret, as it is by the notation "K"?
We have no way of knowing from the text whether this is a proofing error. It
could well be. But, error or not, it could mean just what it says—that Smith,
the reporter, the interviewer, Angela, and Trudi were concerned to ensure that
the subject, K, was identifiable. This, after all, is the sole and final purpose of
measurement: *to make a subject's secrets known against a rule of truth.*

Measurement is, therefore, at one and the same time, a straightforward and
complicated activity, yet one fundamental to any sociology. Smith, however,
makes it much more complicated than most people think it already is. How
and why she does this can be seen in the additional sense of the concept subject apparent in Smith's paper. As we have seen, nothing actually is said—by
Angela, Trudi, the interviewer, or Smith—of K's subjective view on the subject
of her mental illness. In a certain sense, Smith's sociology is devoted to correct-
ing this systematic error in the normal business of sociological research. But,
as in the ambiguous line about ensuring the subject's identity, Smith seems to
make ambiguous her sense of the problem associated with the recovering of a
subject's true experience. Just before presenting the interviewer data, Smith
says of them: "It is important that I convey to the reader *that the data the paper
is concerned with are wholly present to her—just as they are to me—in the type-
script of the interview which she will find below.*"[17] It is important to note that
the passage is emphasized by the author and that the "her" in question is the
generic "reader" of Smith's article, which was published first in 1976. In the use
of the "her" Smith is not being politically correct (a notion that did not exist in
its present sense in 1976). She is appealing strongly to those in a presumably
weak position and, at the same time, attacking conventions (like Durkheim's)
whereby woman does not exist on the pages of scientific documents.

The most general point of Smith's work over the past quarter-century has
been to establish a feminist sociology of women's experience and, thereby, one
at odds with traditional, objectifying sociology that conspires with the "relations of ruling," as Smith puts it. From which critical beginning she builds her
sociology from women's experience:

> My project is a sociology that begins in the actualities of women's experience. It builds on
> that earlier extraordinary moment, unlike anything I've experienced before or since, a
> giving birth to ourselves—slow, remorseless, painful, and powerful. It attempts to create
> a method of inquiry beginning from the site of being that we discovered as we learned to
> center ourselves as speaking, knowing subjects in our experience as women.[18]

Smith's sociology, thus, is founded in the moment in which the secret was told
that women too are speaking, knowing *subjects*. Yet, interestingly, in one of
Smith's most brilliant empirical studies, K, the woman who is principally in

question, is excluded. Her subject secret is kept silent, unintelligible. Smith realizes this, of course, and knows that the dumbing of K presents problems for her social theory. But she does not know what exactly to do about it. The problem is already evident in Smith's assumption that "the data the paper is concerned with are wholly present to" the generic reader, "her." Thus the enigma: If data of any kind are "wholly present," then how does one measure the secret truths of the subject of those data?

Measurement is always a question of getting at subject secrets. So is feminism. How the two sides of Dorothy Smith's sociology pull and tug at each other explains a great deal about the professional sociology against which Smith wants to rebel without leaving sociology altogether. In our day, feminist sociology, though it was significantly invented within sociology, has become a critic of sociology.[19] Feminism's complaint against sociology is that sociology has paid too little attention to the secret differences of women's experience from men's. Or, by evident implication, her complaint is that in sociology it is men's experience that is measured as though it were the universal human experience. Yet, as we see from Smith's account, her attempts to cook sociological data in a better way do not necessarily result in a measurement.

Ironically, Dorothy Smith, the critic of sociology, runs up against the very dilemma that all professional sociologies face: What to do with the fact that even when we cook our data carefully and well, the rawness with which they began cannot be entirely cooked away?

▼▼▼▼▼

The reason raw data cannot be cooked according to recipe is that research subjects keep their secrets. Since at least the generation of Durkheim and Weber, professional sociologists (and most practical ones) believed that the truth of social things can be measured. Weber's last words before dying were, "The Truth is the Truth."[20] Though, at the precise moment, he may have been understandably overwrought, one cannot read much Weber without admiration for his dogged determination to find just the right way to get at the secrets of the modern world. Much the same can be said of Durkheim, as of course it can be said of Dorothy Smith and many others.

Dorothy Smith wants to get at the truth of differences, which, she rightly argues, traditional sociology cannot. Yet, with all her well-placed rage against the "relations of ruling" in which official sociology is implicated, she shares its naive last word on Truth. In "K Is Mentally Ill" Smith seems to believe that the secret truth of K's subjective character is sufficiently well described by a sensitive description of the odd way it became a fact. Like the official sociology she rebukes, she too is unable to put just the right question. She, like those whose perspectives she roughly shares,[21] is fiercely critical of those official measurement practices that follow Durkheim in naively taking the very existence of social facts as though it were a matter of fact. Facts, as it is said today, are indeed constructed. But this is where Smith falters. She does not seem to see that taking a critical attitude toward the construction of facts is insufficient to the salvation of the subjective secrets of those subjects she most wants to bring into sociology. If her sociology is to be a sociology of women's experience,[22] then a sociology with such a purpose must give more serious critical attention to a prior question.

What if the very idea of subjectivity, from the beginnings of modern culture, has served to conceal, not reveal, differences among human subjects? K, whatever was going on inside her, was evidently different from those about her. Their human and sociological sympathy for her did nothing, as it turned out, to produce the secret of that difference. K was, to be sure, well measured by the norms of Trudi and Angela and the others and judged "mentally ill." But the secret of K's radically different attitudes toward swimming, the movies, and writing essays told her sociological judges nothing specific about Angela's hunch: "I think there is something wrong with her" (lines 37 and 38). No one truly knows what exactly was wrong with K. According to Smith's raw data, no one asked. Perhaps, if they had, K might not have told. But the fact of the social fact of K's mental illness is that no one asked. Why not? Perhaps because the question cannot be well asked from within sociologies, whether official or critical, that fail to examine with sufficient curiosity the deeper mysteries of social differences.

It is not that Dorothy Smith does not experience the difference it makes to be a woman. Rather, the trouble lies in the way she sets about defining and affirming that difference. In believing that women's experience is different in kind and, thus, superior to the experience of men,[23] she leaves herself in much the same position that Durkheim and Weber were in with respect to the crucial differences made by women and the East in their sociologies. Like Durkheim and Weber, she saw, so to speak, the differences. But also, like them, she defines them as "other," thus, in some important sense, as insufficiently real social things. Like Weber and Durkheim, Smith's sociology is intent upon encouraging the more true experience. For Durkheim and Weber the "more true" was the progress of morality in the West. For Smith it is the progress of women's experience. There is little good reason to suppose that any of them were wrong to believe in such truths. The only question is the one of sociology: Can it survive the crisis of social differences by staying within modernity's brazen insistence on the final triumph of some whole and single, final word of Truth?

Another way is suggested by turning to a practical sociologist who lived with social differences in a definite historical way and lived to tell the story.

In 1892, the year before Durkheim published *Division of Labor,* an American wrote a work that much later became a classic of a different kind. Had things been different, she might have become a sociologist. Even today, not many professional sociologists would recognize her name.

Anna Julia Cooper's *A Voice From the South* is today considered a classic work in the tradition of Black feminist social thought.[24] Though Cooper would live another seventy-two years, she would not duplicate the special brilliance of her first book in 1892. (She died in 1964 at about 104 years.) During her long life Cooper enjoyed many personal and professional successes. Born probably in 1858, the daughter of a slave, Cooper lived a productive life equal to the best accomplishments of any American of her time—as a graduate of Oberlin College; as a young teacher and the principal of the M Street School in Washington, D.C.; as adoptive mother of five children, a responsibility she assumed at age fifty-four; as a successful doctoral student at the Sorbonne, to which she commuted summers while teaching in Washington, D.C.; as translator and scholarly interpreter of medieval French texts; as president of an evening college for working-class adults (which she founded and organized after retiring from the teaching profession). All this, but never after would she publish a work like *Voice From the South.*[25]

When we look backwards from a century's perspective, Cooper's 1892 book seems to put the words to social worlds that would not exert their influence until the right time. It has become a classic today because, among the many other works of that era of Black feminist writing, none put a basic principle of social theory nearly so memorably as did Cooper's. The most famous line from *Voices* she derived from a surprising context. Though it might today appear as an affirmation of Black pride, it was in fact a criticism not of white society but of the men of her own race. Commenting on the proud declaration of one of the most distinguished and powerful Black men of the day, Cooper said: "Only the BLACK WOMAN can say 'when and where I enter,' in the quiet, undisputed dignity of my womanhood."[26] Martin R. Delany had once used the words "when and where I enter" to claim the right to represent his race in the powerful circles of world politics in which he moved. Against the Black man, Cooper meant to assert the prior moral and historical authority of the Black Woman. Later, in *A Voice From the South,* in an essay titled "Woman Versus the 'Indian,'" Cooper criticized the ideal of Woman as the embodiment of civilized virtue. With particular subtlety, Cooper drew attention to the

Reverend Anna Shaw's use of the title "Woman Versus the 'Indian'" in a paper delivered at the National Woman's Council in 1891, thus firmly calling attention to the limitations of a feminist principle that could think of the Native American as though she were the savage opposite to true womanhood. Though Cooper does not say it in so many words, it is clear that she means the white woman, from whom she does not exclude the leading feminists of the day. Here Cooper defines the social space of the woman who is neither savage nor white, as earlier she defined the place of the Black who is not man. *A Voice From the South,* thus, took up the tradition of Sojourner Truth's famous 1851 "Ar'n't I a Woman?" speech in order to assert patiently the unique vocation of the Black Woman in America.[27]

Like others of her generation—and of her social experience then and now—Cooper used personal stories to make a theoretical claim. At one point in the "Woman Versus the 'Indian'" essay, Cooper told a story that might today seem all too familiar—a story of injustices encountered by Blacks traveling in public conveyances. But what the reader might think of it as a precursor to the legend of Rosa Park's refusal to sit in the back of a Montgomery bus is something else. Cooper did not protest. She chose the path of quiet, cultured dignity. From which perspective she made a telling observation, juxtaposing the moral inferiority of the whites to the signs of social structures enforcing her reality and theirs:

> And when farther on in the same section our train stops at a dilapidated station, rendered yet more unsightly by dozens of loafers with their hands in their pockets while a productive soil and inviting climate beckon in vain to industry; and when, looking a little more closely, I see two dingy little rooms with 'FOR LADIES' swinging over one and 'FOR COLORED PEOPLE' over the other; while wondering under which head I come.[28]

In this expression of her theoretical repose, Cooper said what others knew but seldom put into so many words with such elegance. In observing that even the discrimination of American society left no categorical place for her, she identified a critical instability in the wider social order, thus defining the moral and social reality of the Black Woman in America. Though she spoke out of historical experience, her words advanced the invention of a category of social theory.

Needless to say, her method was not Durkheim's. Nor was it Dorothy Smith's. Cooper's definition, put in narrative form, drew the lines of the categorical contradictions in the public signs of a deep structural discrimination in her society. She did not, of course, define a science. People who did not readily come under some official heading were not then (and are barely so today) real subjects of a social science. For all intents and purposes, the Black Woman had *no* scientific reality because those of her racial kind had no social status in the eyes of the dominant society, just as those of her racial gender had an inferior status in the eyes of men of both races. In 1892, it would have been inconceivable, even perhaps to Cooper, that a century later there would be a field of writing and knowledge in and of the name of the Black Woman in America—a literature that came into its own in the larger society because those of and for whom Cooper wrote have become a cultural and political force. They had been such a force in Cooper's day, of course. How and why they, and others of similar position, became a *public* reality the presence of which could not be denied is a question of major historical importance for the fate of sociology.

At the least, Cooper's quiet sociology of the Black Woman puts a unique twist on the realities with which social theories now contend. Since Durkheim, sociology has been unable to provide a plausible resolution of the classic question, *Who am I if things social are different?* Even the current generation of sociological theorists of structures has not succeeded where others failed. From the point of view of Cooper's formulation, written at the time of Durkheim's first major formulation of his sociology, it is possible to see where the sociological tradition may have gone wrong.

Cooper puts into perspective the wisdom of the recursivists who want to get around the dualism of subject and object. Though, in *A Voice From the South,* she did not use the formal language of the dualities of modern social thought, her education at Oberlin College assures what is evident in every page of her book—that she both understood and approved of the values of modernity. This is well illustrated by the way she speaks of the Black Woman's moral responsibility in "The Status of Woman in America":[29]

> Everything to this race is new and strange and inspiring. There is a quickening of its pulses and a glowing of its self-consciousness. Aha, I can rival that! I can aspire to that! I can honor my name and vindicate my race! Something like this, it strikes me, is the enthusiasm which stirs the genius of young Africa in America; and the memory of past oppression and the fact of present attempted repression only serve to gather momentum for its irrepressible powers. Then again, a race in such a stage of growth is peculiarly sensitive to impressions. Not even the photographer's sensitized plate is more delicately impressionable to outer influences than is this high strung people here on the threshold of a career. . . . What a responsibility then to have the sole management of the primal lights and shadows! Such is the colored woman's office. She must stamp weal and woe on the coming history of this people. May she see her opportunity and vindicate her high prerogative.[30]

Though her attention is on the "colored woman's office," the language and moral hope could then have been taken, with minor substitutions, from any place in the then-white-dominated culture of America. In the 1890s, after the wounds of the Civil War had begun to heal for some and the closed frontier's promises loomed ahead, many Americans believed more than ever in progress. They felt that America, and its people, were destined to stamp weal and woe on all human people, as Cooper believed the colored woman would for her people. Cooper was very much an American modernist. If anything, she was, like most Americans, more the enthusiast for progress than Durkheim. Somehow Jim Crow did not dim her faith. Cooper believed that historical progress built new social worlds out of the moral actions of individuals, including those who would take responsibility for the management of "the primal lights and shadows!"[31]

But Cooper's theory of the Black Woman differs from the then, and still, dominant convictions of modern sociology. The difference is not merely that she includes what it excludes: race and gender. Cooper thought differently about the relations between moral subjects and the constructed historical structures with which they live. That difference is not readily apparent. Perhaps she wrote as a storyteller because this then was the only way to express a theory appropriate to the social reality of which she wrote. At the least, Cooper's idea of the Black Woman as a decisively distinct, but historically real, social individual is not conveniently thought within the formal categories of subjects and objects. If the categories of modern sociology are analytically unstable in their own right, then the nature of their instability may be evident in their inability to conceive of the Black Woman.

Cooper's Black Woman fits neither under "LADIES" nor "COLORED" because she cannot be reduced to any conceivable universal subject. Neither her race nor her gender is sufficient to account for her social reality. She is not, therefore, any one subject because she is not subject to any one general category. The historical conditions of her exclusion define her reality, which is not accountable to any manipulation of the classic terms of modernity. The Black Woman, as Cooper and others write of her, is not, for example, merely a gendered or racialized double man. By contrast, Durkheim's double man, like modernity's, was Universal Humanity caught in the duality of his existence—moral subject with a nature, historical yet animal, free but finite. Though Cooper does not subject her to analytic examination, the Black Woman would seem to be an historical individual whose nature resists reduction to the categories of modern thought. In the most exact historical sense, women doubly excluded—by men of their race, by women not of their race—are not *human* in the sense in which modern culture means that term. Anyone faced with a choice between two categorical doors—LADIES/COLORED, or others of similar effect, neither of which apply to her—is put outside the categories of Western culture. The discrimination behind the exclusion is real, but the sociological insistence of the historical experience goes beyond any particular discrimination.

What Cooper does is to express the moral purpose in the unique historical category. She, thus, reformulates even Rousseau's classic invention of the morally unique modern. Rousseau described the specialness of his personal moral history in order to demonstrate the universal truth of his character. But Cooper, while still a believer in Rousseau's culture, does what Rousseau could not (as he did what she could not). Rousseau took his personal history with utter seriousness, as does Cooper hers. But Rousseau, having been a cultured European man, was, by that fact, a natural member of what modernity considered the universal human social group. It was Rousseau's nature to be the uniquely honest man. Only a member of a universal category can possibly believe that the truth of his private confessions is of public value. Nothing in Cooper's experience compares. She, like others in a similar position of structured exclusion, lacks the natural qualification of universal humanity that Rousseau and other European gentlemen, before and since, took for granted. It is not by chance that a common discriminating weapon against those thus excluded is the claim that "they" (a "they" applied to any number of individuals) are not fully human.

Thus, the boldness of Cooper's idea of the "colored woman's office" is in its understated challenge to the same modern culture in which she still believed. Modernity believed, and believes, that humanity is the culture of the European male—the culture of Rousseau and the Encyclopedists, Jefferson and the American fathers, and all their kin. How else could there ever have been a universal culture based on the rights of man? How else could Rousseau, among others, have ever conceived of the audacious project of writing the unique truth himself? How else could it have been possible, in language and in moral thought, for the name of one category of the human species to serve, as if by right, as a synonym for modern culture? Social ideas of any kind and, most of all, those more sensitive ones meant to express the deepest convictions of a culture, could hardly serve their purpose without some real, empirical reference. It is a common insight, but a powerful one, that the invention of modern culture, having been executed by a social class dominated by European men, would learn to think of its culture as the culture exhibited by those men. Rousseau did not merely *tell* his personal story. He displayed it in his travels throughout Europe, in the courts and salons of France, and at the table he shared with Diderot and Voltaire at the Procope, once their habitual cafe in Paris. Anyone passing by the Procope in those days could have known, and probably did know, who these men were, what they thought, and thus what they represented. They were, in effect, the coming universal subjects of Modern Man.

What Cooper did unselfconsciously was to call out of the shadows an historical subject who, upon reflection, confounded the very idea of *the* historical Subject. Thus began, or continued, a tradition of sociology that today is not at all restricted to the Black Woman. Cooper's "the colored woman's office" gave moral authority to a social category comprising millions of women of color for whom, in America in the 1890s, the Black Woman was but one powerful instance. In her gentle criticism of Anna Shaw, Cooper clearly intended, at least implicitly, to include the Native American woman with the Black Woman. Though today that voice is more complicated, less naively progressive, the woman of color expresses those social truths that cannot be held firmly within the categories of modern thought.

Typically the woman of color position, like Cooper's, is one that recovers the silenced voice of those who by virture of racial, gendered, and sexual differences (among many others) were silenced by those long-dominant categories. Gloria Anzaldúa—Chicana, Indian, lesbian, feminist—is one example:

> The odds were heavily against her. She hid her feelings; she hid her truths; she concealed her power fire; but she kept stoking the inner flame. She remained faceless and voiceless, but a light shone through her veil of silence. And though she was unable to spread her limbs and though for her right now the sun has sunk under the earth and there is no moon, she continues to tend the flame. The spirit of the fire spurs her to fight for her own skin and a piece of ground to stand on, a ground from which to view the world—a perspective, a home ground where she can plumb the rich ancestral roots into her own ample *mestiza* heart. She waits till the waters are not so turbulent and the mountains not so slippery with sleet. Battered and bruised she waits, her bruises throwing her back upon herself and the rhythmic pulse of the feminine. *Coatlalopeuh* waits with her.[32]

Like Du Bois, Anzaldúa uses the veil metaphor. Like Cooper she speaks of the latent power of recovering the repressed and oppressed feminine. Though more radically than either, Anzaldúa and other women of color define a tradition of practical sociology in explicit and direct opposition to the traditional—a tradition that unsettles the already unstable analytic categories of classic sociology.

These are also the unstable categories that unsettle Dorothy Smith's theory of measurement. Smith could not measure the secret of K's difference because, in spite of her critical intentions, she accepted the traditional conviction that social measures are made against a shared standard of the normal. Ironically, any critical theory like Smith's that constructs its measures against a counternorm (in her case woman's experience) will have a difficult time escaping the problems faced by the methods it opposes. Just as Durkheim could not measure the difference of women, so Smith was unable to measure the difference of a different woman. Durkheim failed because he believed too earnestly in the universal value of the West's moral progress. Smith failed because she believed too simply in the ability of woman's subjective experience to get at and thus calculate the truth of, at least, another woman's secret. Anna

Julia Cooper, and those in her tradition, would have disputed both Durkheim and Smith.

Cooper, like Du Bois, held that the final measure of the secret of human subjects cannot be universal. Just as there is no universal truth to Black experience, nor is there any single essence to the truth of woman's experience. The measure of all things social is the colored woman's office. Though, to be sure, Cooper referred to the specifics of her proper historical condition at a definite time, it is possible to generalize cautiously. What makes Cooper's theory of the colored woman's office applicable to the circumstances of others is the boldness of its gentle critique of the culture she believed in. In striking contrast to Du Bois, she seemingly took the bitter pill of Jim Crow and the failure of Reconstruction with less discomfort. This was perhaps because she did not set the responsibility for racial uplift solely on Black shoulders alone. She was, in effect, defining a uniquely different social space—different even from Du Bois's. In effect, Cooper took Josie with even greater seriousness than did Du Bois!

"How shall man measure Progress where the dark-faced Josie lies?" Cooper would have agreed in general but might have added, in effect: It is not simply that Progress is measured against Josie's heartfuls of sorrow but that Josie is the measure of Progress. "What a responsibility," said Cooper, "to have the sole management of the primal lights and shadows!" Only she who knows firsthand all the engendered and racialized secrets of the West can know the truth of the West. By implication, if the West, if America, does not manage *both* the primal lights and shadows, there can be no standard by which to judge its progress.

From the facts of today's crisis it would be perfectly possible to look back to Cooper's faith in progress as naive. But such a judgment does not change the value of her theoretical contribution. No universal principle—neither Durkheim's nor Smith's nor any similar—is sufficient to the task of measuring at once the shadows and the lights. Measurement, in its modernist form, fails because of its triumphal faith in true, objective, unassailable standards. Ultimately such a perspective can never gather the dark secrets of Western civilization—those of its foundations in the slave trade and expansion in a vast colonial system in which all who were different by any racial, gender, or sexual standard were seen as one, and Other—and forced to act as such. It is not, of course, that these facts are secrets any longer but that the effects on those who are not descended from the white European and American explorer fathers are not accessible from any place uncritically within the West's colonizing culture.

Differently put, the classic formula of social measures—that *subjects apprehend objects* (and all its substitutes and correlates)—works only in a world that believes in universal social truth. A world can thus believe only if its structures (whether real or virtual) support the formula. Here is where the sociology of measurement rejoins the sociology of structures. Strictly speaking, the duality of subjects and objects cannot be used to apprehend a world comprising subjects whose objective worlds are inherently different, as surely Josie's and Cooper's were. Thus, it can be seen that the limitations on the modernist sociologies of structures, like those of its measurers, are not an accident of any theorist's failure "to think things through well enough." The reason all sociologies of structures fail to accomplish *their* own theoretical purposes is that those purposes are products of a culture that no longer enjoys the broad popular support of a human community. In the absence of historical conditions necessary to the idea of a Universal Humanity, it is not possible to think of social structures as articulated products of human subjects, nor to measure them as though their secrets were readily available to good intentions. It is not even possible to think of structures as complex recursive relations without the thinker of the thought forcing himself into a virtual world recursing to the point of theoretical exhaustion.

In modern sociology, structures serve the historical purpose of structuring away the differences of the modern world. In like manner, measurement controls the outlying variances of social differences. This is what Durkheim did with the Jew and Woman, what Weber did with the East, and what American sociology at the turn of the previous century did with those like Anna Julia Cooper, Du Bois and Josie, and others who thought as they did. They all thought, one supposes, from the other side of a veil, drawn precisely in order that their truths would remain in the dark.

▼▼▼▼▼

Anna Julia Cooper represented, in effect, an ideal type of practical sociology— she put words to the inconvenient realities of her time and circumstances. By the same token, she was not a professional sociologist, and for reasons that go beyond the vicious discriminations of post-Reconstruction America. Du Bois was of course similarly excluded and might have been a professional sociologist had professional sociology permitted.[33] Yet, one supposes, even Du Bois would never have been a professional sociologist in the sense that his contemporaries Durkheim and Weber were then dreaming of sociology. Like Cooper's, Du Bois's sociology was rooted in the practical realities of his life and history, of which he was not afraid to speak.

In 1892, the year Cooper published *A Voice From the South*, W.E.B. Du Bois interrupted his graduate studies at Harvard University for two years of independent study in Europe, during which he lived principally in Berlin. At

Harvard, Du Bois had already grown close to one of his most influential teachers, William James. While in Germany, he heard Max Weber lecture and, very probably, was familiar with Weber's early writings.[34] In that same year, 1892, the University of Chicago founded the first major department of sociology. At the time of Du Bois's graduate work, Harvard did not offer work in sociology. Just the same, after completing his doctoral studies in 1895, Du Bois accepted a position as "assistant instructor of sociology" at the University of Pennsylvania. The position provided no office and permitted no teaching.[35] It served merely as a base for Du Bois's famous sociological study, *The Philadelphia Negro,* for which the university was willing to take credit of sponsorship without having given Du Bois the customary credit of identification with it. *The Philadelphia Negro* remains a masterpiece of thorough sociological field research and is still cited for its insights into the life of urban Blacks in America. It did not, however, become his best-known book partly because professional sociologists have been slow to read it, and partly because it was soon eclipsed by an even greater book.

Du Bois's *Souls of Black Folk* was published in 1903, the year before Weber wrote the first of the studies that became *The Protestant Ethic.* Though Henry James considered this work the only truly great southern literature of the time, *Souls* was recognized and widely read mostly by Blacks around the world. *Souls of Black Folk,* however, is the source of a sociological turn much like Cooper's (and may have been partially influenced by her[36]). But Du Bois's idea of the "double consciousness" of the Black American, while in its way less complicated than Cooper's ideal of the Black Woman, is a particularly interesting illustration of the analytic failures of the social theory written by the professional sociologies that were just then taking their definitive academic shape. Most notably, Du Bois's famous idea of the double conscious self of the American Negro, like Cooper's of the colored woman's office, indicts the analytic incapacities of official social thought. The fact is all the more poignant in Du Bois's case because his most famous idea is clearly borrowed from the official social science of his day—directly from the theories of the social self of William James, indirectly perhaps from Weber's idea of the double-sided nature of modern life.[37] Yet, whatever its professional sources, Du Bois's theory, like Cooper's, makes sense only with reference to the specific practical experiences of American Blacks.

Du Bois's doubly conscious American Black was *not* a mere variant on sociology's different theory of the double man. His idea conveys more and different social meanings:

> After the Egyptian and Indian, the Greek and Roman, the Teuton and Mongolian, the Negro is a sort of seventh son, born with a veil, and *gifted with second-sight in this American world,—a world which yields him no true self-consciousness, but only lets him*

see himself through the revelation of the other world. It is a peculiar sensation, this double-consciousness, this sense of always looking at one's self through the eyes of others, of measuring one's soul by the type of a world that looks on in amused contempt and pity. One ever feels his twoness,—*an American, a Negro; two souls, two thoughts, two unreconciled strivings; two warring ideas in one dark body, whose dogged strength alone keeps it from being torn asunder.*[38]

Though Du Bois in 1903 was more sober than Cooper a decade earlier, still, like her, he defined the social space of the American Black as unique. The famous doctrine of twoness, of the double consciousness of the American Negro, is more complicated than at first it may appear. It is not just that Black Americans see both sides of social reality but that they see through the veil through which they are seen.[39] The veil segregates the Negro American, but the segregation is as much a cultural and moral discrimination as a physical and legal one. Whenever a veil is imposed it serves a double purpose, one unintended: to keep those enveiled out of sight, to provide those enveiled with a mask behind which they can see without being seen. Veils establish a strange confusion in the communication between the two sides. He who does not want to see is blinded; those he does not want to see, see some things more clearly than he.

Thus, just as Cooper's Black Woman sees her unique place both against and between LADIES and COLORED, Du Bois sees the Black American seeing himself through the eyes of those who insist on the discriminating signs. From one point of view, Cooper's idea is the more subtle; from another, Du Bois's is. Hers defines the positive purpose of the excluded against the multiple axes of exclusion—thus turning an absence into a presence, an exclusion into power. Du Bois, though his idea ignores Woman (a symptom perhaps of his sociology), defines the space of the Black American with the greater regard for the ways in which the structures of the world define and complicate the structures of perception and self-consciousness. If Cooper's figure is just *there* to be drawn from the shadows, Du Bois's is never quite there even to himself even though his double awareness is his moral strength.

Though it is easily overlooked, the most telling aspect of Du Bois's is in that line, "*gifted with second-sight in this American world,—a world which yields him no true self-consciousness.*" Du Bois describes a structured world that structures away the American Black's self-consciousness—and not just the consciousness *of* self, but Self itself. As a student of William James in 1890, the year James published *The Principles of Psychology,* which includes his classic description of the social self, Du Bois could not possibly have used the term "self" in any of its variants without meaning to say what he says. He meant, thereby, to define an historical American individual whose world structures away the self—"two souls, two thoughts, two unreconciled strivings; two warring ideals in one dark body." Though the Negro longs for what Du Bois calls "a better truer self," he is what he is because of a double consciousness that leaves him self-less.[40]

Du Bois's man with two souls yet without a self is not, however, man oppressed. Like Cooper in 1892, Du Bois in 1903 believed in Progress. In fact their common belief united them at a distance. *Souls of Black Folk,* a collection of essays, includes his first and most famous attack on Booker T. Washington. Washington was then the most powerful Black man in America, in part because his philosophy of industrial education was more convenient to white society's vision of the Negro's[41] lowly status. Du Bois's idea of the "talented tenth" was a vision of the higher education of the most talented American Blacks, who then would lift the race. It was, of course, a vision consistent with his own background; even more, it fit Anna Julia Cooper's experience. She, as much as he, was the embodiment of the talented-tenth principle, thus both were noxious to Booker T. Washington's philosophy.

Cooper in her early years as principal of the M Street School in Washington, D.C., had succeeded in placing a number of her students in the best white schools in the East and in supplementing M Street's traditional curriculum with college-oriented courses. This earned her the hostility of Washington's local operatives, who in 1905 conspired against her, concocting a story of sexual promiscuity, to force her from the principalship and, for several years, from M Street altogether. Earlier (in 1900) the same forces had blocked the appointment of Du Bois as the assistant superintendent for colored schools in the District of Columbia. Cooper and Du Bois both suffered in the struggle within the Black community, a struggle that could be viewed as a reflection of the Negro's doubled circumstance in white America. In one sense Washington's power lay in his readiness to accept the veil, thus to encourage Blacks to remain in agricultural and industrial vocations, excluded from the highest social positions in the society.

Against Booker T. Washington, Du Bois had a definite idea of social progress. Like Cooper, though less enthusiastically, the Du Bois of *Souls* believed that double consciousness may have uniquely suited Blacks for the advancement of the American civilization. Though in later years Du Bois would abandon his youthful faith in American progress, in *Souls* he was as clear as Cooper:

> Merely a concrete test of the underlying principles of the great republic is the Negro Problem, and the spiritual striving of the freedmen's sons is the travail of souls whose

burden is almost beyond the measure of their strength, but who bear it in the name of an historic race, in the name of this the land of their fathers' fathers, in the name of human opportunity.[42]

The measure of the American way is, as it was in regard to Josie, its capacity to know the true, secret meaning of the subject of its founding discriminations. In the retrospect of subsequent history Du Bois and Cooper may seem naive in their beliefs about the progress of Americans. If so, they were never as blindly naive as the keepers of the American way who denied altogether that the evil of racial discrimination was the central fact of the republic.

Before entering the technologies of professional sociologists, social measurement was the decisive act whereby the cultural meaning of the West was determined. In modern culture, measurement is first and foremost the determination of the precise meaning of world structures to social subjects. Before the research subject, there was the historical Subject of modern culture. Without Him there could be no standard, hence no measurement of any kind.

As Erving Goffman once observed, in social life there are two constitutive secrets: strategic and dark.[43] Strategic secrets cover those aspects of social information that are meant to be revealed in time as the progress of things unfolds. In a certain sense, one could say that America was the European West's strategic secret. As George Berkeley, the eighteenth-century English philosopher, put it,

> Westward the course of empire takes its way;
> The first four acts already past,
> A fifth shall close the drama with the day;
> Time's noblest offspring is the last.[44]

From Berkeley to Crèvecoeur to de Tocqueville, early modern Europeans came to look upon America as the fulfillment of that which was left incomplete in Europe, as the secret of the future of historical Man—which was, of course, nothing less than European man.[45] The gradual manifestation of the secret over several centuries of the American destiny was due to the strategic leaking of the dawning truth of progress that, in Europe, failed to present itself.

But it was another European who much later was among the first to say what had long been denied. In another, deeper sense America held the *dark* secret of the West. Dark secrets, Goffman taught, are those that dare not be told. Telling a dark secret risks the destruction of cultural meanings. Gunnar

Myrdal, however, began *The American Dilemma*: "The American Negro problem is a problem in the heart of the American."[46] One could say the American dilemma is that of keeping the secret that this shining light of republican virtue was founded on the dark secret of racial hatred and abuse. America was not alone in this fact, but it was, among the European peoples in diaspora, the people to whom all looked for perfection of the dream of human progress. Though race hatred was not the only form of this dark secret, it was the most visible and, thus, the most difficult to deny.[47]

It would not be wrong to say, therefore, that the dark secret of the West was that its strategic secret was not what it promised to be. Theories of the West's structures were, therefore, necessarily intent upon structuring away real differences, the truth of which would destroy the social whole. Likewise, measurement was understood as the act of investing the central tendency of progress with formal verification. The standard of structuring and of measuring was, with little exception, the abstract emerging truth of the idealized progress of Man, the universal human Subject.

The crisis after which sociologies must learn to define themselves is nothing less than the insistent evidence that there is, contrary to Lincoln's oft-quoted line, no one "last best hope" for the ideal of the historical Subject. As a consequence, everything must be rethought. As they were a century ago when the dark secret was widely kept, sociologies are means whereby people tell the truth of the present.

The opportunity of the present is that of telling a truth fully. Whatever the dark secret of the present is, it is not what it once was. Sociologies, practical and professional, should begin anew, here and now.

Chapter 9

The Future of Sociologies

M ore or less a generation ago, when Alvin Gouldner wrote *The Coming Crisis in Western Sociology,* neither he nor his readers could have anticipated just how severe that crisis would be. It is far from clear that the crisis will ever end. It may, perhaps, be the way the world is. The very lack of any strong, coherent voice announcing anything like a crisis-free future in this world suggests we may be in this for the long haul. The more confident voices today are fundamentalisms, religious and secular, of various kinds. They denounce the corruptions of the present time and, very often, as evangelicals always have, call their followers to another world. Few are called to praise the present world.

These are the conditions that separate today's sociologists, practical and professional, from those of that earlier era—from Gouldner, C. Wright Mills, many of the sociologists of structures, and the thousands of practical sociologists in the 1960s who were convinced that new knowledge, or new consciousness, would be sufficient to the making of a new world. None were more eloquent than the founders of SNCC, whose words were quoted at the beginning of this book. Their words are worth repeating, if only to remind us how much less confident we are today. In 1960, with simple eloquence, they dreamed a world in which

> through nonviolence, courage displaces fear. Love transcends hate. Acceptance dissipates prejudice; hope ends despair. Faith reconciles doubt. Peace dominates war. Mutual regard cancels enmity. Justice for all overthrows injustice. The redemptive community supersedes immoral social systems.[1]

196

A beautiful and compelling moral vision, true. But, it is hard to look back at such a sociological imagination with any real conviction that it applies to our near future. Indeed, only a few years after SNCC had begun in this hope, it gave up on the dream of a single, integrated, redemptive community. The founders of SNCC were not alone in dreaming of a new world, nor alone in changing their minds about its prospects.

In 1961, Frantz Fanon was among those who saw the crisis that would come from the first instances of a worldwide withdrawal of confidence in the old order. Fanon's words, also quoted in the first chapter of this book, bear repeating alongside those of SNCC's founders. Though the two visions were written nearly at the same time in the early 1960s, Fanon's told more of what came to pass:

> Decolonization never takes place unnoticed, for it influences individuals and modifies them fundamentally. It transforms spectators crushed with their inessentiality into privileged actors, with the grandiose glare of history's floodlights upon them. . . . Decolonization is the veritable creation of new men. . . . In decolonization, there is therefore the need of a complete calling in question of the colonial situation.[2]

Fanon's was, indeed, a different moral vision. His "new men" would, in words of the book's English edition subtitle, "change the shape of the world." Fanon's was the more perspicacious vision because, as things turned out, the old order, though it endured the political turmoil of the 1960s, has never recovered from effects of the reversal of the "grandiose glare of history's floodlights." Once it and all the consequent and subsequent movements in its aftermath took notice of the world colonial system, decolonization not only "transformed spectators" into "new men" but called the entire world situation into question. By the mid-1960s the truth of political and moral differences asserted itself.

Hence the strange effect of the crisis that does not present itself *as* crisis, at least not to those in positions of relative comfort. To them the world is not burning as it did daily, seemingly everywhere, in the late 1960s. To them the crisis appears as crisis only in awkward moments when they try to talk confidently of the world and find themselves in the strange situation of President Bush—unable to find the right words, unable to get the story straight, unable to chant the old litanies in strong voice. It is not, of course, that the terrors of the world are any less for those who suffer most. Children struggling to grow and survive in Mozambique, Belfast, Cambodia, South Chicago, the West Bank, know the crisis of violence and deprivation firsthand.[3] It might be said that the true nature of the world crisis lies in the fact that those, like President Bush, who seek to speak the general truth of the world cannot account for those, like the millions of starving and violated children worldwide, who know its specific, bitter realities.

Fanon had it exactly right. Yet, in the last generation, the floodlights of history have also had the surprising effect of blinding the actors who had formerly assumed the right to represent humankind. After the collapse of the colonial system, those who once built the world could neither see nor say the world as such—except dimly, stuttering. It may not be possible, from any position within the deep culture of modernity, to see these realities truly.

Forty percent of elementary schoolchildren growing up in urban Chicago have witnessed a shooting; 25 percent have witnessed a murder. Forty-five percent of women and 19 percent of child refugees who are from Mozambique have witnessed or known someone injured by political violence. Until just recently, twelve-year-old Palestinian boys in the West Bank and Gaza thought of themselves as warriors under moral obligation to attack Israeli forces, hurling stones at great risk against the armaments of modern warfare. Some still do.[4] These facts of violence against the world's children only begin to tell the story, the implications of which are more terrifying than any prior holocaust if only because of the lack of a moral narrative with which to account for them. The cruelty of what Hitler and Stalin did could be explained by the West's story of itself as an unleashing of the evil the modern world thought it would overcome. Before the shape of the world changed there were certain widely shared moral truths that allowed those on the side of the good to identify evil, and to dream of superseding moral communities, as did the young founders of SNCC and many others of their time. Today, dreams of a moral society are at best the local hopes of those who suffer, at worst platitudes hiding the meanness of arrogant men. When will we again become decent and whole? Perhaps never again.

The crisis, therefore, is one facing those who accept a responsibility to tell the truth of the world in order to imagine a better one. Where this crisis began is hard to say. It may well have been there buried deep in modernity's steady denial of its other side—in its bold, one-sided attempt to define itself as humanity's truth and the world's best hope. That hope was just as much the foundation of the world's colonial system as it was the inspiration of modern progress and culture. Thus, beginning most notably with Gandhi's challenge to British colonial rule and continuing through the decolonizing struggles of the 1950s in Algeria and the rest of Africa, China and Asia, Cuba and Latin America, the world changed its shape. Each of the decolonizing movements called notice to the modern West's blindness to its own inherent capacity for destruction. That notice did not, of course, fail to inspire those who felt their circumstances suited the decolonizing realities—American Blacks, feminists, and, later, gays and lesbians. Fanon's question of the colonial system was also the question of the racist, patriarchal, and heteronormative foundations of

Western culture. Though the revolutions against that culture took different, and sometimes conflicting directions, their collective effect was to change the world's shape.

The veil of which Du Bois wrote a century ago has been rent asunder. There is, to be sure, still a color line, and multiple other excluding lines of division. But they are not so simply drawn as they once were. With rare exception, those in positions of privilege today are still extravagantly ignorant of the racial, gendered, sexual, or postcolonial others they hate or fear. But today this ignorance is unstable; it decomposes under multiple exposures to encounters with those others who, to use the expression, put their differences "in the face" of those who scurry for the shelter of a false privilege.

The color line was, we now know, never just a color line but a moral barrier drawn by the deep principles of Western culture against all those whose services were required for the building of its global colonial system. Color was, certainly, the first and most insidious of the West's principles of exclusion and suppression. It was, in this sense, the most visible form of the veil and most effective as an ugly justification for the taking of lands, resources, and people into the emergent capitalist world system. After the establishment of the North Atlantic culture as a world colonial structure in the early sixteenth century,[5] the slave system established the color line from which "right of exclusion" other lines of separation gained legitimacy. Just as the modern world economy was predicated on the moral "necessity" of enslavement and the displacement of African and other peoples of color from their native lands, so the emergent bourgeois culture depended on the patriarchate (to use Charlotte Perkins Gilman's word). The unpaid or underpaid labor of women in the household, as wives or domestics, and in marginal positions in the industrial workforce constituted a savings on capital expenditures that fueled the expansion of industrial capitalism out of agricultural economies.[6] And, though it has been less closely examined until recently, it is evident now that the exclusion of women from positions of economic and political power was tied to an irrational desire to contain feminine sexuality, which in turn was fundamental to the still strong desire to suppress and oppress those who digress from the strict, punitive heteronormativity governing sexual life in the West.[7] Racism, sexism, and homophobia—though they have independent histories and differential effects—are part of the same system. The West required the veil of race—or, as Henry Louis Gates puts it, the trope of race[8]—from which all other lines of exclusion, whether overt or covert, derived their power.

It would not be far wrong to say that the modern culture of the West was essentially an exclusionary culture. Its grand promise of social hope based on progress for all was the general dream that could not be dreamt without the already decided fact that great numbers of human beings would be excluded by their very natures. The dream was too grand to be offered to everyone without qualification. Even as a dream—a grand myth of a great civilization—such largesse would have entailed the promise of polities with power for all and economies without scarcity. No one ever truly believed this possible. From Hobbes to Ricardo, the grand theorists of modern social life knew full well, against their fondest hopes, that the war of all against all in the struggle against starvation lurked in the wilderness just beyond the civilized consciousness of the good society.

If the world of the North Atlantic peoples was thus constituted, then the powerful, if weird, effect of decolonization makes better sense. The breaking up of the West's world-colonial empire in the two decades following World War II broke the world's classically modern shape. The transformation was not, as it is sometimes thought, that the Euro-American Center lost its political and economic grip on the world. If anything, its iron fist, now fortified by almost miraculous military finesse, is stronger than ever. The West's ability to destroy its opponents is more perfect than ever. Though its economies are less discrete than before, they are as busy as ever, now cannibalizing the markets in the Pacific Basin with products fashioned from labor and materials appropriated from the African, Latin American, and Asian hinterlands. Yet, the power of the West is weaker than it ever was in the most important respect. Hardly anyone believes in, or trusts, the West to be what it once believed itself to be.

In a certain sense the political right and the more conservative elements in the American military establishment of a generation ago were correct when they said that America failed in Vietnam because it lacked the political will to win. The only thing wrong with this conviction is its assumption that political will can today be expressed directly through the technology of modern warfare.[9] The Americans lost in Vietnam for the same reason the Soviets lost in Afghanistan. The refusal of people in these, as it is said, "primitive" regions to believe in the might of the West not only encouraged their own successful resistance movements but fed the political doubts of the invading soldiers, their families and friends, and the body politic that must will the military actions. Whether on playgrounds or in world politics, when the bully is called out for what he is, he shrinks—imperceptibly at first, to be sure; but he shrinks, if only by pulling the punch that exposes a flank to an exhausting assault of tiny hits. Over time these small batterings of the body weaken it. He may retreat for a while to take up the attack elsewhere—in the Falklands, Grenada, or Iraq—where his prowess is exhibited but with meager results. Whatever the gains, it is evident that Iraq remains Iraq, much as it was before the American attacks. It seems, today, that all it takes is a few SCUD missiles outside Baghdad, secondhand rifles in Somalia, or street sweepers in South Chicago to hold the great powers at bay.

If the great powers cannot win their wars against their designated enemies—whether regional tyrants or the system of drug-based violence—then the world is changed from what it was. The change, of course, is a complex relation between loss of faith and the shocking spread of miracle technologies. Power could still the regional rebels and urban gangs if they believed in, or trusted, Power's promises. But not even the proponents of Western power believe as they once did. Former President Bush is not the only one unable to get the story straight. No one gets it quite right because so few in power know quite what to say.

The ironic fact that changed the world's shape was that the very idea of *world* was itself called into question. In the modern sense, the idea of a coherent world order was a variant of the dream of unity of all of mankind. In the current situation, whatever remains of the imaginary of universal Humanity, the predominant fact of the times is that of differences. It is not simply "diversity" or "pluralism" within some overarching moral accord. Today, the situation is one in which, whatever men and women share, they increasingly see themselves, and their circumstances, as the reality of their differences from others. This is not necessarily a cause for celebration. The spread of ethnic wars within and between deteriorating nation-states is a tragedy few but the most cynical could enjoy.

Yet, just as the seed of destruction was sown along with the dream of moral unity, so the kernel of social hope can be nurtured in the rocky ground of social differences. This is the first historical condition sociologies must consider if they are to live with, or get beyond, the world crisis.

▼▼▼▼▼

The future of sociologies is the present. One of the enduring strengths of the earliest sociologists was their regard for such a principle. Though they failed in other ways, Marx, Weber, and Durkheim, three of the greatest founders of professional sociology, thought in and of their present. Marx wrote of the alienating effects of industrial capitalism in the 1860s, when industrial capitalism was first developing. Weber and Durkheim wrote of the overrationalizing and anomic effects of bureaucracy and the modern division of social labor just as Germany and France were struggling (vainly as it turned out) to find a new, humane solution to their transitions from traditional social and political cultures while avoiding the terrible costs of world war. Each of these writers helped invent some crucial aspect of sociology's classic culture by living in and thinking through the world before them.

Du Bois, Cooper, and Gilman, contemporaries of the founders of professional sociology, were among the most accomplished of practical sociologists of their day. Each was excluded, or chose to be excluded, from professional sociology. Yet each wrote of his or her time and wrote with a definite sociological interest. Against the culture of those times, they were, if anything, more astutely critical of the powers of modernity than were Marx, Weber, and Durkheim. Surely, to again use a Du Boisian line, they were, in their different ways, gifted with a second sight. This is not that they saw things perfectly but that at least they saw the world more clearly—more clearly even than those, like Marx, who dreamed of the future free of class conflict; or those, like Durkheim, who trusted in sociology to shape the moral heart of modernity; or those, like Weber, who were to some uncertain degree baffled by the mixed blessing of modern reason. But, like the founders of professional sociology, they too thought with respect to their present—and, perhaps, thought more clearly because they had no good reason to long for the lost past Durkheim left with his rabbinical ancestors and most men and women in bourgeois European culture lost in some similar fashion. The generation of the 1890s was a generation vexed with its present, with the conflicting realities of progress and loss.

The generation of the 1990s is in a very different circumstance, though not so different as some might suppose. Young people worldwide (those who actually survive their childhoods) will come to the full promise of their adult lives without ever having known firsthand *any* of the golden ages between which the history of modernity has been strung. The last such moment, depending on one's age and perspective, was either the years just after World War II in America or, for those born during or just after that war, the exhilarating moments of the 1960s. But both were golden ages of sad, inconclusive endings. The parents, many of them veterans of World War II and the Great Depression, believed in the American century in the days when the United States was the unchallenged leader of the world. They tried as well as they could to deny the reality of the Cold War while also ignoring the first signs of revolt within. But already by 1950 and decidedly by the beginning of the civil rights movement in Montgomery in 1955, these denials of the changing world order were shattered. The only thing they could not see clearly enough was that the more fundamental challenge to Western dominance was not the USSR but the growing rebellions in the colonial system, of which the civil rights and student movements were but an internal reverberation. Yet, the children's generation was no less naive. Among them were those, including many who would become today's professional sociologists, who believed deeply that the revolution would soon come. It did not, of course. Something changed, but that change was one that rendered their own best ideas as futile as the naively optimistic and chauvinistic principles of their parents' generation.

Today's new generation was bred in less assurance of comfort than was its predecessor in the 1960s.[10] Most notably, today's youth are the only generation in this century to have *never* experienced the exhilarating effect of widely shared enthusiasm for a good future based on present realities. Even those who came of age in the 1930s knew something of the false promises in the decade after the First World War, and many lived to enjoy the benefits of the years after the Second. Today's youth grew up with an experience much closer to that of those who suffered the Holocaust and the Gulag. This does not diminish the far greater horror the latter faced. I mean only to suggest how few are those in this last generation of the century who have known a childhood and youth anything like the relatively more hopeful formative years of their mothers, their mother's mothers, and most of those who came before them in the West's twentieth century.

This is not to say, of course, that most people in the century since the beginnings of institutional sociology enjoyed the benefits of life in a present society that promised a hopeful future. Hardly. The numbers of those excluded from and actually deprived of even the most meager crumbs of modernity's extravagant promises have always been greater by far than the numbers of those who believed that their good fortune was humanity itself, normal and universal. This gross ratio has been modernity's moral nightmare. But now the most fundamental cultural change in the world's shape is more than a mere lack of confidence in the West. It is more likely to be a devastating collapse of the delicate capacity for self-deception whereby the normal is, now, decisively more a matter of exclusion than inclusion.

Nor is this to suppose that the formerly excluded suddenly have the upper hand; nor that privilege has disappeared from the moral landscape. If anything, exclusions are enforced more harshly in proportion to the dramatic visibility of the excluded and the increasingly greater knowledge of the social mechanisms of their exclusion. How else to explain one of the most bewildering facts of the past thirty years? In this time it has come to be reasonably common knowledge that imperialism worked its way all too easily by complicity with popular racial and sexual phobias. More is known and said today about the centrality of racism, sexism, and homophobia to the great metropolitan cultures than at any time in the half-millennium history of the modern world. Yet, though much has been accomplished in the raising of liberal consciousness—and some gains have been made in the political inclusion of people of color, gays, and women—the hard reality is that by the crucial measures little has changed. In the United States, women on the average hold economic positions only barely improved in relative terms since the late 1960s. The overall economic situation for Blacks, especially Black men, is worse by far. Violence against women and gays has not diminished. Economic exploitation of people in the former world colonies moves inexorably ahead, abated only where drought and starvation are killing those not already slain in civil and ethnic conflict. One thinks, by comparison, of Marx's powerful line at the beginning of the *1844 Manuscripts*: "We proceed from an *actual* economic fact. The worker becomes all the poorer the more wealth he produces, the more his production increases in power and range."[11] In like manner we could say of the present situation that the excluded of the world, especially their children, lose ground in proportion to an increased knowledge of their number and circumstance in a world of plenty. This is the world reality into which today's younger generations have been born and bred. Whatever might be an individual's relative danger or immunity, the looming social salience of the world's excluded is inescapable. In this respect those who will be in full power of adult life in 2000, at the exact end of the millennium, know a world very different from that at the end of the nineteenth century.

As strange as it may seem to say it, this is a world from which *everyone* is excluded. When privilege and authority no longer enjoy an exemption from close scrutiny of their accounts, they may hold their positions, but never as they once did. Cultural privilege and political authority, today, must continually assert their claims to attention and power against a rapid regress of popular attention to the harsh reality on the streets or in the media. When George Bush began his public life in those blue skies over the Pacific war, the world still longed for heroes and golden ages. When Presidents Clinton and Yeltsin assumed the powers of their offices they, like leaders everywhere, enjoyed not the least relief from public skepticism. If men and women in public life are to hold positive attention for more than a passing moment, they must avoid the temptation to face the world as its heroic saviors. This applies even more particularly to individuals contending with uncertain job prospects and the certain prospects of violence that constitute the normal of daily life. Whether one's estate is high or low, the norm of daily life is so far from what it was in the 1890s that one can hardly think of oneself as of the same world.

"Keep hope alive" rings in vain because it concedes hope's declining fortunes. Yet, there is reason for hope—or, if not hope exactly, a maturely cautious sense that life with others can be understood and worked through to some more than simply satisfactory solution. At the least, it seems reasonable to conclude that the terrible grip of denial and resistance to the reality of differences constituting ordinary social life has been broken. If the cost of this social working through of the West's ignorance of itself is the loss of universal visions of social hope and liberation, then the cost is more than bearable if new sociologies can learn to tell the story of the world as it is, thus to encourage a new realism in world affairs.

Modernity was what it was. In many respects it was just fine. It has assuredly given humankind precious gifts, from literatures to technologies, that have vastly enriched the average woman and man in comparison to their counterparts in, say, 1500, at the midpoint of this millennium. This almost goes without saying. But it must be said, with conviction, for these are the resources out of which, and against which, the new sociologies will learn to rethink and retell a new world.

In this one crucial respect, today's youth enjoy a circumstance not that different from their counterparts in the previous *fin de siècle*. They too must face the present for what it is. Very few of the old dreams have more than metaphoric value today. This is the consequence of a weakened sense of the world's future. Social dreams, like individual ones, are projections of the unconscious onto an imagined future that, in the dream state, seems as real as life itself. Yet, when we wake, the dream dissolves into tenuously remembered fragments. Good psychoanalytic work encourages the patient to work through back to what was lost in order to face the present. Sociology, like psychoanalysis, therefore, begins in the present in the reporting of the first impressions, impulses, events of daily life, that form the crust covering deeper reflections. When it goes well, over much time, social analysis supports individuals, and their communities, in a thoughtful journey back and deep into a sense of how things once were. In this way, as in a curing analysis of an individual's unconscious, social analysis encourages a patient, daily working through of all that was forgotten.[12]

If, as I believe, the West was founded and has endured on the basis of the grand denial of the reality of its own aggression and evil, the modern West must be considered a good candidate for such an analysis. In order to work through to the present, it is necessary to remember. In order for the West to give up the compulsion to repeat its habitual exclusions of those who constitute the Other to its sense of the normal, in this last generation of the modern world there must be a disciplined restraint against acting and acting out. Thus can we leave emotional, intellectual, and political energy for a good sociology of the world.

Sociology, in this sense, is, as I have suggested from the beginning, the ubiquitous (though not universal) human capacity to tell the story of the world. In this respect there ought not be any difference of kind between practical and professional sociologies. At least, the difference ought not apply when professional sociology accepts its classical obligation to study and analyze the character of the world.

The debate over postmodernism that has been raging in the last decade or so is, very probably, poorly named. I do not, myself, have any doubt that the world has changed. But, even if I and others who think this way are correct, then it is still, as Talcott Parsons once said with a different purpose in mind, a bit premature to speak of postmodernism. There can be no "post" to the modern world until the modern world works through its own history. Then, it may perhaps be able to live in the present, whatever it is.

The world can be neither late-modern nor postmodern until it faces itself. This is a task currently undertaken by numerous sociologists one of whose most interesting characteristics is that they seldom identify themselves as professional sociologists.

Before the coming crisis of which Alvin Gouldner wrote, he and many others believed with good reason that sociology was a subject of general interest and central importance to the world at large. He meant, of course, professional sociology. Neither he nor C. Wright Mills could have anticipated the terrible reputational state into which the profession would fall in the 1980s. Though Gouldner saw intimations of it, he would almost certainly be shocked to learn that today sociology has lost its way in the public imagination not simply because of the collapse of the welfare state, which bankrolled the profession's golden age, but because the crisis he and others predicted was so severe that it caught the profession unawares.

Yet, what was then true about sociology is still true. It remains an endeavor of, if anything, ever more urgent centrality to worldly affairs. But its centrality is not that which it once imagined. Sociology is not so much the good, technical purveyor of the last word on the world's structures. Nor is it the decisive measurer of social facts. However well it does these things, they are not its reason for being. Likewise, the contributions it makes to the description of the social order are exceedingly important and may be sufficient justification for its institutional existence in the universities and colleges, but these descriptions are not sufficient unto sociology's moral responsiblities. In the long run, these reponsibilities are the more critical consideration. For, no more matter how authoritative sociology's descriptive work may be, it will lose its voice among the coming generation of young people if it fails to relinquish its rigid adherence to the traditional disciplinary standards.

The new generation of students, many of whom come to colleges and universities as survivors of gang warfare, apartheid, drug addiction, street violence, civil war, and worse, has no enduring need of measures well done and structures finely defined if those measures misrepresent the world they know well.[13] They, after all, grew up in a world with no central tendency and very little structure. Their survival into young adult life was in fact a matter of their learned capacity to fashion a strong sense of themselves as subjects owing allegiance to no one universal principle. They were born into weak worlds and learned to understand the structures of those worlds as structures that enforced social differences. The very idea of a reality in which sociologies of whatever kind could structure away social differences in order to provide a strong world that nurtures the universal human Subject is ludicrous to them.

But this is still how a great deal of sociology, both professional and practical, thinks. Among professional sociologists the continuing debates we engage in belie our lingering nostalgia for the good times of the classic era. Whether we consider the surprising emergence of rational choice theories, on the one hand, or the strong effects of sometimes very classically Marxist or Durkheimian, or Weberian conceptions, on the other, the fact is that a very great deal of social thought among the professionals remains wedded to its classical, modernist principles. More striking still is the fact, illustrated rather straightforwardly by the sociologies of structures discussed previously, that these differing enterprises are pursued so thoroughly within the most foundational of modernist concepts. The classic dichotomies—subject/object, micro-/macro-structures, agential self/constraining structures, and so on—are not, of course, neat equivalents. They refer to differing aspects of a wide range of sociological problems. But they all refer to those problems as though the world were, somehow, still properly viewed from within the prisms of modernist formulas. It is not that this work is wrong, as certainly it is not. There is much to be learned still from these sources. I am not, therefore, recommending the irresponsibly precipitous course of throwing out the old in favor of some new ill-defined alternative. Instead, my concern is that in the very best work and thinking in sociology there seems to be a reluctance truly to rethink the origins and implications of sociology's way of thinking, and thus the field has been defiantly resistant to the best sociology that is being done today *outside* the organized profession of sociologists.

It has long been recognized that professional sociologists have resisted a serious taking into account of feminism. If anything, their record has been even more dismal in their unwillingness to read with definitive seriousness the writings of other extramural sociologists—the new developments in queer theory and postcolonial studies, the varied and serious work by African

Americanists, the very considerable literature by and about Black feminists and other women of color. Among the human sciences, few other fields so resist these writings as does sociology, and it is not clear why this is so. Once professional sociologists led the way in breaking barriers, reading what others dared not read, rethinking the terms of social analysis. The great classic writers are proof enough of this point. But, somehow, after a period of bold adventure in the 1970s, sociology has largely lost its way.

But sociology is not lost by far. It is a reliable diagnostic judgment that, whenever there is strong resistance, one is getting close to something deeply felt. It may perhaps be that sociologists are caught in a contradiction of the field's own making—that of having banked its self-esteem so much on being the one social science most critical of the modern world (as surely it has been and, relative to the other social *sciences,* still is). Perhaps, having come to enjoy this unique status, sociology now faces the terrifying work of admitting that it did all this good critical work largely from within the culture it was critiquing. This was fine and good so long as there were only modest doubts about that culture. Now that there are not only doubts about that culture's value but also doubts about its very existence, enterprises like sociology with deep stakes in the previous order quite naturally resist the *thought* of that order ending out of fear that the ending entails their own actual loss of stake.

One must be cautious, in saying this, not to assume as a matter of fact that the end is at hand. This cannot be known. But the problem for a field like sociology, which has as its main business knowing what is going on in the world, is that such a prospect cannot possibly be examined from any position with too great an interest in believing the order itself. It is, always, difficult to go back to origins to think things through to the present, but especially so if what is conceivably entailed in the work is the *possibility* that the world in which one believes is no longer. It may be only a possibility, but even the possibility cannot be examined without the courageous first step away from old habits of thought and action.

When they were first making their new sciences, Marx and Weber and Durkheim and others borrowed. They had no choice. They thus drew heavily from others, sometimes even from their opponents—Hegel and the political economists in Marx's case; Nietzsche and Marx and Kant in Weber's; Comte, Rousseau, Montesquieu, and even Spencer in Durkheim's; Weber and James in Du Bois's; Marx in Gilman's; Anna Shaw and Martin Delany in Cooper's— and so on. There is nothing wrong with borrowing from without if borrowing is the way to get back into one's own soul.

Fortunately, for sociologists, whether practical or professional, there is today a frighteningly good number of extrasociological sociologists—many of them, like Du Bois and Gilman, situated deeply in practical sociology but able to speak to the professionals. The list of those in like position today includes, to mention but a few: Gayatri Chakravorty Spivak, Trinh T. Minh-ha, Henry Louis Gates, Toni Morrison, Spike Lee, Patricia Hill Collins, bell hooks, Teresa de Lauretis, Cornel West, Mary Daley, Andrea Dworkin, Kate Millett, Judith Butler, Donna Haraway, Gloria Anzaldúa. They do not speak as of one voice. But each of them and others of like experience with histories of exclusion are, in a most definite way, writing the sociologies of our time. To a very large extent these are the sociologists who tell the story of the world as it is. Each tells a different story thus to affirm the necessary recognition of the unstructured and unstructurable differences of a world wherein the power of inclusion slips behind the authority of those excluded. That each tells a different story does not, however, mean there is no story of the world as such to tell. It only means that, as has been said many times, that story is not the story of one world progressing toward a better day when all men will be free and good. Practical sociologists like these truly do not, for the most part, believe the world is One. Nor, however, do they believe it is hopelessly many. Rather, theirs is more a sometimes awkwardly shared sense that in their differences from each other, and collectively from the drawers of the veils, there is a surprisingly hybrid (or, in Donna Haraway's word, cyborg[14]) quality to life in the world.

The world is without any clear, assertive normal. It is a world in which what would have formerly been considered deviant is now uncomfortably more real. As a result, wherever those with wide-awake hearts begin to think through the nature of the world, they tend to come back to others in like position. Cornel West, for example, in his description of the world's transformation from 1500 through the era of the West, now into the postcolonial period, defines the new cultural worker as, to use my words, the sociologist who studies the Other and the Other's differences:

> Black culture workers must investigate and interrogate the Other of blackness-whiteness. One cannot deconstruct the binary oppositional logic of images of blackness without extending it to the contrary condition of blackness-whiteness itself. However, a mere dismantling will not do—for the very notion of a deconstructive social theory is oxymoronic. Yet social theory is what is needed to examine and *explain* the historically specific ways in which "whiteness" is a politically constructed category parasitic on "blackness," and thereby to conceive of the profoundly hybrid character of what we mean by "race," "ethnicity" and "nationality." For instance, European immigrants arrived on American shores perceiving themselves as "Irish," "Sicilian," "Lithuanian" and so on. They had to learn that they were "white" principally by adopting an American discourse of positively valued whiteness and negatively charged blackness.

This process by which people defined themselves physically, socially, sexually and even politically in terms of whiteness or blackness has much bearing not only on constructed notions of race and ethnicity but also on how we understand the changing character of US nationalities. And given the Americanization of the world, especially in the sphere of mass culture, such inquiries—encouraged by the new cultural politics of difference—raise critical issues of "hybridity," "exilic status" and "identity" on an international scale. Needless to say, these inquiries must traverse those of "male-female," "colonizer-colonized," "heterosexual-homosexual," and others, as well.[15]

Though West begins with a sociology of race in the world, he argues that race is never one—a position that Anna Julia Cooper first began to argue more than a century ago. But not only is it not one, it is necessarily transgressed and joined to all the other differences by which we now know social life is organized. These are not variables or concepts or propositions of which West speaks. They are the languages the world speaks of its very being.

These are not so much languages framed in the promises of a perfect future but—and contrary to their popular reputations—relatively modest languages. As West states clearly, it is not a question of dismantling but of examining and explaining the history of these things. Such a phrase should warm a professional sociologist's heart. It might, were it not that West means that the new cultural workers need to lead their investigations back into the origins of all those false differences, like blackness/whiteness or hetero-/homosexual, that served to organize modernity's denial of the very Others who now interrogate it. This is the social analysis with which the future sociologies should be preoccupied. It is the social analysis of where we came from—where *all* of us came from and how we came to be what we are—through those tragic histories of denial and exclusion.

Gloria Anzaldúa, who starts from a considerable number of differences from West, makes a startlingly similar statement:

For the lesbian of color, the ultimate rebellion she can make against her native culture is through her sexual behavior. She goes against two moral prohibitions: sexuality and homosexuality. Being lesbian and raised Catholic, indoctrinated as straight, I *made the choice to be queer* (for some it is genetically inherent). It's an interesting path, one that continually slips in and out of the white, the Catholic, the Mexican, the indigenous, the instincts. In and out of my head. It makes for *loquería,* the crazies. It is a path of knowledge—one of knowing (and of learning) the history of oppression of our *raza.* It is a way of balancing, of mitigating duality.[16]

Not many have had that experience; and many have experienced nothing like it, and never will. But, the fact of the world is that those in the new generation at the end of the millennium understand it better than any previous generation in the long history of modernity. They do because many of them have become practical sociologists able, like Cornel West and Gloria Anzaldúa, to work through their own personal histories by working through the histories of their races, in Anzaldúa's words. Neither race nor sex nor gender nor class nor postcolonial position is one. Even those who are not prominently touched or marked by a history of exclusion, by a line drawn through one or more of these personal histories, understand them, often against their deepest wishes.

If sociology is to serve more than its institutional purposes in the universities, it needs to face the world. This, very often, begins with facing our students. They are more likely to understand writers like West and Anzaldúa, even if to disagree with them, because they are the first generation that includes so many brought up after the mystical veils were torn.

The crisis may outlive us, but people can learn to think and feel and act their lives and their worlds just the same. It may be that the crisis is only a crisis when it is measured by the universal standard of modern progress. When modernity entered its highest cultural moment in the Enlightenment, Kant defined its moral culture as "daring to know"; but he also said that enlightened daring would bring mankind out of its immaturity. In the end, this may be what enlightened social maturity is: accepting the world for what it is, and learning to speak of it in its particular, differential details—without denying anything, without leaving oneself out, no matter how painful it might be to be there.

This once was what sociologies thought they were, and what they tried to do.

After those terrible moments when the dream fades, the world dawns just as it is. Then, morning rituals completed, sociologies begin their work. They can, if only they will.

Notes

Chapter 1

1. Quoted in Todd Gitlin, *The Sixties* (Bantam Books, 1987), p. 409.

2. Alvin W. Gouldner, *The Coming Crisis in Western Sociology* (Basic Books, 1970), p. vii.

3. Also in 1950, Erik Erikson published *Childhood and Society,* the first in a long series of critical studies of the role of youth in modern society (a theme that would become particularly salient in the 1960s). On the role of social and cultural critics in the 1950s, see also Winifred Breines, *Young, White, and Miserable* (Beacon Press, 1992); John D'Emilio, *Sexual Politics, Sexual Communities* (University of Chicago Press, 1993), especially part 2; John Patrick Diggins, *Proud Decades: America in War and Peace, 1941–1960* (W. W. Norton, 1988), part 2; Barbara Ehrenreich, *The Hearts of Men: American Dreams and the Flight from Commitment* (Anchor Books, 1983); David Halberstam, *The Fifties* (Fawcett Columbine, 1993); Andrew Ross, *No Respect: Intellectuals and Popular Culture* (Routledge, 1989), esp. ch. 3. As the publication dates of these books suggest, there has been a resurgence of critical interest in the 1950s, which in itself suggests that those who attempt to understand the current situation (late in the history of the crisis) must return to its origins early in the post–World War II period.

4. C. Wright Mills, *The Sociological Imagination* (Oxford University Press, 1959), p. 3.

5. Ibid., p. 5.

6. Gouldner, *The Coming Crisis,* p. 489. Emphasis added.

7. In 1962, *The Port Huron Statement* (the founding document of the student movement in the United States) made famous the phrase "participatory democracy," then already current in political discussions. The statement's principal author, Tom Hayden, and its principal coauthor, Richard Flacks, both acknowledged the influence of Mills on their thinking. Thus, *The Port Huron Statement* was, in many ways, a working out of a New Left social theory along the lines of Mills's sociological imagination — that is, uniting concern for the person with an historical critique of political and economic structures. For a discussion see James Miller, *Democracy Is in the Streets* (Simon & Schuster, 1987); also Richard Flacks, *Making History: The American Left and the American Mind* (Columbia University Press, 1988), and Tom Hayden, *Reunion: A Memoir* (Random House, 1988).

The phrase "personal politics" is, however, more precisely associated with the early years of the feminist movement in protest of the treatment of women in the early student movement. See Sara Evans, *Personal Politics: The Roots of Women's Liberation in the Civil Rights Movement and the New Left* (Vintage Books, 1980). Thereafter, personal politics evolved into the movement's defining theories of gender and sexual differences. See Alice Echols, *Daring to Be Bad* (University of Minnesota Press, 1993). Personal politics, and sexual politics, thus became central themes of both early feminism (Patricia Clough, *Feminist Thought* [Blackwell, 1994]) and the gay-lesbian political movement that emerged after the Stonewall

Rebellion in 1969 (Steve Seidman, *Embattled Eros: Sexual Politics and Ethics in Contemporary America* [Routledge, 1992]).

8. Though they were of the same age and generation, both died young of heart attacks—Mills in 1962 (at 43 years), Gouldner in 1980 (at 60 years).

9. On Mills, see Irving Louis Horowitz, *C. Wright Mills: An American Utopian* (Free Press, 1983); and Charles Lemert, "Whole Life Social Theory," *Theory and Society* 15 (1986):431–442. On Gouldner, see *Special Memorial Issue of Theory and Society* (vol. 11, November 1982), including Charles Lemert and Paul Piccone, "Theoretical Method and Reflexive Sociology" (pp. 733–748). To the end of his life, Gouldner sometimes distributed along with his curriculum vita a one-page prose resume of his professional accomplishments that included reference to his origins as a street-tough kid from the Bronx.

10. Talcott Parsons, *The System of Modern Societies* (Prentice-Hall, 1971), p. 143.

11. Mills (in *The Sociological Imagination,* p. 9) considered this distinction "an essential tool of the sociological imagination and a feature of all classic work in the social sciences." Obviously, Mills, like Gouldner, was a serious believer in the social *sciences,* notwithstanding the practical ideal of sociology.

12. For example, see David Caute, *The Year of the Barricades: A Journey Through 1968* (Harper & Row, 1988).

13. "SNCC Founding Statement," in Judith C. Albert and Stewart E. Albert, eds., *The Sixties Papers* (Praeger, 1984), p. 113.

14. Though he had been influenced by Gandhi's ideas in his student days, King was not alone in advocating, or even the principal source of, nonviolent methods in the early civil rights movement. See Taylor Branch, *Parting the Waters: America in the King Years* (Simon & Schuster, 1988).

15. Hayden, *Reunion,* part 2. Hayden's first marriage to Sandra Cason was short-lived. Casey Hayden and Mary King, later, were among the first to protest the treatment of women in SNCC. See Mary King, *Freedom Song* (William Morrow, 1987) and Evans, *Personal Politics.*

16. "The Port Huron Statement," in Albert and Albert, *The Sixties Papers,* p. 176.

17. Frantz Fanon, *The Wretched of the Earth,* trans. Constance Farrington (Grove Press, 1968 [1961]), pp. 36–37. See also Aimé Césaire, *Discourse on Colonialism,* trans. by Joan Pinkham (Monthly Review Press, 1972 [1955]); and Albert Memmi, *The Colonizer and the Colonized* (Beacon Press, 1967 [1957]).

18. "SNCC Speaks for Itself (1955–66)," in Albert and Albert, *The Sixties Papers,* p. 125.

19. Anna Grimshaw, ed., *C.L.R. James Reader* (Basil Blackwell, 1992), p. 367. Those mentioned (in addition to Fanon) were among the greatest twentieth-century Pan-Africanists and all were born in the Americas: Garvey (1887–1940) in Jamaica, Padmore (1903–1959) in Trinidad, Du Bois (1868–1963) in Massachusetts.

20. "The Black Panther Party Platform," in Albert and Albert, *The Sixties Papers,* p. 164.

21. Václav Havel, "The End of the Modern Era," in Charles Lemert, ed., *Social Theory: The Multicultural and Classic Readings* (Westview Press, 1993), p. 658.

Chapter 2

1. Italo Calvino, "Cybernetics and Ghosts," in *The Uses of Literature,* trans. Patrick Creagh (Harcourt Brace Jovanovich, 1982), p. 3.

2. George Bush, "America—The Last Best Hope for Man on Earth," *Vital Speeches of the*

Day 59 (January 15, 1993):194–197. The speech was delivered on December 15, 1992. It is the policy of *Vital Speeches* not to edit the material it prints. Thus the words quoted are relatively close to Bush's own as he spoke them.

3. "An occasional thoughtless thinker asserts that science is a free creation of the human spirit." George Homans, *The Nature of Social Science* (Harcourt, Brace and World, 1967), p. 7. The author of this line is one of a long line of sociologists who consider it thoughtless to construe science as free and human. Against this are social scientists who would agree with Susan Krieger (*The Mirror Dance* [Temple University Press, 1991], p. 52): "A good feminist, like a good social scientist, . . . should try to give others space to speak in their own words and style."

4. For an excellent discussion of just how imaginary a "market" can be, see Charles Smith, *Auctions* (Free Press, 1989).

5. A classic discussion of the first three qualities of social structures is Fernand Braudel, *The Mediterranean and the Mediterranean World in the Age of Philip II* (Harper Torchbooks, 1972 [1949]). Compare Immanuel Wallerstein, *Modern World System*, 3 vols. (Academic Press, 1974, 1980, 1989). On structures in space and time see Anthony Giddens, *The Constitution of Society* (University of California Press, 1984), esp. ch. 3.

6. The classic discussions of the problem of presence are the early writings of Jacques Derrida: *Speech and Other Phenomena* (Northwestern University Press, 1973); *Of Grammatology* (Johns Hopkins University Press, 1974); *Writing and Difference* (University of Chicago, 1969).

7. An important recent discussion of imagination and the structure of the modern world is Benedict Anderson, *Imagined Communities* (Verso, 1983).

8. Some important recent discussions of this principle are Fredric Jameson, *The Political Unconscious* (Cornell University Press, 1981), esp. ch. 1; Hayden White, *Metahistory* (Johns Hopkins University Press, 1973); Dierdre Boden and Don H. Zimmerman, *Talk and Social Structures* (Polity Press, 1990); Erving Goffman, *Interaction Ritual* (Doubleday, 1967).

9. This is the general version of Durkheim's formula for egoistic suicide: "Suicide varies inversely with the degree of integration of [religious, domestic, or political] society." See Émile Durkheim, *Suicide* (Free Press, 1951 [1897]), p. 208. The entire story of this famous book, to say nothing of Durkheim's idea of sociology and modern society, is suggested by and entailed in "s = 1/i." More on this follows, especially in Chapter 3.

10. Jameson (*Political Unconscious*), is particularly astute on this point. Also, Anderson's *Imagined Communities* shows how the nation-state, a most essential structure of the modern world, came to be in this way.

11. According to a 1994 U.S. Department of Census report, "The Diverse Living Arrangements of Children, 1991," only 25.9 percent of Black children and 50.8 percent of all children live in nuclear families comprising both biological parents and full brothers and/or sisters. Between 1970 and 1992, the number of children living with mothers and without fathers (of any kind) has doubled. In 1992, more than half of all Black children lived with mothers only. Between 1970 and 1992, the number of children living with unmarried couples has increased nearly 600 percent, and one of the fastest-growing domestic units is single people who have never married. For data, see *Statistical Abstracts of the United States, 1993*, pp. 54–65. For discussions from various points of view, see Judith Stacey, *Brave New Families* (Basic Books, 1988); Kath Weston, *Families We Choose: Gays, Lesbians, Kinship* (Columbia University Press, 1991); Barrie

Thorne and Marilyn Yalom, eds., *Rethinking the Family* (Northeastern University Press, 1992).

12. Herbert Gans, *The Urban Villagers* (Free Press, 1982 [1962]). For years, sociology students have read of Gans's lost neighborhood as though it were real, which it is, even though it did not survive to see the book published.

13. Lawrence Veysey, *The Emergence of the American University* (University of Chicago Press, 1965). In France, see Terrence N. Clark, *Prophets and Patrons: The French University and the Emergence of the Social Sciences* (Harvard University Press, 1973). Compare to the German case: Fritz Ringer, *The Decline of the German Mandarins* (Harvard University Press, 1969). For the University of Chicago, where sociology was first fully institutionalized, see Martin Bulmer, *The Chicago School of Sociology* (University of Chicago Press, 1984).

14. Émile Durkheim, *The Rules of Sociological Method,* ed. Steven Lukes, trans. W. D. Hall (Free Press, 1982 [1894]), p. 59. Emphasis added.

15. Both Saint-Simon and Comte thought of sociology more as a general social philosophy of modern science than as a scientific field in the academic sense. There is an important disagreement over which of the two was the first to use the term and, thus, who was the real father of sociology. Lewis Coser (*Masters of Sociological Thought* [Harcourt Brace Jovanovich, 1977], p. 3) argues for Comte. Alvin Gouldner ("Introduction," in Émile Durkheim, *Socialism,* trans. Charlotte Sattler [Collier Books, 1958], p. ix) favors Saint-Simon. Gouldner (p. ix) adds that the traditional inclination to view Comte as the true forefather of sociology arises from a desire to suppress knowledge of Saint-Simon's influence on socialism and Marx, thus to discourage the tendency to confuse sociology with socialism.

16. Clark, *Prophets and Patrons;* Charles Lemert, ed., *French Sociology: Rupture and Renewal Since 1968* (Columbia University Press, 1981), especially the chapter by Victor Karady; Steven Lukes, *Émile Durkheim: His Life and Work* (Penguin Books, 1973); Dominick LaCapra, *Émile Durkheim: Sociologist and Philosopher* (University of Chicago, 1972). See also articles in the special issues of *Revue française de Sociologie,* vols. 17 (1976) and 20 (1979), both edited by Philippe Besnard. See also Philippe Besnard, *The Sociological Domain: The Durkheimians and the Founding of French Sociology* (Cambridge University Press, 1983).

17. For example, John Patrick Diggins, *Proud Decades: America in War and Peace, 1941–1960* (W. W. Norton, 1988), pp. 248–249. Feminism, in particular, takes Parsons seriously in this way (for example, Winifred Breines, *Young, White and Miserable* [Beacon Press, 1992], ch. 1).

18. Durkheim, *Rules,* p. 163.

19. Émile Durkheim, *Division of Labor in Society,* trans. George Simpson (Free Press, 1964 [1893]), p. 409. Emphasis added.

20. For example, Durkheim's "Professional Ethics" (*Professional Ethics and Civic Morals,* trans. Cornelia Brookfield [Routledge, 1992]), one of his many essays on ethics, begins: "The science of morals and rights should be based on the study of moral and juridical facts" (p. 1).

21. Durkheim, *Rules,* pp. 51–52.

22. Émile Durkheim, *Montesquieu and Rousseau: Forerunners of Sociology,* trans. Ralph Manheim (University of Michigan Press, 1960).

23. Though neither would put it just this way, see Jeffrey Alexander, "The Centrality of the Classics," in Anthony Giddens and Jonathan Turner, eds., *Social Theory* (Stanford University Press, 1987); and Calvino, *Uses of Literature,* ch. 2, "Why Read the Classics?" Also, there are instances, especially among certain professional sociologists, where the refusal to be known as one who reads any classic is an appropriated identity.

24. Foucault, most significantly in later years, developed the idea of the unthinkable and the unsayable with more or less evident reference to its classic sources, which include Marx, Freud, Hegel, and Nietzsche. See Michel Foucault, *The Order of Things* (Vintage Books, 1970), pp. 322–328. The unthought appears again in this book, Chapter 4.

25. Among those who take Durkheim's *Elementary Forms* as their classic are Claude Lévi-Strauss (for example, see *The Scope of Anthropology*, trans. Sherry Ortner Paul and Robert A. Paul [Jonathan Cape, 1967]); and Michel de Certeau (*The Practice of Everyday Life*, trans. Steven F. Randall [University of California Press], ch. 5). Those who take Durkheim's *Suicide* as their classic include Arthur Stinchcombe (*Constructing Social Theories* [University of California, 1968], pp. 15–18) and James Coleman (*Foundations of Social Theory* [Harvard University Press, 1990], p. 13). Sociologically, the former two have very little in common with the latter two.

26. Émile Durkheim, *Elementary Forms of the Religious Life*, trans. Joseph Swain (Free Press, 1965 [1912]), p. 29.

27. Ibid., p. 79.

28. On the odd juxtaposition of primitives and others see Marianna Torgovnick, *Gone Primitive: Savage Intellectuals, Modern Lives* (University of Chicago Press, 1990), esp. chs. 1 and 11, where the Jew and the primitive in Durkheim's successor, Lévi Strauss, are discussed.

29. See Book 2 of Durkheim's *Division of Labor*.

30. Durkheim, *Division of Labor*, 1964, p. 173. Emphasis added.

31. In French, the crucial phrase "There must, then, be [some other social link]" is *Il faut donc bien*. The English "must" translates the French idiom *il faut*. The French, literally, "it is necessary that," is, in effect, a more forceful locution, consistent with colloquial and logical language in which the speaker wants to say "this *must* follow or else everything else makes little sense."

32. Blaise Pascal, *Pensées*, section 4.

33. Durkheim, *Elementary Forms*, p. 492. Emphasis added. Compare Durkheim and Marcel Mauss, *Primitive Classification*, trans. Rodney Needham (University of Chicago Press, 1963).

34. To speak of the sociological imagination in this sense is not necessarily to reduce social things to the psychological. One such alternative use of the imaginary is Jacques Lacan's *Écrits*, trans. Alan Sheridan (W. W. Norton, 1977), among many others, including those works indebted to Lacan.

Chapter 3

1. Sanyika Shakur, aka Monster Kody Scott, *Monster: Autobiography of an L.A. Gang Member* (Penguin, 1994), pp. 331–333.

2. The story of Martin Guerre (1539–1560) was rediscovered and made known by Natalie Zeamon Davis; see *Return of Martin Guerre* (Harvard University Press, 1983). The story has been made into two recent films, one of the same title and another, set just after the American Civil War, called *Sommersby*.

3. Georg Simmel, "The Stranger," in Charles Lemert, ed., *Social Theory: The Multicultural and Classic Readings* (Westview Press, 1993), p. 200.

4. Blanche DuBois's memorable line in Tennessee Williams's *Streetcar Named Desire* is also the main point of Erving Goffman's important study of social identities, *Stigma* (Simon & Schuster, 1963).

5. That hope was improbably vested in the return of a charismatic authority. This ideal type, borrowed principally from the sociology of religious prophets, appears throughout Weber's writings. See, among other places, Max Weber, *Economy and Society* (University of California Press, 1978), part 1, ch. 1 ("Basic Sociological Terms"); ch. 3 ("Types of Legitimate Domination"); part 2, ch. 16 ("Religious Groups"); ch. 10 ("Domination and Legitimation"). In Weber's *Protestant Ethic and the Spirit of Capitalism* (Scribner's, 1950), something like charisma is the spirit lost to the iron cage; as in "Science as a Vocation" (in *From Max Weber* [Oxford University Press, 1946]), it is the intervening spirit of charismatic grace that grants the scientist his ideas in the midst of routine calculations. Both at the end of *Protestant Ethic* and at the beginning of "Science as a Vocation," it is a charismatic power that gives the individual "personality" and saves him from being a mere "specialist." See, for example, "Science as a Vocation," p. 137.

6. Most famously, this is the crude political ideal behind the 1848 *Manifesto of the Communist Party,* one of Marx's early writings. He did not abandon it in the so-called mature work, *Capital (I),* in 1867. But the idea of lost history is most explicitly expressed in the earliest writings, the *1844 Manuscripts* and *The German Ideology* (1845–1846).

7. See Freud's "Papers on Technique (1911–1915)," in *Standard Edition* (Hogarth Press, 1958), vol. 12, esp. pp. 85–266; and his numerous case presentations, most notably the notorious (but formative) 1905 [actually 1900] case of Dora, "Fragments of an Analysis of a Case of Hysteria," in *Standard Edition,* vol. 7, pp. 3–122.

8. Émile Durkheim, *Division of Labor in Society,* trans. George Simpson (Free Press, 1964 [1893]), p. 173. This is an edited line from the passage discussed at length in the previous chapter.

9. Émile Durkheim, *Suicide,* trans. John A. Spaulding and George Simpson (Free Press, 1951 [1897]), p. 38.

10. Ibid., p. 147.

11. Alex Kotlowitz, *There Are No Children Here* (Doubleday, 1991), p. x.

12. James Garbarino et al., *Children in Danger* (Jossey-Bass, 1992).

13. In a sense Freud's oedipal child was not really a child. He was the projection of adult fears into the child's experience.

14. Durkheim, *Suicide,* p. 213. Emphasis added.

15. Ibid., p. 385.

16. Ibid.

17. Steven Lukes, *Émile Durkheim* (Penguin, 1973), p. 39.

18. Durkheim, *Division of Labor,* p. 64.

19. Ibid., p. 226; emphasis added.

20. The opening chapter of Book 2 of *Division of Labor* is a virtual outline of the argument of *Suicide.*

21. Durkheim, *Division of Labor,* p. 138. The book's empirical section is chapters 4, 5, 6, and 7, which conclude Book 1 (in which the classic distinction between mechanical and organic societies and their laws is made). The passage quoted is in the conclusion to Book 1.

22. Ibid.

23. Exodus 19:5–6. On the centrality of the covenant see George E. Mendenhal, *Law and Covenant in Israel and the Ancient Near East* (The Presbyterian Board of Colportage of

Western Pennsylvania, 1955); and Norman Gottwald, "Israel and the Covenant," in Gottwald, *Light to the Nations* (Harper, 1959), ch. 5.

24. See, for example, Mircea Eliade, *Myth of the Eternal Return* (Princeton University Press, 1954).

25. "Man is a moral being only because he lives in society, since morality consists in being solidary with a group." See Durkheim, *Division of Labor,* p. 399, to which compare p. 403: "To be a person is to be an autonomous source of action."

26. Durkheim, *Suicide,* p. 35.

27. Ibid., p. 276.

28. Ibid., p. 258. Emphasis added.

29. Ibid., p. 169.

30. Ibid., p. 168. In the passage immediately following, Durkheim explicitly describes the Jew as the modern primitive: "This is the reason for the complexity he presents, primitive in certain respects, in others, he is an intellectual and man of culture" (p. 168).

31. A third type, which concerned political disruptions, was weakly developed relative to the other two.

32. The statistical analyses alluded to in the following occur in Book 2 of *Suicide,* chapter 3, for those concerning egoistic suicide, and chapter 5 concerning anomic.

33. Of altruistic, Durkheim says (*Suicide,* p. 373) that it "certainly has no share in the present progress of suicide" and that the egoistic and anomic are the only forms "whose development can be regarded as morbid, and so we have only them to consider."

34. Ibid., p. 383.

35. My interpretation of Durkheim's dealings with women was worked out before I was thoroughly familiar with Jennifer Lehmann's impressive work on the subject. Her studies are far more extensive than mine, especially on Durkheim's attitudes toward feminism. See Lehmann, *Durkheim and Women* (University of Nebraska Press, 1994). The major difference between us is that she tends to see his trouble with women as a series of contradictions in his logic, while I see it more as the inevitable consequence of his modernizing project. The problem was not Durkheim's alone. See also Lehmann's "Durkheim's Theories of Deviance and Suicide," *American Journal of Sociology* 100, no. 4 (January 1994); and *Deconstructing Durkheim* (Routledge, 1993).

36. Durkheim, *Suicide,* p. 258. Here he attempts, vainly, to distinguish the two types after admitting they are "kindred."

37. Ibid., p. 259.

38. Ibid., p. 215. Emphasis added (as though it were necessary).

39. On the issues invoked by this distinction, see (among the many feminist discussions available) Diana Fuss, *Essentially Speaking* (Routledge, 1989), especially chs. 1, 2.

40. Quoted material in this paragraph and the following is in Durkheim, *Suicide,* pp. 269–276, the curious section with which Durkheim concludes his discussion of anomic suicide. Emphasis added.

41. Ibid., p. 272.

42. Ibid., p. 386. Emphasis added. The quotation following is earlier in *Suicide,* p. 379.

43. Ibid., p. 384. Other quotations in this paragraph are in the same place, pp. 384–386. Emphasis, further on, on "psychological inequality" is added.

44. Lévi-Strauss, *The Scope of Anthropology,* trans. Sherry Ortner Paul and Robert A. Paul (Jonathan Cape, 1967). See also Charles Lemert, "Canonical Limits of Durkheim's First Classic," *Sociological Forum* 9 (1994):87–92.

Chapter 4

1. The play on the term *man,* in this and the previous paragraph, is intended. The question "Who is man?" may be the central founding question of modern culture. The question has been asked in various ways of the human and social sciences, including: Michel Foucault, *The Order of Things* (Vintage Books, 1973), especially chs. 9, 10; Jacques Derrida, "Structure, Sign and Play in the Human Sciences," in Derrida, *Writing and Difference* (University of Chicago Press, 1978 [1967]); Jean François Lyotard, *The Postmodern Condition* (University of Minnesota Press, 1984); Richard Rorty, *Philosophy and the Mirror of Nature* (Princeton University Press, 1979); and Charles Lemert, *Sociology and the Twilight of Man* (Southern Illinois University Press, 1979).

2. *New York Times,* September 13, 1992, p. 31.

3. Chip Brown, "I Now Walk into the Wild," *New Yorker,* February 8, 1993, p. 40.

4. Ibid., p. 44.

5. On the relation between death and modern culture see Zygmunt Bauman, *Mortality, Immortality and Other Life Strategies* (Stanford University Press, 1992), esp. chs. 3, 4. Death as a matter of social life is seldom discussed by sociologists. Compare Sogyal Rinpoche, *The Tibetan Book of Living and Dying* (Harper/San Francisco, 1993).

6. Still today, there is no better definition of modern moral culture than Immanuel Kant's (1724–1804) opening words to his 1783 essay "What Is Enlightenment?": "Enlightenment is man's leaving his self-caused immaturity. Maturity is the capacity to use one's intelligence without the guidance of another. . . . *Sapere aude* [Dare to know!]." See "What Is Enlightenment," trans Carl J. Friedrich, in *The Philosophy of Kant: Immanuel Kant's Moral and Political Writings* (Modern Library, 1993).

7. See Marianna Torgovnick, *Gone Primitive: Savage Intellectuals, Modern Lives* (University of Chicago Press, 1990).

8. Philosophically, such a conclusion—however tentatively put—is troubling to those disturbed by relativism (Allan Bloom in *Closing of the American Mind* [Simon & Schuster, 1987]). But relativism is a danger only to those who believe a final, or absolute, truth of things is needed. Against this philosophical attitude is another with deep roots in modern thought. In this tradition, the distinction is made between pure and practical truth (Kant). The two attitudes are not completely opposed. From the beginning with Kant, among those who acknowledge the difference between pure and practical truth claims, there have been attempts to construct virtually final truth out of practical reason. In fact, it has been said, with remarkable plausibility, that modern culture itself was founded in the conviction that practical truths could answer the principal philosophical question of modern life. If that question is What is Man? then some among the proponents of practical reason have answered: Man is the practical equivalent to Truth. Against which the first tradition professes a fear of relativism (as in Allan Bloom's horror at the effects of Nietzsche on modern culture) without being willing to defend philosophical absolutism in so many words. Since Bloom that tradition has been every bit as preoccupied with cultural politics as have the relativists (so-called) of the cultural left.

9. In particular, see Durkheim's explicit statements on Kant in *Elementary Forms of the Religious Life,* trans. Joseph W. Swain (Free Press, 1965 [1912]), p. 494.

10. Michel deCerteau, *The Practice of Everyday Life,* trans. Steven F. Rendall (University of California Press, 1984), p. 68.

11. Foucault, *The Order of Things,* p. 312.

12. Kant took up the philosophical problem of the proofs of God's existence in two early (1763) writings: *The Only Possible Proof for Demonstrating the Existence of God* and *Inquiry*

into the Clearness of the Principles of Natural Theology. For a discussion see Carl J. Friedrich ("Introduction," in *The Philosophy of Kant* [Modern Library, 1993], pp. xxiv–xxvii), who views these works as "set[ting] the stage for [Kant's] own monumental work" (p. xxvii). Kant frequently referred to God and religion in general in his writing on metaphysics and moral philosophy. See, notably, subsection 57 in *Prolegomena to Every Future Metaphysics* (1783) and *Religion Within the Limits of Reason Alone* (1793). His famous "Fundamental Law of Pure, Practical Reason" was "Act so that the maxim of your will can be valid at the same time as a principle of universal legislation." To which the corollary asserts that "pure reason is practical by itself alone and gives man a universal law we call moral law" (*Critique of Pure Practical Reason,* subsection 7). Here Kant founded reason in practical morality. Later, in *Religion Within the Limits,* he did the same for God (see especially the striking final paragraph). Quotations from selections in Friedrich, *The Philosophy of Kant,* pp. 245, 246.

13. Durkheim, *Elementary Forms,* p. 466.

14. Foucault, *The Order of Things,* p. 326.

15. See Derrida, "Structure, Sign and Play."

16. He is, in this sense, an unwitting participant in orientalism. See Edward Said, *Orientalism* (Pantheon, 1978) and *Culture and Imperialism* (Knopf, 1993).

17. Max Weber, *The Protestant Ethic and the Spirit of Capitalism,* p. 182.

18. See Alan Sica, *Weber, Irrationality, and Social Order* (University of California Press, 1988).

19. Weber suffered an extended period of mental illness from 1897 to 1903 that eased just as he resumed work on the essays that became *The Protestant Ethic.* See Marianne Weber, *Max Weber: A Biography,* trans. Harry Zohn (Transaction, 1988), ch. 8; and Dirk Kaesler, *Max Weber: An Introduction to His Life and Work,* trans. Philippa Hurd (University of Chicago Press, 1988), pp. 10–13. After a comprehensive account of the organic and psychodynamic bases for Weber's long illness, Kaesler unaccountably concludes that it was "certainly not" a "mental illness" (p. 12). Sociologists tend to resist the inhibiting power of the unconscious.

20. See Sigmund Freud, "Two Classes of Instincts" (1923), in "The Ego and the Id" (part 4), in *Standard Edition* (Hogarth Press, 1958), vol. 19. Though the idea of the mental life as a continuous struggle appears throughout Freud's writings (beginning prominently with *The Interpretation of Dreams* in 1900), its most visible expression is in the central concept of his clinical work, resistance. See Freud, "Resistances to Psychoanalysis" (1924), in *Standard Edition,* vol. 19, pp. 213–222; and "Remembering, Repeating, and Working Through" (1914), in *Standard Edition,* vol. 12, pp. 145–156. For a history of the concept resistance, see R. J. Marshall, *Resistant Interactions* (Human Sciences Press, 1982), ch. 1.

21. This famous passage appears in *Capital (I)* just at the end of part 2, where he makes the transition to the analysis of how surplus value is extracted, not in market exchange, but in the structure of capitalist production.

22. The camera obscura metaphor appears in Marx's *The German Ideology* and is discussed further on. The metaphor draws on the basic fact of visual perception that everything seen by the eye, as by the photographic camera, is inverted.

23. George Kennan, *Memoirs 1925–1950* (Pantheon, 1967), p. 550.

24. A concise list of possible definitions is provided by Chaim Waxman in his introduction to Waxman, ed., *The End of Ideology Debate* (Funk & Wagnalls, 1969), pp. 3–4. For more discursive studies of the concept, its history and meanings, see Hans Barth, *Truth and Ideology,* trans. Frederick Lilge (University of California Press, 1976); Terry Eagleton,

Ideology: An Introduction (Verso, 1991); John B. Thompson, *Studies in the Theory of Ideology* (University of California Press, 1984); John B. Thompson, *Ideology and Modern Culture* (Stanford University Press, 1990), chs. 1, 2.

25. This is from the camera obscura passage previously referred to (and discussed further on), quoted from Marx, *The German Ideology,* in Robert Tucker, ed., *The Marx-Engels Reader* (W. W. Norton, 1978), p. 154.

26. Karl Marx, "Theses on Feuerbach," in Tucker, *The Marx-Engels Reader,* p. 145.

27. Most notably, see David Harvey, *The Condition of Postmodernity* (Blackwell, 1989), esp. part 1; and Marshall Berman, *All That Is Solid Melts into Air* (Penguin, 1988). Compare Malcolm Bradbury and James McFarlane, *Modernism, 1890–1930* (Harmondsworth, 1976); Barry Smart, *Modern Conditions; Postmodern Controversies* (Routledge, 1992). For analytic discussions, see (among numerous sources) Jürgen Habermas, *The Philosophical Discourse of Modernity* (MIT Press, 1987); Martin Jay, *Fin de Siècle Socialism* (Routledge, 1988), especially the discussions (chs. 7–11) of Gouldner, Habermas, and Hans Blumenberg's *The Legitimacy of the Modern Age.* The most brilliant recent discussion of related issues is, in my opinion, Martin Jay, *Downcast Eyes* (University of California Press, 1993).

28. Karl Marx, "Manifesto of the Communist Party," in Tucker, *The Marx-Engels Reader,* p. 476.

29. Among numerous sources, see Gloria Anzaldúa, *Borderlands/La Frontera: The New Mestiza* (Spinsters/Aunt Lute Press, 1987); James Baldwin, *Notes of a Native Son* (Beacon Press, 1955) and *Fire Next Time* (Dial, 1963); Cherríe Moraga and Gloria Anzaldúa, eds., *This Bridge Called My Back* (Kitchen Table/Women of Color Press, 1981); Patricia Nelson Limerick, *The Legacy of Conquest* (W. W. Norton, 1987); Richard Slotkin, *Regeneration Through Violence* (Wesleyan University Press, 1973) and *The Fatal Environment* (Wesleyan University Press, 1985); Ronald Takaki, *A Different Mirror* (Little, Brown, 1993).

30. It is far from clear that there has even been a postmodern era. If there has been, and this is it, one might imagine that the Velvet Revolutions and the Persian Gulf exercise were its manifestations. In the former, political creativity took the form of reinventing an odd mixture of social democracy and state capitalism in the heart to Europe. In the latter, the destructive potential of world politics is precariously displaced from Europe into the new semiperiphery, and a worldwide Eurocentric social contract against the supposed Hitlerian devil in Iraq is held at bay by the utter uncertainty of the drift of Arab brotherhood and the weird inability of world power to pay the cost of intervention.

31. See Hans Barth, *Truth and Ideology* (University of California Press, 1976), ch. 1. Compare Alvin Gouldner, *The Dialectic of Ideology and Technology* (Seabury Press, 1976), pp. 11–14.

32. Marx, *The German Ideology,* part 1. See Martin Jay, "Ideology and Ocularcentrism: Is There Anything Behind the Mirror's Tain?" in Charles Lemert, ed., *Intellectuals and Politics* (Sage, 1991) and, for the complete discussion of ocularcentrism, see Jay, *Downcast Eyes.* The quote just following is in Marx, "Manifesto," p. 488.

33. It could be said that the camera obscura metaphor leads directly to the possible unification of a sociology of knowledge with the psychoanalytic interpretation of dreams—a prospect only partly explored in Althusser's Lacanian reading of ideology in the 1960s. See Louis Althusser, "Ideology and Ideological State Apparatuses," in *Lenin and Philosophy,* trans. Ben Brewster (Monthly Review Press, 1971), pp. 127–188.

34. Karl Mannheim, *Ideology and Utopia,* trans. Louis Wirth and Edward Shils (Harcourt Brace & World, 1985 [1936]), p. 265. Compare Robert K. Merton, *Social Theory and Social Structure* (Free Press, 1957), chs. 12, 13.

35. Nonetheless, the two sides of Marx's original formulation remained, though highly refracted, in the curious ability of the Mertonian tradition to give intellectual safe haven to political radicals during the McCarthy era. Alvin Gouldner, whose 1976 book *The Dialectic of Ideology and Technology* was an important contribution to current thinking on ideology, was the most notable of those protected, and inspired, by Merton.

36. Seymour Martin Lipset, *Political Man* (Doubleday, 1960). Quoted here from a selection in Waxman, *The End of Ideology Debate*, p. 69.

37. Cited in Elaine Tyler May, *Homeward Bound: American Families in the Cold War* (Basic Books, 1988), p. 17.

38. From *The Port Huron Statement*, end of the section "The Society Beyond," reprinted in James Miller, *"Democracy Is in the Streets"* (Simon & Schuster, 1987), p. 336.

39. Jean Baudrillard, *Selected Writings*, ed. Mark Poster (Stanford University Press, 1988), p. 167.

40. Ibid., p. 171.

41. Guy Debord, *Society of the Spectacle* (Black and Red Press, 1977 [1967]), paragraphs 1, 3, 4. For a discussion see Sadie Plant, *The Most Radical Gesture: The Situationalist International in the Postmodern Age* (Routledge, 1992).

42. The roots of radical postmodernism in modernist thought are explicit. See Plant, *The Most Radical Gesture*, on the Marxist roots of Debord and the situationalists. Also see Douglas Kellner, *Jean Baudrillard: From Marxism to Postmodernism and Beyond* (Stanford University Press, 1989), on the Marxist, and other, backgrounds to Baudrillard. One of the most interesting cases in the intellectual heritage of radical postmodernism is Umberto Eco's *Travels in Hyperreality* (Harcourt Brace Jovanovich, 1983), which appears to be a kind of traveler's fantasy (much like Baudrillard's *Cool Memories* [Verso, 1990]). But Eco's *Travels* can be directly traced to his early, formal Piercean and Saussurean theory of semiotics, in particular his theory of lies (Umberto Eco, *A Theory of Semiotics* [University of Indiana Press, 1976], pp. 6–7).

43. Debord, *Society of the Spectacle*, para. 213.

44. See, for example, Jay, "Ideology and Ocularcentrism," which appears in Martin Jay, *Force Fields* (Routledge, 1993), as well as in Lemert's *Intellectuals and Politics*. Compare John B. Thompson, *Studies in the Theory of Ideology* (University of California Press, 1984), chs. 1, 3.

45. The term "radical modernism" is taken loosely from Anthony Giddens, *The Consequences of Modernity* (Stanford University Press, 1990). Though Habermas has been the leading proponent of this position, Giddens and Pierre Bourdieu are among its most important representatives in academic sociology. Properly speaking, both C. Wright Mills and Alvin Gouldner should be considered radical modernists. For a recent attempt to rethink the critical side of radical modernism, see Craig Calhoun, *Critical Social Theory: Culture, History, and the Challenge of Difference* (Blackwell, 1995).

46. Jay, "Ideology and Ocularcentrism," p. 154.

47. Dorothy Smith, *The Everyday World as Problematic* (Northeastern University Press, 1987), p. 225. For a discussion of Smith see articles by Patricia Hill Collins, R. W. Connell, and Charles Lemert in a special symposium in *Sociological Theory* 10 (1992), edited by Barrie Thorne and Barbara Laslett. On Smith and Hartsock, see Patricia Clough, *Feminist Thought: Desire, Power, and Academic Discourse* (Blackwell, 1994), ch. 3.

48. Among the strategic postmodernists, Foucault has been the target chosen most often by postmodernism's opponents. This is perhaps because his writing is perceived to be more accessible than either Derrida's or Jacques Lacan's. Whether good enough or not, these are the reasons I have chosen Foucault for discussion here. I take the view that, on the essentials, among the variety of poststructuralisms, the similarities are greater than the differences. See Charles Lemert, "The Uses of French Structuralisms in Sociology," in George Ritzer, ed., *Frontiers of Social Theory* (Columbia University Press, 1990), pp. 230–255; and Lemert, "General Social Theory, Irony, Postmodernism," in Steven Seidman and David G. Wagner, eds., *Postmodernism and Social Theory* (Blackwell, 1992). As for the Derridean line, the sources are too numerous to list, though Christopher Norris, *Derrida* (Harvard University Press, 1987), is still the most reliable secondary introduction. As for the third line of strategic postmodernism, the most salient are the varieties of rereadings of Freud inspired by Jacques Lacan, which have had a major impact on film, literary, feminist, and cultural theory. Few of the attempts to make Lacan accessible succeed, though Jane Gallop's *Reading Lacan* (Cornell University Press, 1985) comes close.

None of these three traditions has made major impact on academic sociology, though important beginnings have been made in Patricia Clough, *The End(s) of Ethnography* (Sage, 1992); and Steven Seidman, *Contested Knowledge* (Blackwell, 1994), especially part 3. Compare Charles Lemert, "Social Theory at the Early End of a Short Century," *Sociological Theory* 12 (1994):140–152.

49. Michel Foucault, *Archaeology of Knowledge,* trans. A. M. Sheridan Smith (Pantheon, 1972), and *Order of Things* (Vintage, 1973) are the two works in which Foucault presented his ideas in a structuralist mode, thus creating the false impression of an ahistorical theoretical attitude. All of his important empirical studies are attempts to reformulate concrete histories of modernity.

50. Michel Foucault, "The Subject and Power," reprinted in Hubert Dreyfus and Paul Rabinow, *Michel Foucault* (University of Chicago Press, 1983), p. 211.

51. Ibid., p. 212.

52. Michel Foucault, *History of Sexuality, Vol. I* (Pantheon, 1978), pp. 30–32. Whether the bucolic pleasures were inconsequential to the little girl is another matter.

53. Ibid., p. 10. Marcuse's discussion of repressive desublimation is in *One Dimensional Man* (Beacon Press, 1964).

54. Louis Althusser, "Ideological State Apparatuses and the State," in *Lenin and Philosophy,* trans. Ben Brewster (New Left Books, 1971), esp. pp. 162–177. The application of Lacanian psychoanalytic theory is, in fact, very short of being either Lacanian or psychoanalytic (as Althusser himself comes close to admitting in the appendix following "Freud and Lacan," in *Lenin and Philosophy,* pp. 189–219). For years this essay has been inappropriately used as a shortcut to reading Lacan, much to the detriment of an honest interpretation of either Lacan or Althusser. Althusser's famous essay on ideology is much closer to Marx's thinking in *The German Ideology* than to Lacan's theory of the mirror stage and the imaginary. Thus, the irony that Althusser's essay served to call attention to Lacan and psychoanalysis while itself remaining fundamentally Marxist.

55. Foucault, *History of Sexuality, Vol. I,* p. 12.

56. Nancy Hartsock, "Foucault on Power: A Theory for Women?" in Linda Nicholson, *Feminism/Postmodernism* (Routledge, 1990), p. 163.

57. See Nancy Fraser, "Michel Foucault: A Young 'Conservative'?" in *Unruly Practices* (University of Minnesota Press, 1989), ch. 2. Quotes following are on p. 32, same source.

For a related discussion of Fraser on Foucault, see Charles Lemert, "Social Theory at the Early End of a Short Century," pp. 142–144.

58. The wild card figure is after Alvin Gouldner, especially his idea of the new class as a flawed universal class in *The Future of Intellectuals and the Rise of the New Class* (Seabury Press, 1979).

59. Elaine Tyler May, *Homeward Bound* (Basic Books, 1988).

60. Ibid., p. 190.

Chapter 5

1. In all the reports from August 19, 1992, through late September 1993, though mention is often made of repeated shovings and insults, no indication is made of assault charges brought or sustained against Hogue. When, finally, he was taken into custody, a criminal mischief charge for damage to an automobile, previously held in abeyance, was reactivated ("Homeless Man of West Side Is Held Again," *New York Times*, September 26, 1993).

2. But a traditionally high road media source, CBS News, also used the savage theme in "Wild Man of West 96th Street," *60 Minutes*, August 15, 1993 (a rebroadcast).

3. In August 1993, Hogue was granted release from a New York City psychiatric facility to live in Bridgeport, Connecticut, with his son. Freedom was on the condition that "he stays drug free and does not cause trouble" (*New York Times*, August 25, 1993). Hogue, it turned out, received a monthly disability check (owing to a head injury while in the navy). It seems that he had carefully saved the proceeds. At the time of release he was reported to have enjoyed a perfect credit rating and $30,000 in the bank (*New York Post*, August 11, 1993). By late September 1993, Hogue had relapsed and was once again held for violating the terms of his release (*New York Times*, September 26, 1993). The year following, his status uncertain, Hogue had become a virtual symbol of the supposed "benefits" of involuntary confinement for the mentally ill. Beginning with "Mental Hospitals for Unwilling Gain Support" (*New York Times*, June 17, 1994), the journalistic accounts no longer question that Hogue's problem is mental illness. The "Wild Man" had become, in just a little more than one journalistic year, a "patient."

Among recent sources on freedom and the savage in Western culture, see Marianna Torgovnick, *Gone Primitive: Savage Intellectuals, Modern Lives* (University of Chicago Press, 1990). One of the basic variants of the theme is that which associates savage with Black, for which see also Mary Ann Doane, "Dark Continents," in *Femmes Fatales* (Routledge, 1991).

4. Jonathan Raban, "The Next Last Frontier: A Newcomer's Journey Through the Pacific Northwest," *Harper's*, August 1993.

5. *Thomas Jefferson, Writings* (Library of America, 1984), p. 1130.

6. *The Oxford English Dictionary* (Oxford University Press, 1971) lists twenty-five groups of meanings for "world," of which the two most familiar modern meanings rank no higher than ninth, "The material universe as an ordered system," and tenth, "The sphere within which one's interests are bound up." By comparison, the first of the definitions listed ("The earthly state of human existence; the present life") is decidedly archaic.

7. Sigmund Freud, *Civilization and Its Discontents*, trans. James Strachey (W. W. Norton, 1962 [1930]).

8. This basic metaphor appears in the original theory of dreams (*Interpretation of*

Dreams, trans. James Strachey (Avon Books, 1965 [1900]) and his many lectures and comprehensive summaries of psychoanalysis, including: *Introductory Lectures on Psychoanalysis,* trans. James Strachey (W. W. Norton, 1966 [1917]) and even the posthumous *An Outline of Psycho-analysis,* trans. James Strachey (W. W. Norton, 1969 [1940]).

9. Weber's most memorable statement of the problem, the famous iron cage passage at the end of *The Protestant Ethic and the Spirit of Capitalism,* trans. Talcott Parsons (Scribner's, 1958), turns on the mysterious quotation from an unidentified source: "Specialists without spirit; sensualists without heart: this nullity imagines that it has attained a level of civilization never before achieved" (p. 182). Alan Sica makes a convincing case that the words are Weber's but put in the manner of Goethe to heighten their literary force and legitimacy. See Alan Sica, "Reasonable Science, Unreasonable Life: The Happy Fictions of Marx, Weber, and Social Theory," in Robert J. Antonio and Ronald Glassman, eds., *A Weber-Marx Dialogue* (University of Kansas Press, 1985), pp. 73–75. Another possible source is Nietzsche, for which Sica finds little evidence (personal communication, Alan Sica, October 10, 1994).

10. Referring evidently to Marx's camera obscura metaphor in *The German Ideology,* Gouldner remarked: "Where did the *theorists* of this class struggle fit into the supposed cleavage between proletariat and capitalist class? When the question is raised, there is only embarrassment covered over by a silence. (One is not supposed to ask the television audience, 'Where does the cameraman fit in?')." See Alvin Gouldner, *The Future of Intellectuals and the Rise of the New Class* (New York: Seabury Press, 1979).

11. In his 1911–1915 papers on technique, Freud is remarkably confident; for example, "Not only *some* but *all* of what is essential from childhood has been retained in these memories. It is simply a question of knowing how to extract it out of them by analysis." See Sigmund Freud, "Remembering, Repeating, and Working Through," in *Standard Edition* (Hogarth Press, 1958), vol. 12, p. 148.

12. See discussion of Foucault's unthought in the previous chapter. Compare Charles Lemert and Garth Gillan, *Michel Foucault: Social Theory and Transgression* (Columbia University Press, 1983).

13. Hence Durkheim's influence on subsequent sociology, which was never, as some think, simply that of being the first thoroughly "empirical" sociology. The two founders of mid-twentieth-century sociology both, notably, took the main premises of the moral elements in their sociologies from this theme in Durkheim: Talcott Parsons in *Structure of Social Action* (1937) (Free Press, 1949); and Robert K. Merton in "Social Structure and Anomie" (1938), in *Social Theory and Social Structure* (Free Press, 1957). More on this is in Chapters 6 and 7. The "he," by the way, is meant to be Durkheim's.

14. Thus, Weber's insight that the decisive feature of modern moral life was not at all the practices used to pursue moral purposes but the ethical orientation developed through those practices. Therefore, to use his most famous example, asceticism was practiced both by the medieval monastic and the modern entrepreneur. What distinguished them was that the former was oriented away from this world, the latter toward it.

15. Georg Simmel, "The Metropolis and Mental Life," in Donald N. Levine, ed., *Georg Simmel on Individuality and Social Forms* (University of Chicago Press, 1971), p. 327. Simmel's essay is possibly the most vivid, and for this reason famous, description not just of modern life but of its differences from traditional life. Both in this, and the line about calculations, Simmel's view was virtually the same as Weber's.

16. William James is the classic source of a comparison of self to soul. In *Varieties of*

Religious Experience (Fontana, 1960), for example, he describes the soul as "the hot place of a man's consciousness" and "the habitual center of his personal energy" (p. 200). Curiously, and conversely, when James wrote formally of the self, in *Principles of Psychology* (Harvard University Press, 1981), he stipulated the "Spiritual Self" as one of the structural features of consciousness of self.

The equation of self to soul is made in so many words by Allan Bloom in *Closing of the American Mind* (Simon & Schuster, 1987), p. 173. Compare Charles Taylor, *Sources of the Self* (Harvard University Press, 1989), and Charles Lemert, "Dark Thoughts about the Self," in Craig Calhoun, ed., *Social Theory and the Politics of Identity* (Blackwell, 1994), ch. 3.

17. Most recently, see Charles Taylor's remark: "But Descartes gives Augustinian inwardness a radical twist and takes it in a quite new direction, which has also been epoch-making. The change might be described by saying that Descartes situates the moral sources within us" (*Sources of the Self*, p. 143). Yet, Taylor argues that the line of influence from Descartes to Locke to Kant was that of "the developing power of disengaged, self-responsible reason [which] has tended to accredit a view of the subject as an unsituated, even punctual self" (p. 514). On the other hand, as I argue in "Dark Thoughts about the Self" (pp. 116–121), Taylor's view is insufficiently sociological. In fact, it could be said that, as right as Taylor is about the punctual self, it remained for sociology to reformulate modern philosophy's self along the lines of popular nineteenth-century moral concerns about world structures.

18. Descartes's *Discourse on Method* followed by about a century Martin Luther's *Treatise on Christian Liberty,* in which the theological idea of the "inner Christian life" could be viewed as a precursor of what Descartes developed systematically. Of course, Descartes no less than Luther thought within the broader culture of a then-fading medieval religious world. Luther's formulation, for quite obvious reasons, remained less explicitly developed as a theory of self even though, significantly, in using the language of inner life of the Christian, Luther began the break with otherworldly convictions about the moral soul. Luther stood, therefore, more in the tradition of inwardness, the repressed Neoplatonic culture traceable back through Augustine to the Pauline fathers of the early Christian church to the pre-Christian Neoplatonists of late-postexile Israel and even certain of the eighth- and sixth-century B.C. prophets (Jeremiah and the second Isaiah, in particular). Inwardness was, therefore, always a kind of cultural left doctrine of heretical gnosticisms. One could say, therefore, that the moral revolution of modernity was in the reversal of the fate of these classic heterodoxies.

19. One sees here precisely the influence of Descartes on Durkheim, as on most modern thinkers who investigated the original, elemental state of things social.

20. René Descartes, *Discourse on Method,* trans. John Vietch (Open Court Classics, 1962), p. 35 (in part 4). In the translation of *cogito, ergo sum,* I have substituted the more familiar "therefore" for the translator's "hence." In the French text presented by Étienne Gilson (Paris: J. Vrin, 1947), the word here properly rendered "dream" is *songe,* which in French refers particularly to dreams of distinctive incoherence, like those of the ancient prophets. The parenthetical "presentations" are introduced by the English translator.

21. In the famous *1844 Manuscripts* the self (so to speak) was dismissed because, under conditions of actual history (in particular capitalism), the self was alienated from itself because "man (the worker) no longer feels himself to be freely active" (in Robert Tucker, ed., *The Marx-Engels Reader* [W. W. Norton, 1978], p. 75). In not feeling himself freely active, man does not, in the modern sense, feel himself at all. Here begins the line of argument that, in the early manuscripts, appears as self-alienation or estrangement and, in *Capital (I),* appears as the fetishism of commodities. Though the moral point of Marx's theory was to free man back to himself, the scientific means was through the structural

analysis of the mode of production that produced the unfreedom in the first place and was thus conducted as though the self were not there at all because, according to the theory, it was not. This was, in these general terms, a strategy remarkably similar to Durkheim's.

22. The poignancy of Weber's Hobbesian attitude owed to the terrible disruptions in his world—political discord in Weimar Germany and world war. "When and why do men obey? Upon what inner justifications and upon what external means does this domination rest?" See Max Weber, "Politics as a Vocation," in Hans Gerth and C. Wright Mills, eds., *From Max Weber* (Oxford University Press, 1946), p. 78.

23. Weber was not, of course, the first to ask the more general question, which was obvious from the very beginning. Rousseau, for example, concluded his "Discourse on Inequality" with "It follows from this account that inequality, being almost nonexistent in the state of Nature, owes its force and growth to the development of our faculties and the progress of the human Mind, and that it finally becomes stable and legitimate by the establishment of property and Laws." Jean-Jacques Rousseau, *First and Second Discourses*, trans. Victor Gourevitch (Harper and Row, 1986 [1754]).

24. Weber, "Politics as a Vocation," p. 78.

25. This was, of course, the question that stood behind the important studies of authority in Max Weber's *Economy and Society* (University of California, 1978) and, thus, the whole of Weber's political sociology, which has been contemporized by Jürgen Habermas in *Legitimation Crisis* (Beacon Press, 1975) among other places.

26. *The Protestant Ethic* originally appeared in 1904 and 1905 as two articles in *Archiv für Sozialwissenschaft und Sozialpolitik*. The English translation by Talcott Parsons is of a subsequent (1920–1921) revised edition.

27. Alan Sica has done more than any other scholar to demonstrate the centrality of the irrational in Weber's thought in *Weber, Irrationality, and Social Order* (University of California Press, 1988).

28. For example, "The Indian geometry had no rational proof; that was another product of the Greek intellect, also the creator of mechanics and physics. The Indian natural sciences, though well developed in observation, lacked the method of experiment, which was, apart from the beginnings in antiquity, essentially a product of the Renaissance, as was the modern laboratory." Max Weber, *The Protestant Ethic and the Spirit of Capitalism* (Scribner's, 1958), p. 13. Evidently, Weber did not allow for the possibility of difference among the kinds of proofs and sciences. Presumably, he could not allow for reasonable differences in proof because, as the passage shows, he thought of rational proof as Western by its original nature. Rationality was occidental, hence universal.

29. Though both Weber and Durkheim clearly understood the differences, in both cases the logic of the argument at particular points requires an unnatural assimilation of real differences. It would be hard to imagine the logical effect of the argument in *Protestant Ethic* had not Weber spent the author's introduction and the first two chapters isolating the unique social and cultural impact of the protestant ethic, first, and the modern ethic he metaphorically called "the spirit of capitalism." Were, in this book at least, traditionalism in the West somehow different from the lesser rationality of the East, then the force of the scientific claim of his historical study, as well as his moral concerns at the end about the iron cage, would be significantly reduced.

30. Weber, *The Protestant Ethic*, pp. 54–55. Emphasis added.

31. The term *habitus* is Pierre Bourdieu's. See, for example, *Outline of a Theory of*

Practice (Cambridge University Press, 1977 [1972]), ch. 2, where he also offers an excellent presentation, in his own terms, of what was already present in Weber.

32. This recursive relation is best described by Anthony Giddens, *Constitution of Society* (University of California Press, 1984).

33. Weber, *The Protestant Ethic,* p. 78. Emphasis added.

34. Ibid., p. 15.

35. Ibid., p. 13.

36. Though methodologically the analysis of the capitalist mode of production required Marx's comparative references to other, non- (and usually pre-) capitalist modes of production, he considered them more as analytic givens than as subjects of serious historical investigation (for example, in the early pages of *The German Ideology,* where Marx contrasts the four historical types of ownership: tribal, ancient communal, feudal, and capitalist). Alvin Gouldner has demonstrated that Marx may have actively repressed certain modes such as the Asiatic. See Gouldner, *Two Marxisms* (Seabury Press, 1980), pp. 257–258, 325–328, 343–346.

37. See George Marcus and Michael Fischer, *Anthropology as Cultural Critique* (University of Chicago Press, 1986), chs. 1, 2.

38. For a fascinating discussion of Freud and the primitive see Torgovnick, *Gone Primitive,* ch. 10.

39. See V. Y. Mudimbe, *The Invention of Africa* (Indiana University Press, 1988), esp. ch. 1.

40. For the best recent discussion of how and why the powerful seldom hear the message of the powerless, see James Scott, *Domination and the Arts of Resistance* (Yale University Press, 1990).

41. One should refer here not to the dedicated right wings of the West but to those of the center and, even, the liberal left who want to believe in the traditional order of things, of which a striking (and touching) example is Arthur Schlesinger Jr., *Disuniting of America* (Whittle Books, 1991).

Chapter 6

1. Wallace Stegner, *Angle of Repose* (Penguin, 1971), pp. 15–16, 18.

2. Russell Jacoby, in *The Last Intellectuals* (Basic Books, 1987), is particularly hard on the sociologists of his generation. A sociologist, Irving Louis Horowitz is, if anything, even more hard on the field as a whole, in *The Composition of Sociology* (Oxford University Press, 1993). Otherwise, the two authors have little in common. Jacoby writes from the point of view of the angry left, Horowitz as a bitterly disappointed and dyspeptic neoconservative.

3. The closed department was at Washington University. Though the university's administration justified its decision to end sociology at Washington University on the grounds that the department's excellence had declined, the story is much more complex than that. It is undoubtedly true that by the time of the closing in 1989, the department was less brilliant than it had been in the 1960s, when it was considered one of the best in the country. Many of its stars from the earlier period had departed, largely due to a number of departmental conflicts (in which Alvin Gouldner was a major player, and in some people's minds the cause of the troubles). At the same time, the university's administration was, at the least, unsupportive of the department during its times of trouble and, at the worst, aggressively hostile to its left-oriented research. In the midst of all this the university had gone

through a period of fiscal crisis, from which it was rescued by the corporate interests of St. Louis, which could not be expected to have been enthusiastic about left-liberal sociology in general, and one study of their own power structure in particular. For discussions of various of these themes, see "Special Section: Closing of the Sociology Department at Washington University," *American Sociologist* 20 (Winter 1989–1990):303–352.

The reference to bad behavior is to Harvard's department which in the 1980s and early 1990s had been involved in two successive, embarrassing controversies: one over the denial of tenure to Theda Skocpol, and another over its loss of undergraduate majors to the interdisciplinary Social Studies Program. Skocpol brought sex discrimination charges and was eventually granted tenure, and the department seems to have stabilized itself and its enrollments. After a number of years of turmoil (including a period in which the department was rumored to have been put in receivership by the university's administration), Harvard's is once again one of the discipline's respected departments. On the Skocpol affair, see, for examples, *Chronicle of Higher Education* 23 (1982) and 19 (1985). I also heard the story of the controversy from Professor Skocpol in an interview on June 22, 1990, after she had returned to Harvard. On the controversy with the Social Studies Program, see, for examples, *New York Times,* April 16, 1990, and *Harvard Crimson,* May 11, 1990.

The reference to the reversed cutbacks are to Yale (for which my information is mostly from personal communications over several years with faculty and students associated with the Yale department, where I taught in 1991 during the crisis). Another reversed cutback was at San Diego State University in 1992 (see *Los Angeles Times,* August 13, 1992).

More generally the field has been subjected to occasional journalistic attacks (notably, "Sociology's Lonely Crowd," *Newsweek,* February 3, 1992), in response to which it has given good account of itself (for example, "Sociologists Confront Questions About the Field's Vitality and Direction," *Chronicle of Higher Education,* August 12, 1992).

4. It is also true that, as Jacoby argues (*Last Intellectuals*), sociologists tend to have grown politically soft in recent years, a point of view reflected, with special effect, in Barrie Thorne and Judith Stacey's "Missing Feminist Revolution in Sociology," *Social Problems* 32 (1985):301–317.

5. Yet, as important as sociology's contributions in these areas are, both have been shared or borrowed. Self-theory was developed as much by philosophers like William James and George Herbert Mead as by sociologists. And, though techniques of social measurement like survey research were largely invented by sociologists like Paul Lazarsfeld and Herbert Hyman, they have been readily borrowed and put to other uses. In the latter regard, see Herbert Hyman, *Taking Society's Measure* (Russell Sage Foundation, 1991).

Some might assume that even structures are more the intellectual property of other fields like anthropology and literary theory, which have borrowed much from structuralism. But, even here, sociologists have done more to apply the structural theories of structuralists like Claude Lévi-Strauss to modern societies. This is so notwithstanding criticisms that could be put to the *way* in which those applications have been made. See, for examples, the essays collected in Peter M. Blau and Robert K. Merton, *Continuities in Structural Inquiry* (Sage, 1981).

6. Charlotte Perkins Gilman, "Women and Economics" (1898), in *The Yellow Wallpaper and Other Writings* (Bantam, 1989), p. 136.

7. Du Bois first encountered the more famous German sociologist during his student days in Berlin (1892–1894), when he attended lectures by Weber. In 1904 Du Bois was among those whom Weber met during his tour of the United States. After reading *Souls of Black Folk,* Weber offered to arrange its translation into German and write an introduction

for it. Though the translation did not take place until much later, Weber did publish, in the *Archiv für Sozialwissenschaft and Sozialpolitik* (1906), Du Bois's article "The Negro Question in the United States." See letter of March 30, 1904, from Weber to Du Bois in *The Correspondence of W.E.B. Du Bois, Vol I* (University of Massachusetts Press, 1973). See also Charles Lemert, "A Classic from the Other Side of the Veil: Du Bois's *Souls of Black Folk*," *Sociological Quarterly* 32 (1994):383–396.

8. W.E.B. Du Bois, *Souls of Black Folk* (Bantam, 1989 [1903]), p. 3.

9. The question of the sources of Du Bois's famous idea of double consciousness is a subject of debate. See Arnold Rampersad, *The Art and Imagination of W.E.B. Du Bois* (Schocken Books, 1976), ch. 4; and David Levering Lewis, *W.E.B. Du Bois: Biography of a Race, 1968–1919* (Henry Holt, 1993), ch. 11. It is almost certain that the idea owes a great deal to Du Bois's teacher at Harvard, William James, who understood the social self as multiple and had his own concept of double consciousness. Notably, Charles Horton Cooley wrote about the "looking glass self" in *Human Nature and Social Order* (1902), the year before *Souls of Black Folk*. (Du Bois's line "a world which . . . lets him see himself through the revelation of the other world" first appeared, however, in 1897.) Also discussed in Lemert, "A Classic from the Other Side of the Veil."

10. From Immanuel Kant, *Fundamental Principles of the Metaphysics of Morals* in *Introduction to Contemporary Civilization in the West* (Columbia University Press, 1960), p. 1171. The quote follows by a few pages the most famous of all Kant's statements, in which his moral code is arrived at by parallel application of Descartes's reduction method: "As I have stripped the will of every impulse which could arise from it from obedience to any law, there remains nothing but the general conformity of the will's actions to law in general. Only this conformity to law is to serve the will as a principle; that is, I am never to act in any way other than *so I could want my maxim also to become a general law*" (ibid., p. 1169). The systematic exposition of practical reason is the famous 1788 *Critique of Pure Practical Reason*.

11. From John Maynard Keynes, "The Psychology of Modern Society," in Lemert, *Social Theory* (Westview Press, 1993), pp. 222–223.

12. Georg Lukács, "History and Class Conciousness," in Charles Lemert, ed., *Social Theory: The Multicultural and Classic Readings* (Westview Press, 1993), p. 225.

13. See, among many other sources, Alvin Gouldner, *The Two Marxisms* (Seabury Press, 1980); and Martin Jay, *The Dialectical Imagination* (Little, Brown, 1973). Compare Craig Calhoun, *Critical Social Theory: Culture, History, and the Challenge of Difference*, (Blackwell, 1995).

14. For example, see Lévi-Strauss's famous remarks on Sartre in "History and Dialectic," the concluding chapter of *The Savage Mind* (University of Chicago Press, 1966 [1962]).

15. Those that preserve the classic formula are most purely represented by standpoint theorists like Nancy Hartsock (discussed in Chapter 4) and Dorothy Smith (to be discussed in Chapter 8). Among the many attempts to rethink the classic language are, notably, Judith Butler, *Gender Trouble* (Routledge, 1990), and *Bodies That Matter* (Routledge, 1993). One should also note the attempts to reformulate a standpoint position in ways that both keep the language and subvert it, such as Patricia Hill Collins, *Black Feminist Thought* (Unwin Hyman, 1990).

16. Merton, "Social Structure and Anomie," in *Social Theory and Social Structure* (Free Press, 1957), pp. 131–132.

17. Talcott Parsons, *Structure of Social Action* (Free Press, 1949 [1937]), p. 44.

18. Anthony Giddens, the leading sociologist of the recursivity of structures, does not credit Parsons on this point. Though he is appreciative of other aspects of Parsons's writings, Giddens began his systematic theory of structures by identifying Parsons's failures in *Structure of Social Action* as the beginning point for theoretical renewal. See *Constitution of Society* (University of California Press, 1984), pp. xiii–xiv.

19. The passages are from the following sources, listed by number of the selection: [1] Peter M. Blau and Otis Dudley Duncan, *The American Occupational Structure* (John Wiley, 1967), p. 23. For many years after its publication in 1967 this book was the most frequently cited book in the field. It remains today a late-modern classic in the study of occupational structures. [2] Harold Garfinkel and Harvey Sacks, "On Formal Structures of Practical Actions," in John C. McKinney and Edward A. Tiryakian, eds., *Theoretical Sociology* (Appleton-Century-Crofts, 1970), p. 339. This article followed by three years Garfinkel's *Studies in Ethnomethodology* (Prentice-Hall, 1967), which first announced the new trend in sociological work that astonished the field. Though some consider ethnomethodology a microsociology, it has been concerned with structures from the first. [3] Mark S. Granovetter, "The Strength of Weak Ties," *American Journal of Sociology* 78, no. 6 (May 1973):1360. [4] Immanuel Wallerstein, *The Modern World System I* (Academic Press, 1974), p. 347. [5] Theda Skocpol, *States and Social Revolutions* (Cambridge University Press, 1979), p. 8. [6] Randall Collins, "Micro-Translation as a Theory-Building Strategy," in Karin Knorr-Cetina and Aaron V. Cicourel, eds., *Advances in Social Theory and Methodology* (Routledge & Kegan Paul, 1981), p. 105. [7] Jeffrey C. Alexander, *Theoretical Logic in Sociology I* (University of California Press, 1982), pp. 114–115. [8] Anthony Giddens, *The Constitution of Society* (University of California Press, 1984), p. 17. [9] Erik Olin Wright, *Classes* (Verso Books, 1985), p. 125. [10] James S. Coleman, *Foundations of Social Theory* (Harvard University Press, 1990), pp. 1, 2. [11] William H. Sewell Jr., "A Theory of Structure: Duality, Agency, and Transformation," *American Journal of Sociology* 98, no. 1 (July 1992):27. [12] Michele Lamont, *Money, Morals and Manners* (University of Chicago Press, 1992), p. 135.

20. Sewell, "A Theory of Structure," p. 18.

21. Among the twelve examples previously cited, the revisionists would be Garfinkel and Sacks [2], Collins [6], Alexander [7], Coleman [10], and, in a sense, Granovetter [3]. From this, and the following lists, it can readily be seen that sociologists grouped according to their views on structures may have little else in common. This, and the two positions following, are discussed at length in Chapter 7.

22. The structure-reductionists in the list would be Blau and Duncan [1], Wallerstein [4], Skocpol [5], and Wright [9].

23. The two most explicit recursivists are Pierre Bourdieu and Anthony Giddens [8], discussed in detail in the following chapter. Sewell [11] and Lamont [12] are less explicit recursivists.

Chapter 7

1. Immanuel Wallerstein, *The Modern World System II: Mercantilism and the Consolidation of the European World-Economy, 1600–1750* (Academic Press, 1980), ch. 2.

2. An alternate interpretation is that the letter and the writing materials on the table invoke a literary world of which the mistress is part. This seems to be the assumption of the

book designers who, without explanation, use this same painting for the cover of an important book on literary theory: Terry Eagleton, *Literary Theory: An Introduction* (University of Minnesota Press, 1983).

3. The three theories of structures are defined at the end of the previous chapter (pp. 128–129) and discussed in detail in this chapter.

4. Jean-Jacques Rousseau, *Confessions*, trans. J. M. Cohen (Penguin, 1953). The preceding lines appear at the end of this edition. The following quotation is at the beginning.

5. From Jefferson original draft of "A Declaration by the Representatives of the United States of America," in *Thomas Jefferson, Writings* (Library of America, 1984), p. 19.

6. The book in which the lecture appears in English announces the author's long-standing commitment to reflexive sociology. The lecture from which these quotations are taken appears as the last chapter in Bourdieu, *In Other Words: Essays Toward a Reflexive Sociology*, trans. Matthew Adamson (Stanford University Press, 1990), pp. 177–178.

7. Ibid., p. 186. Emphasis added.

8. Pierre Bourdieu, *Outline of a Theory of Practice*, trans. Richard Nice (Cambridge University Press, 1977 [1972]). In the late 1950s and through the 1960s Bourdieu went through a number of relatively minor theoretical shifts (including a prominent flirtation with structuralism). The most important book of this period was the one that is said to have energized the student rebellions in 1968, *The Inheritors* (University of Chicago Press, 1979 [1964]), in which his reproduction theory is clearly stated. *Outline of a Theory of Practice* was a rewrite of his early field studies in Algeria, in which Bourdieu provided a clear statement of his important concept *habitus* and of his program of overcoming the classic subjectivist/objectivist dichotomy. Though his empirical research evolved spectacularly (with attendant additions to his theoretical vocabulary), there have been no notable shifts since *Outline* in the general concepts and intentions of the theory.

9. Bourdieu, *Outline*, p. 72.

10. Ibid.

11. Pierre Bourdieu, *Homo Academicus*, trans. Peter Collier (Stanford University Press, 1988), p. 91. For a more detailed discussion of this book, see Charles Lemert, "The Habits of Intellectuals: Response to Ringer," *Theory and Society* 19, no. 3 (June 1990):295–311.

12. Ibid., p. 128.

13. Ibid., p. 143.

14. Ibid., p. 150.

15. Ibid., p. 151.

16. Ibid.

17. Ibid., p. 152.

18. The difference is suggested, for one example, by a comparison of Bourdieu's 1982 inaugural lecture at the Collège de France (referred to previously) with Giddens's inaugural lecture at Cambridge University on January 29, 1986. Bourdieu's was "A Lecture on the Lecture," a play not just on words but on the reflexive character of the sociologist. Giddens's was "What Do Sociologists Do?"—a relatively straightforward public defense of sociology as the "prime medium of [social scientific] reflexivity." In other words, so to speak, both spoke of the reflexivity of sociology. Where Bourdieu tried to exhibit it in his speech, Giddens spoke about it as, yes, a property of the field. See Anthony Giddens, "What Do Sociologists Do?" in *Social Theory and Modern Society* (Stanford University Press, 1987), pp. 1–22.

19. Anthony Giddens, *New Rules of Sociological Method: A Positive Critique of Interpretative Sociologies* (Basic Books, 1976), p. 162.

20. Anthony Giddens, *Constitution of Society: Outline of a Theory of Structuration* (University of California Press, 1984). Thereafter, Giddens extended the general theory in this book in a number of literary directions over several key conceptual topics, including *The Nation-State and Violence* (University of California, 1985); a comprehensive textbook for introductory sociology courses, *Introduction to Sociology* (W. W. Norton, 1991); and a series of essays on themes of modern life and ethics, including *The Consequences of Modernity* (Stanford University Press, 1990) and *Modernity and Self-Identity* (Stanford University Press, 1991). These only suggest the range and number of Giddens's literary output, to which only Bourdieu's is comparable in scope and impact.

21. Giddens, *Constitution,* p. xxvii.

22. Ibid., p. xvii.

23. Ibid., p. 17. Emphasis added.

24. Giddens begins *Constitution* with reference to the "orthodox consensus" fashioned by Parsons and the functionalists in sociology and Marxists in Europe, against which recent developments with the notable exception of structuralism sought to reestablish the "active reflexive character of human conduct" (pp. xiii–xvi; compare pp. 1–4). Compare the earlier *New Rules of Sociological Method,* which was, as the subtitle suggests, "a positive critique of interpretative sociologies"; that is, an attempt to rehabilitate that wing of social thought he considered more sensitive to the reflexive subject of action. For his discussion of rules and resources, see *Constitution,* pp. 17–25 (and elsewhere).

25. The AGIL paradigm is Parsons's most abstract representation of the four basic functional features of all action (including social) systems: Adaptation (A), Goal-attainment (G), Integration (I), Latent pattern maintenance (L).

26. Giddens, *Constitution,* p. 25. Emphasis added. This idea, which is repeated in Giddens's glossary at the end of the book, is the key passage in the best-known attempt to integrate Bourdieu and Giddens. See William H. Sewell, "A Theory of Structure: Duality, Agency, and Transformation," *American Journal of Sociology* 98, no. 1 (July 1992):5.

27. This figure of speech is used in both of Giddens's textbooks: *Introduction to Sociology,* p. 17, to which compare *Sociology: A Brief but Critical Introduction* (Harcourt Brace Jovanovich, 1987), p. 12. By contrast, the formal presentation in reference to the duality of structures in the glossary in *Constitution* (p. 374): "Structure [is] the medium and outcome of the conduct it recursively organizes; the structural properties of social systems do not exist outside of action but are chronically implicated in its production and reproduction."

28. Giddens's words (*Constitution,* p. xxiii): "What agents know about what they do, and why they do it—their knowledgeability *as* agents—is largely carried in practical consciousness. Practical consciousness consists of all the things which actors know tacitly about how to 'go on' in the contexts of social life without being able to give them direct discursive expression."

29. Giddens on discursive consciousness (*Constitution,* p. 374): "What actors are able to say, or to give verbal expression to, about social conditions, including especially the conditions of their own action; awareness which has a discursive form." On both practical and discursive consciousness, see *Constitution,* ch. 2.

30. Ibid., p. 29.

31. For examples (among others), Giddens, *The Nation-State and Violence* and *The Consequences of Modernity.*

32. See chapter 2, "The Unconscious, Time and Memory," in Giddens, *Constitution.*

33. Giddens, *The Consequences of Modernity,* p. 7. See also Giddens, *Modernity and Self-Identity,* where he says (p. 3), with simple elegance, that "trust in this sense is basic to a

'protective cocoon' which stands guard over the self in its dealings with daily life." Though trust is discussed in *Constitution*, the earlier book on structures, it becomes an explicit theme in the later books (*Consequences* and *Modernity*), which address directly the existential reality of modern life—in particular its disembedding nature. The disembeddedness theme is, in turn, dependent on his very influential theories of time-space in the chapter "Time, Space and Regionalization," in *Constitution*. See also *The Transformation of Intimacy* (Stanford University Press, 1992).

34. This paragraph is a free translation of Giddens, *Modernity and Self-Identity*, especially chapter 2.

35. Giddens, at the crucial place, reads Freud through Erik Erikson, from whom he derives the trust/risk dilemma. See "Erikson: Anxiety and Trust," pp. 51–60 in Giddens's *Constitution*.

36. The expression "view from nowhere" is Thomas Nagel's, appropriated most recently, and aptly, by feminist critics of modernist thought. For example, Susan Bordo, "Feminism, Postmodernism, and Gender-Skepticism," in Linda Nicholson, ed., *Feminism/Postmodernism* (Routledge, 1990), pp. 136–145.

37. George Homans, *Nature of Social Science* (Harcourt Brace & World, 1967), ch. 2. See also his *Social Behavior: Its Elementary Forms* (Harcourt Brace & World, 1961). For a discussion see Charles Lemert, *Sociology and the Twilight of Man* (Southern Illinois University Press, 1979), ch. 2.

38. On the sober and playful sides of Homans see Charles Lemert, "Whole Life Social Theory," *Theory and Society* 15 (1986):431–442; and Charles Tilly, "George Caspar Homans and the Rest of Us," *Theory and Society* 19 (1990):261–268.

39. Immanuel Wallerstein, *The Modern World System*, 3 vols. (Academic Press, 1974, 1980, 1989). For modernization theory, compare W. W. Rostow, *Stages of Economic Growth* (Cambridge University Press, 1971).

40. Wallerstein, *The Modern World System I*, p. 8.

41. In fact, the decision to reduce the problem to its structural terms, ignoring the subjectivist question, was one of the most important differences between world systems theory (and other, similar theories of economic development) and the modernization theories they opposed. Modernization theories at the time had been greatly preoccupied with the more Weberian question of the nature of the new modernizing man—where and how he appeared in those areas that were, to use Rostow's classic phrase, ready for "take-off." See Rostow, *Stages of Economic Growth*.

42. Theda Skocpol, *States and Social Revolutions* (Cambridge University Press, 1979), p. xii. Compare Skocpol, "The Uppity Generation and the Revitalization of Macroscopic Sociology: Reflections at Mid-Career by a Woman from the Sixties," *Theory and Society* 17(1988–1989):627–645.

43. See the section "The 1960s and the Sociological Imagination," in Skocpol, "The Uppity Generation," where she says: "Sociology as a discipline . . . has survived the raucous advent of a generation of ex-student protestors. As a result, sociology has much more vivid and interesting things to say about the United States and the world" (p. 632).

44. Skocpol, *States and Social Revolutions*, ch. 1. The quotations following are in *States*, pp. 4 and 5, respectively. Compare Skocpol, "Bring the State Back In," pp. 3–44 in Peter B. Evans, Dietrich Rueschemeyer, and Theda Skocpol, eds., *Bringing the State Back In* (Cambridge University Press, 1985).

45. I might pass over the phrase "modes of explanation used by the currently prevalent theories" if she had not indicated in the preface just who her teachers and influences were. They included George Homans (adviser for her doctoral thesis, from which the book was

built), Daniel Bell, and Barrington Moore Jr.—respectively the greatest of his generation of methodological individualists, the foremost proponent of the end of ideology, and a major social theorist in the tradition of Marx at a time when there were few Marxists anywhere in American universities. That three men of such differing points of view could cooperate in a project that itself differed from, even attacked, some of their opinions is a tribute as much to them as to her. The relation with Homans may be to some the most disconcerting, not just because his ideas on sociology were so at odds with hers but also because he was so much the proponent of explanation based on observations and she wrote a book based entirely on secondary literature. Yet, even today, Skocpol is known to be a structural sociologist strongly opposed to the kind of theorizing Giddens does, and brusquely insistent on the importance of empirical explanation.

46. Skocpol, "Uppity Generation," p. 628.

47. Skocpol, *States and Social Revolutions*, p. 17.

48. The following paragraph summarizes Skocpol's *States and Social Revolutions*, chs. 2 and 5.

49. Skocpol, *States and Social Revolutions*, p. 67.

50. Randall Collins, *Theoretical Sociology* (Harcourt Brace Jovanovich, 1988), p. 2.

51. Jeffrey Alexander, "Action and Its Environments," in Alexander et al., eds., *The Macro-Micro Link* (University of California Press, 1987), p. 290.

52. See Coleman's response to Alexander's critique of Coleman's *Foundations of Social Theory* (Harvard University Press, 1990) in a review symposium on Coleman's book, *Theory and Society* 21, no. 2 (1992):183–284.

53. James S. Coleman, *Foundations of Social Theory* (Harvard University Press, 1990), p. 2. The more detailed accounts of his theory are found in part 4 of *Foundations*, especially (in my opinion) chapter 20, "Natural Persons and the New Corporate Actors," and chapter 24, "The New Social Structure and the New Social Science."

54. Ibid., p. 3.

55. Ibid., p. 29.

56. Marianna Torgovnick, "Taking Tarzan Seriously," chapter 2 in *Gone Primitive: Savage Intellectuals, Modern Lives* (University of Chicago Press, 1990).

57. The expression is from Sandra Harding Press, "The Analytic Instability of the Categories of Feminist Theory," in Sandra Harding and Jean F. O'Barr, eds., *Sex and Scientific Inquiry* (University of California Press, 1987), pp. 183–301.

Chapter 8

1. Mr. Moneybags figured brilliantly in that crucial passage at the end of part 2 of *Capital (I)*, where Marx, having demonstrated that capital profit cannot be explained by reference to the visible aspects of commodity or labor exchange, invites the reader with him into the secrets of production: "Accompanied by Mr. Moneybags and by the possessor of labour-power we therefore take leave of this noisy sphere, where everything takes place on the surface and in view of all men, and follow them both to the hidden abode of production, on whose threshold there stares us in the face: 'No admittance except on business.'" Also, the phrase "must be so lucky as to discover" is Marx's at the beginning of chapter 6, part 2, of *Capital (I)*.

2. For Dora, see Sigmund Freud, "Fragment of an Analysis of a Case of Hysteria," in *Standard Edition* (Hogarth Press, 1958), vol. 7, pp. 3–122. For the Rat Man and other cases see Freud, *Three Case Histories* (Collier Books, 1963).

3. W.E.B. Du Bois, *Souls of Black Folk* (Bantam, 1989), p. 43.

4. Ibid., pp. 47–48.

5. Ibid., p. 49.

6. Ibid., p. 52. Emphasis added.

7. This extract is composed from "Science as a Vocation," in Hans Gerth and C. Wright Mills, eds., *From Max Weber* (Oxford University Press, 1946), pp. 135–137. The omissions indicated are in places whole paragraphs. The sense of Weber's idea is retained. Though he was arguing a definite view of science against the political controversies of his day, the view is consistent with his general view of the modern social world as one in which individuals are caught in endless calculations and "saved," if at all, when some moral idea breaks into the dreary day-to-day. On the political controversies see Alvin Gouldner, "Anti-Minotaur: The Myth of Value-Free Sociology," *Social Problems* 9, no. 3 (1962):199–213.

8. Georg Simmel, "Metropolis and Mental Life" (1903), in Donald N. Levine, ed., *Georg Simmel on Individuality and Social Forms* (University of Chicago Press, 1971), p. 325.

9. For an example: "[A] theory need not account for all the observed variation—even if research conditions are ideal with respect to procedural matters such as measurement error, sampling, respondent availability, and so on." See Stanley Lieberson, *Making It Count* (University of California Press, 1985), p. 98. In other words, if differences in the data are well controlled, then measurement need not account for all possible observations. This, of course, places an enormous burden of responsibility on the measurer, as an earlier, classic theorist of social research observed: "*The use of a particular mathematical model presupposes that a certain level of measurement has been attained.* The responsibility rests squarely on the shoulders of the research to determine whether or not his operational procedures permit the use of certain mathematical operations." Hubert Blalock, *Social Statistics* (McGraw Hill, 1960), p. 17. Compare "Our best bet is to eliminate possible error by careful design." Blalock, *An Introduction to Social Research* (Prentice-Hall, 1970), p. 17. For a discussion see Charles Lemert, *Sociology and the Twilight of Man* (Sourthern Illinois University Press, 1979), ch. 3.

10. Aaron Cicourel, *Method and Measurement in Sociology* (Free Press, 1964), p. 173. See also Cicourel, *Cognitive Sociology* (Macmillan, 1974). For a discussion of Cicourel's theory of measurement in relation to the measurement ideas of other ethnomethodological sociologists see Lemert, *Sociology and the Twilight of Man*, ch. 7.

11. The adjective "artful" is frequently used by ethnomethodologists to suggest, among other things, that measurements, before they occur in sciences, are practical accomplishments (another of their expressions) of daily life. Cicourel enjoys a direct, if askance, relation to ethnomethodology, as does Dorothy Smith (of whom more, soon).

12. Dorothy Smith, "K Is Mentally Ill: The Anatomy of a Factual Account," in *Texts, Facts, and Femininity: Exploring the Relations of Ruling* (Northeastern University Press, 1990 [1978]), pp. 12–52. Originally published in *Sociology* 12 (1976):25–53.

13. This view is shared by one of professional sociology's most distinguished measurers in a reference to the desire to treat nonexperimental data as though they were truly experimental: "The data are sliced, chopped, beaten, molded, baked, and finally artificially colored until the research is able to serve us proudly with a plateful of mock experiment." See Lieberson, *Making It Count*, p. 4.

14. Smith, "K Is Mentally Ill," p. 18.

15. Ibid., p. 27.

16. Ibid., p. 17. Emphasis added.

17. Ibid. Emphasis added.

18. Dorothy Smith, "Sociology from Women's Experience: A Reaffirmation," *Sociological Theory* 10 (1992):88. It is important to state that Smith is not a naive experientialist. Women's experience is the beginning point from which she proceeds toward a sociological analysis of the larger array of social organizations and positions, including most especially the social relations of ruling, that affect the actual lives of subjects. For example, "The knowing subject is always located in a particular spatial and temporal site, a particular configuration of the everyday/everynight world. Inquiry is directed towards exploring and explicating what she does not know—the social relations and organization pervading her world but invisible in it" (p. 91). For a discussion see Charles Lemert, "The Limits of Subjectivity," *Sociological Theory* 10 (1992):63–72.

19. See Judith Stacey and Barrie Thorne, "The Missing Feminist Revolution in Sociology," *Social Problems* 32 (1985); Anna Yeatman, "A Feminist Theory of Social Differentiation," in Linda Nicholson, ed., *Feminism/Postmodernism* (Routledge, 1990). Compare Patricia Clough, *Feminist Thought: Desire, Power, and Academic Discourse* (Basil Blackwell, 1994).

20. Lewis Coser, *Masters of Sociological Thought* (Harcourt Brace Jovanovich, 1971), p. 242.

21. These other perspectives include, of course, other feminisms and other identity-specific social theories critical of traditional official disciplines. But they also include rebellious movements within the traditions—in Smith's case most especially her two most often mentioned sociological resources: Marx and ethnomethodology. Whether she is an "ethnomethodologist" or, for that matter, a Marxist in any normal sense is another question. On the relation between these two sources see, in particular, Dorothy Smith, "The Ideological Practice of Sociology," in Smith, *Conceptual Practices of Power* (Northeastern University Press, 1990), ch. 2 (compare chs. 3, 4). Also, on the relation to Marx see Smith, *Texts, Facts, and Femininity*, esp. chs. 4, 6.

22. See Lemert, "The Limits of Subjectivity," and note 18.

23. In an early essay (1974), Smith describes the superiority of that difference "as an insider's experience, an experience distinctively of women, though by no means the experience of all women." (The essay is republished as "The Disjuncture Between Sociology and Women's Experience," in Smith, *The Conceptual Practices of Power*, pp. 11–28.) More recently, she has said: "My research concern is to build an ordinary good knowledge of the text-mediated organization of power from the standpoint of women in contemporary capitalism." See Smith, "Sociology from Women's Experience," *Sociological Theory* 10 (1992):97. Virtually everything Smith has written on sociological method has been to demonstrate the inherent weakness of sociology done within the ruling culture of capitalist societies and, by direct inference, the superiority of sociologies based on a feminist standpoint.

This involves also the very complicated question of what some would see as Smith's feminist essentialism. In a recent defense of her work, Smith seems to acknowledge this point: "It's true that I begin with what I learned from my own experience of two worlds of consciousness and their relations (so, incidentally, did Descartes), but the formulation of a method of inquiry that I developed in fact works to make a space into which anyone's experience, however various, could become a beginning place of inquiry. 'Anyone' could be an Afro- or Chinese or Caucasian Canadian, an individual from the First Nations, an old woman or man, a lesbian or a gay man, a member of the ruling class, or any other man" (Smith, "Sociology from Women's Experience," p. 90). I do not myself find this convincing, given that one of the premises of her standpoint is that some things cannot be so well known by ruling-class men. I suppose that the confessed similarity to Descartes is not all that incidental after all.

24. See, for examples, Paula Giddings, *When and Where I Enter: The Impact of Black Women on Race and Sex in America* (Bantam Books, 1984); Patricia Hill Collins, *Black Feminist Thought* (Unwin Hyman, 1990); bell hooks, *Ain't I a Woman?* (South End Press, 1981); Hazel Carby, *Reconstructing Womanhood: The Emergence of the Afro-American Woman Novelist* (Oxford University Press, 1987). The most comprehensive anthology is Margaret Busby, ed., *Daughters of Africa* (Pantheon, 1992). The locus classicus may be *The Narrative of Sojourner Truth* (Vintage Books, 1993), especially Sojourner Truth's 1851 "Ar'n't I a Woman?" speech.

25. Anna Julia Cooper, *A Voice From the South: By a Black Woman of the South* (Oxford University Press, 1988). On the book's importance see Carby, *Reconstructing Womanhood*, ch. 5. On Cooper see Louise Daniel Hutchinson, *Anna Julia Cooper: A Voice From the South* (The Smithsonian Institution Press, 1981); and Leona C. Gabel, *From Slavery to the Sorbonne* (Smith College, 1982). See also Charles Lemert, "Anna Julia Cooper: The Colored Woman's Office," in *Dark Thoughts* (forthcoming).

26. Cooper, *A Voice From the South*, p. 31. Martin Robinson Delany, to whom the original use of the phrase is attributed, was one of the first African American Pan-Africanists. For a brief discussion and further sources see David Levering Lewis, *W.E.B. Du Bois* (Henry Holt, 1993), pp. 161–162.

27. Sojourner Truth's short speech was an intervention at the 1851 Women's Rights Convention in Akron, Ohio. See p. 118 in *Narrative of Sojourner Truth*. Cooper's "Woman Versus the 'Indian'" chapter begins carefully by acknowledging that Shaw was no racist: "Susan B. Anthony and Anna Shaw are evidently too noble to be held in thrall by the provincialisms of women who seem never to have breathed the atmosphere beyond the confines of their grandfather's plantation. It is only from the broad plateau of light and love that one can see petty prejudice and narrow priggishness in their true perspective; and it is on this high ground, as I sincerely believe, these two grand women stand" (p. 83). She refers to the occasion when Anthony and Shaw took personal stands against an act of racial discrimination (described pp. 80–82 in Cooper's *A Voice From the South*). Cooper's balanced dignity never failed her. She was making a point not about these particular feminists but about the cultural limitations of white feminism, as earlier she was not attacking Martin Delany but the position he represented in American culture.

28. Cooper, *A Voice From the South*, p. 96. Emphasis in original.

29. Ibid., ch. 4.

30. Ibid., pp. 144–145.

31. Cooper's *Voice From the South* expresses many of the unreserved ethusiasms for progress that made Edward Bellamy's utopian novel, *Looking Backwards*, one of the most popular books of that day. (I owe this observation to Richard Ohmann.) Bellamy's book closes thus: "'Looking Backward' was written in the belief that the Gold Age lies before us and not behind us, and is not far away. Our children will surely see it, and we, too, who are already men and women if we deserve it by our faith and by our works." See Bellamy, *Looking Backwards 2000–1887* (Modern Library, 1951 [1887]), p. 276.

32. Gloria Anzaldúa, *Borderlands/La Frontera: The New Mestiza* (Spinsters/Aunt Lute Press, 1987), p. 23. For a Native American feminist position, see Paula Gunn Allen, *The Sacred Hoop: Recovering the Feminine in American Indian Traditions* (Beacon Press, 1987). For the women-of-color position generally see Anzaldúa, ed., *Making Face, Making Soul: Haciendo Caras* (Aunt Lute Foundation, 1990); and Cherríe Moraga and Gloria Anzaldúa, eds., *This Bridge Called My Back* (Kitchen Table/Women of Color Press, 1981). Other prominent examples are Gayatri Chakravorty Spivak, "Can the Subaltern Speak?" in Carry

Nelson and Lawrence Grossberg, eds., *Marxism and the Interpretation of Culture* (University of Illinois Press, 1988), pp. 217–313; and Trinh T. Minh-ha, *Woman, Native, Other* (University of Indiana Press, 1989). For a discussion in relation to feminist theory, see Clough, *Feminist Thought*, chs. 4, 5.

33. On Du Bois's exclusion from sociology, see Charles Lemert, "A Classic from the Other Side of the Veil: Du Bois's *Souls of Black Folk*," *Sociological Quarterly* 35 (1994): 383–396.

34. Weber and Du Bois were friendly later. Weber had attended Du Bois's Atlanta Conference in 1904 and had offered to arrange the German translation of *Souls of Black Folk*.

35. On this and other details of Du Bois's life, see Lewis, *W.E.B. Du Bois*.

36. The James observation was in *The American Scene*. As an instance of feminist criticism of Du Bois, see Mary Helen Washington, "Introduction," in Cooper, *A Voice From the South*, pp. xli–xlii. The substance of Washington's criticism is that Du Bois slighted Cooper, who had urged him to write *Black Reconstruction* (Harcourt Brace, 1935) and from whom he had quoted the "when and where I enter" line without naming her. The two had a long but not close relation, dating at least from the 1900 Pan African Congress. Their fates were particularly linked, though at a remove, in the struggle against Booker T. Washington.

37. See Lemert, "A Classic from the Other Side of the Veil."

38. Du Bois, *Souls of Black Folk*, pp. 2–3. Emphasis added.

39. For a discussion in relation to William James, G. Herbert Mead, and Charles Horton Cooley, see Lemert, "A Classic," pp. 388–390.

40. For a discussion see Charles Lemert, "Dark Thoughts about the Self," in Craig Calhoun, ed., *Social Theory and the Politics of Identity* (Basil Blackwell, 1994), pp. 100–129.

41. Du Bois frequently used the term Negro and fought a long, and eventually successful, struggle to have the word capitalized.

42. Du Bois, *Souls of Black Folk*, pp. 8–9.

43. Erving Goffman, *Presentation of Self in Everyday Life* (Anchor Books, 1959), pp. 141–144.

44. Bishop George Berkeley, "On the Prospect of Planting Arts and Learning in America," in *The Works of George Berkeley*, vol. 7 (Nelson, 1955), p. 373.

45. The best interpretation of American politics from this point of view is Walter Russell Mead, *Mortal Splendor* (Houghton Mifflin, 1987). The best recent (but uncritical) appropriation of the theme (with particular reference to Crèvecoeur) is Arthur Schlesinger Jr., *The Disuniting of America* (Whittle Books, 1991).

46. Gunnar Myrdal, *An American Dilemma* (Harper, 1994), p. xlvii.

47. The relations among race, gender, and sexual orientation are discussed in the next chapter.

Chapter 9

1. "SNCC Founding Statement" (October 1960), in Judith C. Albert and Stewart E. Albert, eds., *The Sixties Papers* (Praeger, 1984), p. 113.

2. Frantz Fanon, *The Wretched of the Earth: The Handbook for the Black Revolution That Is Changing the Shape of the World* (Grove Press, 1968 [1961]), pp. 36–37.

3. James Garbarino et al., *Children in Danger* (Jossey-Bass, 1992).

4. References for facts are in Garbarino, *Children in Danger*, pp. 46, 29, 36–37, respectively.

5. See Immanuel Wallerstein, *The World-System I: Capitalist Agriculture and the Origins of the European World-Economy in the Sixteenth Century* (Academic Press, 1975). See also Paul Gilroy, *The Black Atlantic: Modernity and Double Consciousness* (Harvard University Press, 1993).

6. See, for example, Heide I. Hartmann, "The Family as the Locus of Gender, Class, and Political Struggle: The Example of Housework," *Signs* 6 (1981):366–394; Claire Brown and Joseph A. Pechman, eds., *Gender in the Workplace* (Brookings Institution, 1987); Alice H. Amsden, ed., *The Economics of Woman and Work* (St. Martin's Press, 1980); Ava Baron, "Gender and Labor History: Learning from the Past, Looking to the Future," and other essays in Ava Baron, ed., *Work Engendered: Toward a New History of American Labor* (Cornell University Press, 1991). See also Charlotte Perkins Gilman, *Women and Economics* (New York: Source Book Press, 1970 [1898]); and Carl Degler, *At Odds: Women and the Family in America from the Revolution to the Present* (Oxford University Press, 1980); among numerous other sources. For the relation between early feminism and women's economic situation, see Nancy Cott, *The Grounding of Modern Feminism* (Yale University Press, 1984), esp. ch. 4. For a current theory of social and economic foundations of the sexual division of labor see R. W. Connell, *Gender and Power* (Stanford University Press, 1987), esp. part 2.

7. See, among other sources, Adrienne Rich, "Compulsory Heterosexuality and Lesbian Experience," in Henry Abelove et al., eds., *The Lesbian and Gay Studies Reader* (Routledge, 1993), pp. 117–154, among other selections in this excellent reader; Steve Seidman, *Romantic Longings: Love in America, 1830–1980* (Routledge, 1991); John D'Emilio, *Sexual Politics, Sexual Communities* (University of Chicago Press, 1983). On the containment of female sexuality and its implications see Elaine Tyler May, *Homeward Bound* (Basic Books, 1988).

8. Henry Louis Gates Jr., "Writing, 'Race,' and the Difference It Makes," in *Loose Canons* (Oxford University Press, 1992), pp. 43–70. Compare, among many sources, Cornel West, "The New Cultural Politics of Difference," in *Keeping Faith* (Routledge, 1993), pp. 3–32, and a very interesting recent discussion by Paul Gilroy, *Black Atlantic* (Harvard University Press, 1993), esp. ch. 1.

9. William Gibson, *The Perfect War: The Technowar in Vietnam* (Atlantic Monthly Press, 1986).

10. The allusion is to the opening line of SDS's 1962 *Port Huron Statement:* "We are people of this generation, bred in at least modest comfort."

11. Karl Marx, "Economic and Philosophical Manuscripts of 1844," in Robert Tucker, ed., *The Marx-Engels Reader* (W. W. Norton, 1978), p. 71.

12. For the psychoanalytic view see Sigmund Freud, "Remembering, Repeating, and Working-Through," in *Standard Edition* (Hogarth Press, 1958), vol. 12.

13. The misrepresentation may only be unintentional, of which the two most famous cases from the previous generation were the well-intentioned liberal purposes behind Oscar Lewis's initial culture-of-poverty arguments and, most especially, Patrick Daniel Moynihan's sympathetic but poorly expressed 1965 statistical report on the Black family in America. The latter still infuriates students who seem to have known about it long before attending college.

14. Donna Haraway, "Manifesto for Cyborgs," in *Simians, Cyborgs, and Women: The Reinvention of Nature* (Routledge, 1991).

15. West, *Keeping Faith,* pp. 20–21.

16. Gloria Anzaldúa, *Borderlands/La Frontera: The New Mestiza* (Spinsters/Aunt Lute Press, 1987), p. 19.

Acknowledgments

UNLIKE SOME BOOKS of several parts, the parts of this book have not appeared in print before. The exceptions are a few pages of Chapter 3 from "The Canonical Limits of Durkheim's First Classic," *Sociological Forum* 9 (1994):87–93; a few pages more in Chapters 4 and 5 from "Social Theory at the Early End of a Short Century," *Sociological Theory* 12 (1994):140–153; and not much more than the title for Chapter 4 from "The End of Ideology, Really!" *Sociological Theory* 9 (1991):164–173. I thank the Eastern Sociological Society and the American Sociological Association for permission, granted by prior agreement, to reformulate and reuse these lines.

Though little has been printed before, much has been aired in public places where by their kindness (and, in some instances, indifference) colleagues and others have alerted me to problems in need of repair. These include gatherings of various kinds at Rice University, UCLA, the University of Kansas (both the Law School and the Department of Sociology), the University of Minnesota, the University of Connecticut, Pennsylvania State University, the University of California at Davis and at Santa Cruz, the Inter-University Center in Prague, Helsinki University (and the Finnish Political Science Association), and the Center for the Humanities at Wesleyan University; with the Faculty of Law and Social Science at Liège, and the members of Pierre Bourdieu's Centre de Sociologie Européenne in Paris; and various meetings of the American Sociological Association, the Eastern Sociological Society, and the Midwest Sociological Society. Some of these talks were given quite a while ago, but each was an occasion on which I learned things that found their way into this book.

I thank especially the following for various contributions ranging from a friendly remark in passing to a poignant critique to a thorough reading of the manuscript as a whole: Jeff Alexander, Sandy Becker, David Brain, Wini Breines, Gary Comstock, Lisa Freeman, Bill Harris, Rich Hilbert, Martin Jay, Richard Lachmann, Barbara Laslett, Edwin Lemert, Elizabeth Long, Phyllis Meadow, Simon Prosser, Dena Reed, Charlie Smith, Alan Sica, Barrie Thorne, and Gaye Tuchman. For many years now Irene Spinnler has worked with me and my colleagues in the Department of Sociology at Wesleyan. I thank her and Connie Colangelo (who has done the same for a fewer number of years) for kind help without which much work might never have seen the light of day.

I could not have had a better editor than Dean Birkenkamp who, among much else, has possibly read this book more times than I. During the past years, especially through the development of *Sociology After the Crisis*, he has also become a friend. Westview is one of those few publishing places where good literary values still live in real human terms.

I am fortunate to have two of the best sociology pals one could hope for. Steve Seidman, Patricia Clough, and I have discussed ideas related to this book in various odd places here and there—bars and museums in New York City, trains in California, cabins in Massachusetts. Patricia Clough is a daring and brilliant, yet respectful, critic of sociology.

There are stretches when it seems I learn from her daily. Steve Seidman has done more than anyone I know to show us the way to a better sociology, and he has done this with the same grace and love I have enjoyed as his friend.

I mention my sons often in what I write. Noah and Matt appear so regularly as examples because they have touched me so deeply by the ways they face the worlds they have both honestly and creatively. Finally, the brief word of dedication to Geri does not begin to express what I would never say in public about all the good things she has brought to my life these past years.

Charles Lemert

About the Book and Author

"How shall man measure Progress there where the dark-faced Josie lies?
How many heartfuls of sorrow shall balance a bushel of wheat?"

—W.E.B. Du Bois

Western societies today are caught in a crisis brought about by the challenge of voices like Du Bois's. Once national states were stable, and their governments and universities the guarantors of social progress. Today they are broken apart by acrimonious confusion over how to respond to the challenges of racial and ethnic minorities, feminists, gays and lesbians, and postcolonials. In clear and convincing language, *Sociology After the Crisis* measures the importance of these new voices, which are both challenges to and opportunities for the sociological imagination.

The crisis-riddled world needs a renewed sociology perhaps even more than it requires economic or political advice. Charles Lemert sees sociology as first and foremost a special type of practical, moral wisdom. Sociology is the way in which individuals try to understand the inner secrets of social life against the embracing structures of the modern world. All professional sociologies build, or ought to build, from this fundamental human attempt to take the measure of one's self in a structured world.

Readers will find *Sociology After the Crisis* an elegant, well-informed, and captivating defense of sociology. It is writing strongly reminiscent of others in sociology's long tradition of morally passionate exposition—writers like W.E.B. Du Bois, Charlotte Perkins Gilman, C. Wright Mills, and Alvin Gouldner.

Lemert's appreciative insights span the historical development of sociology from the days of Durkheim and Weber, through those of Merton and Parsons, to today's sociology influenced by Dorothy Smith, Bourdieu, Giddens, and many more. With uncommon ease the author speaks of writers like these in relation to Gloria Anzaldúa, Cornel West, and others who represent the current wave of practical sociologies.

Sociology After the Crisis invites sociologists, social scientists, and all those concerned with today's world to take up once again their responsibilities as public intellectuals and to begin by recognizing that sociology is most powerful when rooted in the practical work of daily life.

Charles Lemert, professor of sociology at Wesleyan University in Middletown, Connecticut, is the author of many books, including *Social Theory: The Multicultural and Classic Readings* (Westview 1993).

Praise for *Sociology After the Crisis*

"Charles Lemert's *Sociology After the Crisis* is a valiant and valuable effort to recover the moral voca-tion of sociology. Lemert's insistence that sociology be linked to the everyday lives and ethical con-cerns of common people will ensure that it becomes once again a powerful resource for our social ex-istence. And his expansive reimagining of the historical roots of sociological imagination—especially as it embraces voices and visions long lost to our most important national debates—is balm to the fractured soul of American society. Lemert's elegant and passionate volume will aid immeasurably in our nation's search for sane solutions to the crises of purpose and perspective he so skillfully explores."

—Michael Eric Dyson
author of *Making Malcolm* and *Between God and Gangsta' Rap*

"*Sociology After the Crisis* is a stunning book; learned, gracious, passionate, a history of sociological theory and practice and a meditation on the vocation of 'coming to terms with one's social world' when the world no longer harbors such confident singularity. Charles Lemert has produced one of the most thoughtful and compelling books on modernity itself. Every sociologist should carefully read Lemert's arguments for the centrality of our work to worldly affairs."

—Avery F. Gordon
University of California at Santa Barbara

"*Sociology After the Crisis* orchestrates a dialogue between established sociological traditions and the 'new' social knowledges (e.g., postmodernism, feminism, race-based theory, and queer theory). Lemert imagines a sociology respectful of classic traditions, yet engaging questions of social differ-ence, ethics, and politics. In this elegantly crafted, brilliantly argued volume, Lemert establishes him-self as perhaps the preeminent essayist in sociology today."

—Steven Seidman
State University of New York at Albany

"Charles Lemert trains his keen intelligence and state-of-the-art theoretical tools from feminist, post-modernist, postcolonial, cultural studies, and other 'minority' discourses on the canonical works of sociology. In doing so, he enables its holy trinity of dead, white, European men—Marx, Weber, Durkheim—and many of their theoretical ancestors and descendants, to speak *with* the rest of us. The reflexive, critical sociology of C. Wright Mills and Alvin Gouldner has produced no worthier heir than this eloquent, learned, and passionate book."

—Judith Stacey
author of *Brave New Families*

"Once again, Charles Lemert has come to the aid of his discipline with finesse, learning, and a humane sense of humor that makes the book invaluable—for believers and nonbelievers alike."

—Alan Sica
Pennsylvania State University

Index